THE
REAL
BENEDICT
ARNOLD

THE
REAL
BENEDICT
ARNOLD

by

Jim Murphy

CLARION BOOKS
NEW YORK

Clarion Books
a Houghton Mifflin Company imprint
215 Park Avenue South, New York, NY 10003
Copyright © 2007 by Jim Murphy

The text was set in 12-point Weiss.
Maps by Kayley LeFaiver.

www.clarionbooks.com

Printed in the U.S.A.

Library of Congress Cataloging-in-Publication Data

Murphy, Jim, 1947–
The Real Benedict Arnold / by Jim Murphy.
p. cm.
Includes bibliographical references and index.
ISBN: 978-0-395-77609-4
1. Arnold, Benedict, 1741–1801—Juvenile literature. 2. American loyalists—Biography—
Juvenile literature. 3. Generals—United States—Biography—Juvenile literature.
4. United States. Continental Army—Biography—Juvenile literature.
5. United States—History—Revolution, 1775–1783—Juvenile literature. I. Title.
E278.A7M87 2007
973.3'82092—dc22[B]2007005700

VB 10 9 8 7 6 5 4 3 2 1

The reputations of those who shape the fate of nations become historical forces in themselves. They are twisted and turned to fit the needs of those who follow, until, it seems, there is no actual person left.

—Bernard Bailyn

CONTENTS

1

THE MOST BRILLIANT SOLDIER

The road from the visitor center of Saratoga National Historical Park winds along past where John Freeman's farmhouse once stood and then to the handsomely restored Neilson House. Freeman, a Loyalist who supported England's claim to America, joined General John Burgoyne's invading British forces in 1777, while his Patriot neighbor, John Neilson, fought against him as part of the 13th Albany Militia.

The road continues north several hundred yards before it loops around and travels back over a grassy ridge that saw hard fighting in September and October of 1777. British losses were so great that eventually Burgoyne had to admit defeat and surrender his entire army of 6,000 soldiers. All British hopes of possessing the Hudson Valley and thus cutting off New England and New York from the other colonies vanished after this, and when word of the stunning American victory reached Europe several weeks later, France officially sided with the American rebels. Many historians consider the victory at Saratoga the

turning point in the war, leading inevitably to American independence.

Stop Number 7 on the road is the Breymann Redoubt, a fortification named after Lieutenant Colonel Heinrich Breymann. In 1777 it was an imposing line of breastworks some two hundred yards long made of thick timbers eight feet tall. It was there that Breymann's two hundred German riflemen guarded the right side of the British line of battle and where the fiercest fighting took place.

Today the breastworks are gone, and in their place is one of the more curious Revolutionary War monuments. From a distance it looks like an ordinary gravesite, with a wrought-iron fence around it to define the plot. Only on closer inspection does a visitor realize that no one is actually buried there.

One side of the marker, carved out of gray granite in 1887, depicts the battered boot of an officer strapped to a half-buried cannon barrel. The reverse side bears this inscription:

In Memory of
the "most brilliant soldier" of the
Continental Army, who was desperately wounded
on this spot, the sally port of
BURGOYNE'S "GREAT (WESTERN) REDOUBT"
7th October 1777,
winning for his countrymen
the Decisive Battle of the
American Revolution
and for himself the rank of
Major General.

The man who had the monument erected, Major General John Watts de Peyster, made certain that his own name was chiseled prominently above the inscription. But the name of the "most brilliant soldier" does not appear at all.

The soldier referred to but not identified was Benedict Arnold.

De Peyster was a Civil War veteran as well as a military historian,

A present-day view of the restored John Neilson House.
SARATOGA NATIONAL HISTORICAL PARK

writer, and philanthropist who commissioned many sculptures during his lifetime. He was also a bit of an eccentric. He considered Arnold a vile traitor to the American cause because Arnold attempted to surrender West Point to the British in 1780. But while he did not want to glorify a turn-coat's name, de Peyster could not deny Arnold's superior military skills and heroic leadership at Saratoga, or the fact that Arnold's left leg was severely and permanently crippled during the fighting. De Peyster wanted to honor some of Arnold's deeds without honoring the man.

The "Boot Monument" was a clever sleight of hand in stone. Accord-ing to historian Michael R. Lear, de Peyster reasoned that because "the leg was the only part of Arnold not to later turn traitor and since it was sac-

A recent photograph of the "Boot Monument," the only monument in the United States that honors Benedict Arnold's contribution to the Revolution.
SARATOGA NATIONAL HISTORICAL PARK

This etching of Benedict Arnold by H. B. Hall was based on an original portrait by John Trumbull.

THE LIBRARY OF CONGRESS

rificed in winning the Battle of Saratoga, *it* should be commemorated" and not Arnold.

In many ways, Benedict Arnold has come down to us through history in much the same manner. He's there; he's a presence that cannot be denied or ignored. Yet his plot to betray West Point and his fellow Patriots has often overshadowed and in many ways erased the real Benedict Arnold and his many genuine achievements.

This book is in no way meant to underplay Arnold's guilt or to justify his actions. He was indeed a traitor to the American Revolution. Instead, I've tried to expose at least some of the rumors and folktales that have become attached to his life's story so that we can see Benedict Arnold in as fair and as objective a way as possible. In doing so, I hope to highlight his numerous military contributions to the fight for American independence and to discuss some of the complex factors that led to his treasonous schemes.

The task isn't at all easy, because of a lack of key documents. While Arnold's military journal and correspondence survive, he never wrote a personal history and left no diary to fully explain his motivations for switching sides. His second wife, Peggy Shippen Arnold, burned almost all of his private letters after his death. In turn, when she died, Peggy's relatives destroyed all of her letters to them, possibly to erase her involvement in her infamous husband's plot.

The man who emerges from this frustratingly incomplete record is complex and at times elusive—charming and thoughtful one moment, combative and aggressive the next; intelligent and educated, but at the same time politically naïve; charismatic and popular with some, but loathed by others. What sort of person was Benedict Arnold, and what forces drove him to do what he did? The quest for the real Benedict Arnold begins on a bitterly cold January 14, 1741, the day when the future Revolutionary War hero and traitor was born.

2

YOU ARE ACCOUNTABLE

The Benedict Arnold who fought in the Revolutionary War was actually the sixth Benedict born into the Arnold clan. He was destined for greatness—his family's position in their community and church suggested this, as did Benedict Arnold's distinguished bloodline.

The first Arnolds left England to come to New England in 1635. William Arnold settled in Massachusetts with a group of other Puritans escaping the religious persecutions of England's King Charles I. Along with William came his family, including his twenty-year-old son, the very first Benedict Arnold.

A year later, William and family moved to the Pawtucket River region in Rhode Island. Immediately, William began buying up tracts of land, until he had amassed over 10,000 acres. As new settlers arrived, William and then his son Benedict sold them pieces of their real estate empire at a handsome profit. In England the Arnolds had been decidedly middle-class, economically and socially. By the 1640s they were among the wealthiest and most influential settlers in Rhode Island.

This first Benedict was trusted enough by other settlers to be elected governor of Rhode Island ten times, serving for fifteen years (longer than any other colonial governor). His eldest son, also named Benedict, would be appointed to the colony's General Court (which settled disputes between individuals, and negotiated land deals with Native American tribes) and even became speaker of the highest governing body in the colony, the House of Deputies. The Arnold family name was long respected in New England by the time the sixth Benedict came into the world.

A famous name was quite nice, but wealth was even more important. And in this regard, Benedict Arnold's line of the family had been both spectacularly successful and spectacularly unwise.

William Arnold and his son and heir, Benedict (I), accumulated considerable wealth. But before this Benedict died in 1678, he broke with family tradition. Instead of designating his oldest son as his sole heir, he had his estate divided equally among his eight children, a form of wealth distribution called partible inheritance. Most of the land had been sold off by this time, so the second Benedict, in addition to some cash and a few personal possessions, received just over 500 acres. He in turn divided his estate among his five surviving children, so that the third Benedict came away with only 140 acres.

This Benedict took to farming his land, but he died at the relatively young age of thirty-six, survived by his wife, several children, and some worrisome debts. Because he had foreseen that to further divide up his farm would make it impossible for any of his children to make a living from it, he gave his entire estate to his eldest son, Caleb. All that younger son Benedict (IV) received was an apprenticeship to a barrel maker.

By 1730 the Arnold financial fortunes had reached their lowest point in generations, and Benedict's prospects for the future were modest at best. At that time, most individuals would have seen their economic status not only as their place for life but as something ordained by God. As John Winthrop, the colonial governor of Massachusetts, had so bluntly put it: "God Almighty in His holy and wise providence hath so disposed the condition of mankind as in all times some may be rich, some poor, some high and eminent in power and dignity, others mean and in subjection." But Benedict decided to struggle against being "mean and in subjection" in order to better himself. And fortunately he had the ambition, energy, imagination—and good luck—to make it happen.

His first decision was to move to the thriving Connecticut town of Norwich. The town was located on the Thames River some twelve miles inland from the Atlantic Ocean. It was here that the river split in two, with each smaller branch river running farther into the fertile countryside. The chief industries of the town were shipbuilding and trading, both of which required the services of a good cooper, or barrel maker. In those days just about everything was transported in barrels—nails, ships' sails, molasses, whale oil, dried beef, beer, and wine. The list is endless, and so was the need for a barrel maker in a bustling town.

Benedict (IV) set up a cooper's shop, but he had no intention of spending his entire life enclosing wood staves in iron hoops. He worked hard for three years and prospered in the booming economy, all the while awaiting a break in his fortunes. That came in 1732, when one of Norwich's richest merchants, Absalom King, was drowned in a storm while on a trading voyage to Ireland. King left behind a thriving business and a young widow, Hannah Waterman King.

It's possible that Benedict was working for King at the time of the tragedy, which would account for how two people from such widely different economic spheres came to know each other. However they met, Hannah was able to look past Benedict's humble position and fall in love with him. Benedict's honored family heritage, along with his solid work habits and rising prospects, couldn't have hurt the relationship, either. After a respectable period of mourning, the two were wed in November 1733.

Benedict sold his barrel-making shop and assumed control of Absalom King's extensive trading business. Soon he was sailing to the islands of the West Indies and bringing back such goods as pewter, linen, glassware, and books to trade all along the New England coast. He rose in stature in the community, eventually holding a number of elected offices, including surveyor, constable, and selectman. His days as a humble cooper were behind him, and friends and relatives took to calling him Captain Arnold.

When Hannah married Benedict, she brought to the marriage more than just a handsome estate. Her paternal grandfather, Thomas Waterman, had been one of the original founders of Norwich in 1659, while her mother was from the prominent and extremely wealthy Lathrop family. Added to a family background every bit as honored as the Arnolds' was a leading position in the Congregational Church. Pews were assigned according to rank in the community, and when Hannah attended services, she sat in the front row.

The marriage of Benedict and Hannah appears to have been a happy one from the beginning. The couple prospered, eventually moving into a fine two-story house on five acres of land just outside the village. The first of their six children was born in August 1738. He was named Benedict (V), but this infant would die before reaching his first birthday, borne off by one of the many fevers that struck during the summer months.

This, then, was the family history into which the Arnolds' second child was born in 1741. Even though the emotional pain of their firstborn's death still lingered, they named their new son Benedict (VI) as well. Such a naming practice wasn't unusual in eighteenth-century New England; when a child died, his or her name was used again in four out of five families. By keeping the genealogical chain of name identity going, Benedict's parents were honoring his father and past Benedicts, and also, according to historian James Kirby Martin, "stressing the importance of family lineage."

Many if not most historians have pointed to a number of Benedict's alleged childhood incidents to show the origins of his ultimate treachery. It was claimed, for instance, that as a boy he liked to trap and kill birds for pleasure, that he challenged the town constable to a fight, and that he liked to show off by grabbing hold of a spinning water wheel and riding it all the way around. The impression conveyed by such tales was that Benedict was hell-bent from birth, a reckless, aggressive ringleader who led other children astray and constantly challenged adult authority. One nineteenth-century historian, Jared Sparks, dismissed the young Benedict Arnold as having "an innate love of mischief, [to which was] added an obduracy of conscience, and a cruelty of disposition, an irritability of temper, and a reckless indifference to the good or ill opinion of others." In case his point had been missed, Sparks added that all these personal flaws "left but a slender foundation upon which to erect a system of correct principles or habits."

Jared Sparks was a respected historian and an avid collector of first-hand accounts of the Revolution. This is how he looked in 1832, when he was thirty-nine years old.
THE NEW YORK PUBLIC LIBRARY

Just about every one of these stories was invented after Arnold had turned traitor and fled the country, mostly by people who openly disliked the man. The truth is that we have almost no confirmed details about his childhood or what he was really like. The scant information available suggests that Benedict had a typical active boy's childhood. "There were horses to ride," writes Arnold scholar Audrey Wallace, "ice skating on the nearby ponds, swimming, and sailing small boats on the river."

There is no detailed description of what Benedict looked like as a boy. Because he was never described as being of more than "middling height" as an adult, a term which probably meant he was at most five feet five inches tall, we can speculate that he was on the small side. That he was naturally athletic and hardy is borne out by descriptions of him when he was older.

We know that his first formal schooling took place in the Montville section of Norwich, at Dr. Jewett's one-room school. Here he was taught his numbers from Edward Cocker's *Arithmetic* and reading and writing from Thomas Dilworth's *A New Guide to the English Tongue*.

When he was eleven, Benedict was sent to a boarding school fifteen miles from home that was run by one of his mother's cousins, the Reverend James Cogswell. Cogswell had graduated from Yale College and was by all accounts a well-educated and demanding teacher. In addition to English and mathematics, young Benedict studied the Bible, the laws of the Puritan God, history, Greek, and Latin, as well as public speaking.

Education for the average American child of that time was haphazard at best and had limited objectives. The child was to be taught to read well enough to understand the Bible, and to add and subtract in order to help with the family business. Clearly, Benedict's studies were intended to achieve much more—to insure he got into college (probably Yale), to help him fit into the upper levels of society, and to mold him into a strong, upright Christian gentleman.

The latter was particularly important to Benedict's mother, as is clear from a letter she sent Cogswell on her son's first day at school. "It is with a great deal of satisfaction that I commit my uncultivated child to your care under God," Hannah Arnold wrote. "Pray don't spare the rod and spoil the child. . . . If you should find him backward and unteachable, pray don't be soon discouraged but use all possible means, again and again."

To Hannah Arnold, "under God" was more than just a conventional phrase in a letter. Judging from the five surviving letters she wrote to her son, she was a loving but morally strict parent. Each letter warns young Benedict to protect "your precious soal [sic] which once lost can never be regained." These letters must have been very important to Benedict; he kept them with his personal possessions for the rest of his life.

A number of Arnold's biographers have pointed to his mother's deep concern for her son's moral well-being as proof that the boy was rebellious and difficult. Cogswell did write to Hannah once about an incident involving Benedict—he balanced on a barn's ridgepole while the building was burning—but there is nothing in the words or tone of his letter to suggest that Benedict was in any way a chronic troublemaker. One such incident could be tolerated as a boyish prank, but Cogswell wouldn't have allowed a repeat offender to remain long at his school, whether he was a relative or not.

We can infer that the source of Hannah's concern was not so much her son's behavior as her own fear. At the time, the American colonies were experiencing a strong revival of religious feelings, spearheaded by traveling preachers, among them the charismatic George Whitefield. Citizens were exhorted to renew their faith in God if they hoped to avoid the fires of eternal damnation. Hannah, a pious person by nature, took the preaching of what came to be called "the Great Awakening" to heart and made it a daily part of her and her family's life.

Family, wealth, education, and religion. All of these automatically placed Benedict Arnold above all other children in the village—above the sons and daughters of bakers, sailors, seamstresses, cobblers, and, yes, coopers. In many ways his social position even placed him above their parents. He was expected to grow up to take over the family business, to become, like the successful Arnolds before him, a leader of his community and church.

It was a blessing to have the path to a successful and powerful life so clearly defined. It was also a great burden. No matter where young Benedict went, he would be reminded of his elevated position in the world. He would hear it in the way workers and sailors addressed his father; in the way his mother interacted with the household servants. His teachers would mention the names of his ancestors when discussing regional history. Even entering his church and walking to the very front of the congregation suggested that he and his family were different.

Such an elevated social position put a great deal of pressure on a young person of that time. Historian Steven Mintz notes that "no earlier people had ever invested greater responsibilities or higher expectations in their children than did the New England Puritans," adding that "this heavy investment produced intense anxiety. . . . Young people were made to carry an awesome psychological burden. Morality, religion, indeed the future, depended on them."

Whatever burden Benedict may have felt was counterbalanced by his parents' love and encouragement. Once when Benedict wrote home request-

Traveling preachers, such as George Whitefield, had a great deal of influence over America in the mid-eighteenth century.

ing spending money, his mother sent him fifty shillings, to which Captain Arnold added another twenty. This came to three pounds ten shillings (or approximately $264 in today's dollars), an extremely generous amount. But his father was often away for long stretches on trading journeys, and much of Benedict's upbringing was left to his mother.

Hannah was skilled at running her household and at raising her children, though it appears that her rigid sense of moral order was never far from the surface. After sending Benedict his requested spending money, for instance, she felt compelled to warn him to spend the money "prudently, as you are accountable to God and your father." She was always there to admonish young Benedict for his every error—for not paying stricter attention to their minister's sermon, for speaking too loudly when playing, or for being thoughtless to someone who might be considered socially below him, such as a servant or an apprentice. "Nobody can be anything . . . but what God makes or permits them to be," she would remind him. "Fix your dependence on Him alone, who is all in all."

Over time her constant worrying and warnings took a toll on the developing boy. "His budding self-confidence was constantly undermined," historian Clare Brandt concludes, "by his mother's stern piety."

There is nothing wrong with this sort of upbringing. Benedict might have grown up with a strong desire to succeed in school or in his religion in order to please one or both of his parents. Sometimes, however, the need to be successful dominates a person's life, though it is usually triggered by some sort of extremely upsetting event. And it was just at this very vulnerable time in Benedict's life that his world began to fall apart.

3

BE YE ALSO READY

*D*eath was always lurking nearby during colonial times, even for those who lived in or near the relative safety of a city or town. A drought or a flood could damage crops and cause shortages of food; a slight cut might very well lead to infection and death. And people could catch deadly fevers and diseases of all sorts—smallpox, scarlet fever, yellow fever, measles, typhus, influenza, camp fever, and the bilious remitting fever, to name just a few. Ten percent of all children died before reaching their first birthday; thirty percent were dead before turning twenty-one.

Benedict Arnold grew up in the shadow of sudden death. His older brother, Benedict, had succumbed to a summer fever as an infant. When Benedict was nine years old, his younger brother, Absalom, died of a mysterious illness. These family tragedies were constantly reinforced by his religious instruction, which admonished children to be good at all times, because death could take them away in an instant. One well-known preacher whom Benedict's mother had studied, Cotton Mather, once gave this advice: "Go into Burying-Place, CHILDREN; you will there see *Graves* as short as your selves. Yea, you may be at *Play* one Hour: *Dead, Dead* the next."

Then in 1753, when he was away at Reverend Cogswell's, troubling letters began arriving from his mother. "My dear child," one begins, "deths [sic] are multiplied all round us and more daly [sic] expected and how soon our time will come we know not. Pray my dear . . . do not neglect your precious soul which once lost can never be regained your uncle Zion Arnold is dead."

A diphtheria epidemic was sweeping across New England. The disease, at the time commonly called the "throat distemper," began as a mild sore throat and then slowly worsened day by painful day, gradually choking its victim to death. There was little that loved ones could do for victims except offer them medicinal teas, read to them from the Bible, and provide whatever comfort was possible. Hannah's letter to Benedict ends with a grim postscript: "Captain Bill has lost all his sons. John Post has lost his wife. John Lathrop and his son Barnabas are dead."

Two weeks later Benedict heard from his mother again and learned that other members of his family had taken ill. "I but wright [sic] to let you know that your poor sisters are in the land of living. But for 3 or 4 days past we looked on Mary as one just stepping off the banks of time, and to all appearances, [your sister] Hannah just behind. . . . Hannah is waxing weak and weaker, hath not got up one hour this seven days past, and her distemper increasing. What God is about to do with us I know not. Your father is very poor. Aunt Hyde is sick and I myself had a touch of the distemper."

What must the twelve-year-old boy have felt after reading these dire reports? Did he worry about his family and friends while waiting for another letter? We can't be certain because, again, Benedict left no written account. Theirs was a close-knit family, so we can assume he must have been upset and terrified for them. He may have even written his mother asking if he was needed at home; one of her letters ends with "I must not have you come home for fear that should be presumption."

In the end two sisters, Mary, who was eight, and Elizabeth, who was almost three, died. His sister Hannah eventually recovered, as did his mother and father. It would have been very natural for young Benedict to feel some degree of guilt over escaping the disease completely while others suffered and died. How much worse must he have felt to read these words written by his own mother: "My dear, god seems to be saying to all children, Be ye also ready. Pray take ye exhortation, for [God's] call to ye is very striking: that God should smite your sisters and spare you as yet." Life is indeed fragile and fleeting, she seems to be telling her son, but the Supreme Being has singled you out as special.

In a subsequent letter she made clear that Benedict's first concern should be "to make your peace with God," because "death may overtake you unprepared, for his commission seems sealed for a great many, and for ought you know you may be one of them." She then went on to remind him he was indeed flawed and needed to better himself. "Keep a steady watch over your thoughts, words and actions. Be dutiful to your superiors, obliging to your equals and affable to inferiors, if any such there be. Always choose that your companions be your betters, that [from] their good examples you may learn."

There is no telling how much of a burden Benedict felt as a result of his mother's directions. It must have been considerable, however. With their siblings dead, all of their parents' concerns, hopes, and dreams were now focused on Hannah and Benedict. The future of the family rested on their young shoulders, especially Benedict's, since he was the sole surviving son.

Before the Arnolds had time to fully grieve the loss of two daughters, more trouble descended upon the family. First, England and France declared war on each other.

The French and Indian War (also known as the Seven Years' War) began when French and English colonists clashed over control of the fertile Ohio Valley in 1754. While English forces outnumbered those of their opponent, the French scored a series of stunning victories because they

During the French and Indian War, fighting often took place in heavily wooded forests.
Seeing the enemy was made more difficult by the thick smoke that accompanied musket fire.
THE NEW YORK PUBLIC LIBRARY

had the backing of Native American nations in the region, who had decided that French settlers were less likely to disrupt their lives. For three years the French dominated the fighting, and eventually the war spread to Europe, with England and Prussia battling France, Austria, and Spain.

While the French were pushing English settlers from their farms in the west, French warships cruised the Atlantic coast of the American colonies, disrupting trade with the West Indies. This virtual blockade seems to have seriously hurt Captain Arnold's trading ventures there, and gradually he fell more and more deeply into debt.

The loss of four children, plus his deteriorating financial situation, began to eat away at him. Like most Anglo-American men at the time, he consumed alcohol regularly and sometimes heavily, but it did not threaten his ability to work until 1754 or 1755. After this, Hannah's letters to Benedict frequently refer to the Captain as being "in a poor state of health." Because she never provided specific symptoms for this illness or even a name, most historians believe she was making veiled references to his alcoholism.

Several of his efforts to put their financial situation right failed, and eventually a warrant was issued for the Captain's arrest on the grounds that he was evading his creditors. Finally, in February 1755, money was so scarce that Hannah Arnold had to reluctantly withdraw Benedict from the Reverend Cogswell's school.

Young Benedict's future was now entirely bleak. The business, which he would normally have taken over when older, was bankrupt; the formal education that would have been an immense advantage in his life was ended. He had seen his family go from the wealthiest and most respected in town to being humiliatingly poor and pitied.

The Arnolds continued living in their big house in what historian Willard Sterne Randall has described as "genteel poverty, still trudging down the aisle to their front-row pew on church days even as their clothes grew obviously older." The Captain's drinking problem worsened. Finally, to remove her son from the corrosive atmosphere at home and give him a way to earn a living, Benedict's mother had him apprenticed to two of her Norwich cousins, Daniel and Joshua Lathrop. Benedict left his home and moved into Daniel Lathrop's sprawling white house on Norwich's village green.

The Lathrops were both Yale graduates and had prospered as partners in a combined apothecary shop/trading business. The war that had ruined Benedict's father turned out to be a great boon to the Lathrops. Theirs was the only apothecary shop between New York City and Boston, and they were given the contract to supply surgical equipment, medicine, and other items to the British army in that region.

Benedict seems to have impressed his cousins with his energy and quick mind. He learned something about doctoring and medicine from Daniel Lathrop, who was a trained physician as well as a shrewd business-man. In addition, the shop sold wine, fabric, dried fruits, perfumes, pow-ders, musk, and even embalming fluid. Daniel's wife, Jerusha, treated young Benedict as a son, teaching him his lessons and instructing him in how a young man should act in proper society.

As always with Benedict Arnold, there are unflattering stories about this phase of his life. The most persistent has it that Benedict ran away, not once but twice, to fight in the French and Indian War. The first time, he was sent home when his minister intervened on behalf of his distraught mother; the second time, he deserted, either because he was bored with camp life or be-cause he'd heard that his mother was ill. In other words, the young Bene-dict Arnold was an unreliable apprentice who lusted to fight, was greedy for the bounty money given enlistees, and was a deserter as well.

While these stories make for neat moral lessons, they aren't true, or at least aren't about our Benedict Arnold. It seems there was a Benedick (also spelled "Bowdick" and "Benidick" on different enlistment rolls) Arnold who enlisted three times in the New York militia. This "Benedick" came from Norwalk, Connecticut, and not Norwich; he was also said to be five feet nine inches tall, which was more than the "middling height" ascribed to Benedict. Besides, the Lathrops were tough businessmen and not likely to welcome back a runaway apprentice, especially one who had run off twice.

One other fact suggests that Benedict Arnold did not rush off to fight. When he was in his thirties, Arnold described himself as being "a coward until he was fifteen years of age." It's hardly likely that such a boy would dash headlong into a bloody fight.

Evidently, members of the Arnold family did live in Norwalk at the time, so Benedick Arnold was probably a distant relative of Benedict. In the end, though, it's a case of mistaken identity that is used to paint our Benedict Arnold in as unflattering a light as possible.

It does appear that young Benedict Arnold mustered arms at least once with the Norwich militia. In August 1757 the French Canadian governor, Marquis Louis-Joseph de Montcalm-Gozon, and a raiding force of French settlers and Native Americans captured Fort William Henry, near Lake George, from the British. Connecticut militiamen joined forces to halt an anticipated French invasion to take Albany, and Benedict, who was sixteen at the time, was just old enough to serve. This was a general call to arms for all able-bodied men, and the Lathrops would have seen it as their civic duty to release their apprentice for military service. Fortunately, the French retreated and Benedict returned to the Lathrops without ever firing a shot.

Benedict's duties at the Lathrop businesses expanded after this. He began negotiating for the purchase of their goods, and even traveled to the West Indies and London as their representative. As such, he came into contact with a variety of people, from common sailors to dignified businessmen, and learned to interact and negotiate with them in an effective way. He must have been very successful in these activities, because when his apprenticeship came to an end in 1761, the Lathrops set him up as a business partner in New Haven, backing his venture with credit worth £500 sterling (approximately $20,000 in today's dollars).

Although Benedict steadily advanced in business, his final years with the Lathrops were anything but tranquil. In 1759 his mother died at the age of fifty-two, carried off by an unidentified illness. After this, his father's continued drunkenness culminated in his arrest on May 26, 1760. The warrant stipulated that Captain Arnold "was drunken in said Norwich so that he was disabled in the use of understanding and reason, appearing in his speech, posture and behavior, which is against the Peace of Our Lord, the King and the laws of this colony."

The court fined Captain Arnold for his unacceptable behavior and warned him to avoid such displays in the future. But the Captain's (and his family's) embarrassment wasn't to end there. Members of his church—the church where he occupied a front-row pew—complained about his unseemly conduct, and Deacon Ebenezer Huntington demanded that he publicly confess his sins and beg forgiveness for "drunkenness in diverse instances."

The Captain refused to appear, and a committee of church leaders marched to his house for a meeting—only to be turned away. "They had not recovered him to his duty," they would report. "He was still impertinent and refused to make a public confession." Next, the full church congregation "voted a public admonition which renders him incapable of communion in special circumstances."

The Captain still defied his church, and church members began discussing the harshest penalty possible: excommunication. At this point, the minister stepped in to ask his parishioners to show charity toward the Captain due to "his great incapacity." Before the close of 1761, Captain Arnold died of acute liver failure.

Benedict was only twenty years old when he took over as head of the family. He had spent his teenage years watching every aspect of his family unravel. Both parents and all but one sibling were dead; the family business was gone, and instead of a handsome inheritance he was left with his father's debts; his very name, once honored and respected, was now in ruins.

These years of struggle and heartache must have taken a terrible toll on him. Arnold scholar Clare Brandt finds a direct relationship between the economic and social downfall of his family and his personality. "His humiliation was severe," she states, "but like many adolescent agonies it remained buried, working its destruction secretly, silently and slowly, deep beneath the skin." As a result, she believes, "Benedict Arnold was a hollow young man, driven by a craving for reassurance and confirmation that could never be satisfied, even by his own well-earned triumphs." No doubt, as historian James Kirby Martin notes, Benedict "harbored feelings of indignation toward those Norwichites who looked at him sanctimoniously . . . as if they were measuring his worth by the failures of his namesake." Martin goes on to suggest that Benedict's strong will and tendency to challenge authority developed because he rejected the severe religious upbringing of his childhood. "He would show little tolerance for those who, like his mother's wrathful Calvinist God, expected complete obedience to their will but demonstrated little or no beneficence toward others. He would challenge arbitrary power wherever it lurked, especially when directed against his person, character, and reputation—and those whom he loved."

Benedict also seems to have made up his mind to return his family name to its once-honored position. As Martin puts it, he determined to "confront anyone, however high or low in birth, who questioned his honor, reputation, or family name. Those with the temerity to do so would find him unrelenting in challenging their slurs."

There was nothing left for Benedict to do but sell the family house and start all over again.

4

A REPUTATION OF UNSULLIED HONOR

*I*n 1761, Benedict moved to the bustling town of New Haven, where he rented a small shop on Chapel Street and hung out his sign. In bold letters it stated:

> *B. Arnold Druggist*
> *Book Seller, Etc.*
> *From London*
> *Sibi Totique*

The Latin motto means "For himself and for all." Some historians have claimed that the motto's meaning shows who always came first for Benedict. One writer even mistranslated it as "wholly for himself." A different interpretation is offered by James Kirby Martin. Martin suggests that Benedict wanted patrons to know he was "a person who was astute enough to appreciate that serving himself depended on his being of service to them."

In short order Benedict had his shelves stocked with a wide variety of medical products, such as Turlington's Balsam of Life, James's Fever Powder, and Spirits of Scurvy Grass. He also sold an impressive list of books, the latest cosmetics from London, plus necklaces, earrings, buckles, and, as one of his advertising broadsides promised, "a very elegant assortment of mezzotint pictures, prints, maps, stationery . . . and paperhangings for rooms."

New Haven was in the midst of a population boom when Benedict opened his doors to the public. Between 1750 and 1775 the town grew from two thousand individuals to eight thousand, becoming the third largest in Connecticut. Many of these people were regular customers of Benedict Arnold. His trade was so brisk that he was forced to move twice into larger stores.

Within the space of three years, Benedict formed a partnership with another prospering New Haven merchant, Adam Babcock. Together they purchased three large sailing vessels. Benedict held on to his apothecary shop, but he hired someone to manage its day-to-day operations. Freed of this responsibility, Benedict spent as much time as possible sailing between the West Indies and Canada, trading in horses, rum, molasses, pork, grain, and timber.

A mark of his skill in business and the growing respect of the community is that customers at his shop began addressing him as Dr. Arnold, while the merchants he dealt with referred to him as Captain Arnold. As his father had before him, Benedict had tapped into the growing economic energy of a boomtown to reverse the sinking fortunes of the Arnold family. He was even able to repurchase his family's home in Norwich, though it isn't clear why he wanted a second house in a town that he rarely visited. It's possible that he bought it to show his former neighbors that he was economically successful, which may have helped erase some of the shame he felt over having had to give it up. Then, just six months later, he turned around and sold the same house for a considerable profit. Again, we can only guess at why he did this. One reason might have been that as a young businessman he needed the profit from the sale to finance further growth in his New Haven business. It's also possible that by selling the house, he was able to summarily reject the community that he believed had wronged his father and family.

His remaining sister, Hannah, came to live with him in New Haven. Her few surviving letters suggest she was an intelligent and caring individual, but little else is known about her. She never married but remained devoted to her older brother for the remainder of her life. Even after he married, Hannah stayed in his house, becoming his chief business assistant and helping to provide him with a comfortable home.

There are a number of unsubstantiated stories about Benedict and Hannah that cast him in a negative light. According to one, Arnold forced his sister to leave Norwich and her friends against her will so she could care for his home at no cost to him. Another has him forbidding her to marry. In one often-repeated tale Hannah was being courted seriously by a French dancing master (though in some versions he's either a French dueling master or a French adventurer, while in others he's simply referred to as a "young foreigner"). Benedict, the story insists, detested the man because he was French and ordered him to stay clear of his sister. When the lovers persisted in their romance, Benedict drove the suitor off by firing a musket at him. Then later Benedict accidentally met the man in the West Indies and severely wounded him in a duel.

These tales probably originated with two elderly men from Norwich,

James Stedman and James Lanman. In 1834 historian Jared Sparks made it known he was planning to write a major biography of Benedict Arnold, and both Stedman and Lanman sent him letters filled with local gossip and legends, including the story of Hannah's supposed romance. Sparks was a serious and respected historian, but he repeated the stories without checking to see if they were authentic. Other writers after him picked them up and reworked them to fit their needs.

It is true that several members of New Haven's established families considered Benedict an arrogant upstart. One man, Rutherford Cook, remembered that Benedict spoke too often of his famous ancestors. Another suggested that he was pushy and lacked the proper "social standing" in the community. When asked if reputable citizens ever invited Arnold to their homes, the man replied, "My father invite Arnold to his house? No, sir; the extent of their acquaintance was 'Good morning, Captain Arnold.'"

No one else ever accused Benedict of talking too much about his famous ancestors, but even if he did, it would be understandable. A great deal of his self-esteem rested on his family background and his hope of one day restoring the Arnold name to a place of prominence. It's also possible that his personality did offend some people. He was, after all, a captain-merchant, comfortable with the rough language of seafaring life and the constant haggling over prices and delivery dates, and accustomed to having his orders obeyed immediately. What made him a success in business may not have worked so well with genteel society.

Still, he seems to have been fairly well accepted by a good many people in New Haven, well enough to become a Freemason. Freemasonry was a secret association that sought ways "to help all human beings to unite and work together for the perfection of Humanity." While it freely used ancient mythology, secret handshakes, and occult knowledge to create a pseudo-religious atmosphere, the society also had a deep interest in learning and philosophical discussions. Many of the leading citizens of the Revolutionary era were drawn to Freemasonry, including George Washington, Paul Revere, John Hancock, and Benjamin Franklin.

Masonic philosophy, which was quite enlightened for the eighteenth century, incorporated many ancient symbols and rituals. This mid-nineteenth-century picture shows Masons in their elaborate uniforms and hats, and, onstage, two men greeting each other with a secret handshake. THE LIBRARY OF CONGRESS

Entry into the Masons was open to all males, regardless of their religious affiliation, occupation, economic circumstances, or place in the community. Even so, applicants had to meet high standards. "Each mason . . . must live honorably, practice justice, love his neighbor, work unceasingly for the true happiness of humanity and help human beings to emancipate themselves from the thralldom of passion and ignorance." This was a lofty set of requirements, but one stood out above all others: "From the first to the last . . . the first condition to be fulfilled is to have a reputation of unsullied honor and probity." That Benedict Arnold was accepted into this select group early in 1765, when he became an initiate of New Haven's Hiram Lodge No. 1, indicates that at age twenty-four he may have been brash, but he was also an upstanding citizen and well respected in his town.

A more important indicator of Arnold's acceptance was that a fellow Mason, Samuel Mansfield, took a personal interest in him. In addition to being a successful merchant, Mansfield served as New Haven County's high sheriff, an appointed position that, among other things, made him responsible for the arrest and imprisonment of wrongdoers. Mansfield invited Benedict to dinner on a number of occasions, and soon the young man was courting Mansfield's twenty-year-old daughter, Margaret. No portraits of Margaret (Peggy) Mansfield survive, though histories of the Mansfield family suggest she was handsome, if frail and painfully shy. She was also a lifelong member of the conservative First Church and held religious views similar to those of Benedict's late mother.

Benedict seems to have been smitten by Peggy and she with him, and he visited and dined with her family regularly and wrote her romantic letters. It is very unlikely that either the devout Peggy or her sheriff father would have allowed this to happen if Benedict had been as arrogant or crude as some historians have painted him.

It is true that a number of people in New Haven didn't like Benedict, but the cause of this hostility wasn't so much the young man's personality. Rather, it was the rigid structure of the community in which he lived and his reaction to it.

Most people then living in America understood and accepted that they lived in a class-oriented society that favored old, established families and prized deference to one's betters. Benedict would have felt that this attitude was perfectly normal—he was, after all, from one of those old families, though not from New Haven. He asked only to trade and profit and rise in the community without interference.

The old New Haven families weren't at all pleased with newcomers like Benedict, no matter what their family history. Before the town's population shot up, the established families controlled the town politically, economically, and socially. But after 1740 the new arrivals had gradually increased in numbers and amassed a great deal of economic and social clout. The 250 old families still had political control of the town. They dominated the town meetings, appointed all local officials, sent representatives to the colonial assembly, and organized and led the local militia. But the old families were beginning to see their decisions questioned and their influence in church matters and the local economy decline. This effectively divided New Haven society into two powerful camps that interacted in a civil but strained way.

This façade of good manners began to disintegrate when the French and Indian War ended in 1763 and the British government found itself deeply in debt. The amount—£137 million sterling—was staggering, more than 1.3 billion of our dollars. The debt was doubly galling to many British legislators in Parliament, who pointed out that the colonial governments had emerged from the war without any debt at all. In addition, the British were still paying to maintain 8,000 to 10,000 troops to guard settlers near the Appalachian Mountains from attacks by Native American tribes.

Some in Parliament suggested that the colonies needed to pony up a portion of the cost of their own defense. One representative in Parliament's House of Lords, Thomas Whately, wondered if those in America really appreciated what had been done for them, saying that "the colonies . . . have been of late the darling object of their mother country's care." The head of the king's cabinet, George Grenville, wasn't convinced the colonists comprehended that the parent nation "had run itself into an immense debt to give them protection."

This very measured language concealed a well of pent-up anger. Grenville and the cabinet, the king, and a majority in Parliament looked on the North American colonists as spoiled and misbehaving children who had to be brought into line. Grenville may have summed up this resolve best when he stated, "Great Britain protects America; America is bound to yield obedience."

To cope with the massive debt, between the years 1763 and 1773 the British government passed a series of acts and laws aimed at either reducing expenses or raising money. One of the first changes took place in 1763, when British naval vessels were ordered to hunt down suspected smugglers in American waters. The action was originally intended to stop colonial merchants from trading with France or Spain during the French and Indian War. There is no evidence to suggest that Benedict or his Lathrop cousins ever traded with the enemy during wartime, but events following the war soon drew all three into such illegal activity.

At the close of the war, the troops were moved to the western territories, and Britain abruptly canceled most of its legal agreements with American merchants on the east coast to supply the army's needs. This led to a deep economic depression in America that lasted almost five years. At the same time, the British government began imposing tariffs, or taxes, on items being imported to America. The list of such legislation was long and included the Sugar Act (1764) and the Stamp Act (1765). In order to survive financially, Benedict and the captains of his trading ships began avoiding these new taxes. In short, they went into the business of smuggling.

Nowadays smugglers are considered criminals. But prior to the American Revolution almost every smuggler was a respectable merchant importing everyday commodities such as molasses or china or tea. In Boston, for instance, a system called "compounding" existed as far back as 1720. For a fee paid directly to port officials, a merchant was allowed to declare anywhere from one tenth to one fifteenth of the actual value of his cargo, thus paying only a small fraction of the real import duty owed. Boston's John Hancock was probably the most famous merchant-smuggler at this time.

The stepped-up efforts of the British to collect import duties, plus the failing economy, forced more and more merchants into "compounding," and now entire cargoes arrived without being declared. A study of the records of the Colonial Office in London reveals that absolutely no duties were paid for the import of molasses, a key ingredient in the making of rum, into Connecticut and Rhode Island between 1733 and 1765, even though "all the northern provinces . . . were most dependent on the French sugar islands."

These God-fearing, law-abiding citizens were able to rationalize their illegal activities in two ways. First, they claimed that the duties had been imposed unfairly by a distant and unfeeling British government. Second, they argued that in order to pay the duties, they would have to increase the price of their goods at home, which would in turn kill off local business. "Smuggling," historian Willard Sterne Randall observes, "had become an economic necessity on which depended the welfare not only of shipowners but of farmers and merchants and virtually anyone else doing business in colonial America."

Benedict's smuggling finally revealed him to be an opponent of British policy and the old families of New Haven. In late January 1766 he had just docked one of his ships, the *Fortune,* in New Haven. The crew managed to unload the cargo—probably West Indian molasses—without paying the three-pence-per-gallon duty. At this point a crewmember, Peter Boles, approached Arnold and demanded an increase in his wages. If he did not receive more money, Boles threatened to report the smuggling.

Benedict told Boles he thought his request was nothing more than blackmail and suggested the man leave town. Instead, Boles rushed to the customs house to turn in Arnold, hoping to receive a reward after the smuggler's ship was seized and sold at auction. The collector wasn't there, so Boles left, intending to return in the morning.

Word of what Boles had done reached Arnold, who sought out and confronted the would-be informer and "gave him a little chastisement." Boles agreed to leave, but two days later Benedict learned that he was still in town. Arnold rounded up a group of his men and once again sought the man out. Boles's word was no longer good enough for Arnold. He had prepared a document stating that Boles was "instigated by the Devil" to inform on Arnold and that he "justly deserve[d] a halter [that is, a noose] for [his] malicious and cruel intentions."

The document also had Boles swear that he would "leave New Haven and never enter the same again. So help me God." After forcing Boles to sign it, Benedict and his men went home. Boles, on the other hand, decided to stay where he was despite the two warnings he had been given and the oath he had sworn.

When Benedict heard that an unrepentant Boles was still in New Haven, he hurried off to confront the man for a third time. In addition to members of his crew, other men (possibly members of the Sons of Liberty, a secret group opposed to British policies) joined with Arnold to drag Boles from the tavern where he was living and tie him "to the whipping post where he received near forty lashes with a small cord." After this, he "was conducted out of town," very likely straddling a split fence rail. This time Boles took the hint and never returned to New Haven.

Thus far, the Boles-Arnold dispute had been essentially a personal matter. It might have passed into history and been forgotten except for some very nervous town elders, most of whom came from old families.

Politically, the country was up in arms over the various taxes the British government kept trying to impose. The most contentious had been the Stamp Act. It required that special stamps be purchased and affixed to all court documents, deeds, liquor licenses, certain contracts, calendars, and even newspapers.

Even before the law went into effect, crowds gathered to protest and demand its repeal. In New Jersey eight hundred angry citizens pressured the courts to close, while Massachusetts' Governor Thomas Hutchinson had his house pillaged and literally pulled to the ground by a nighttime mob. In Virginia, New York, Rhode Island, and Massachusetts, the colonial assemblies were hastily called into session to formally protest the tax.

By comparison, the protests in Connecticut were orderly and genteel. When a highly respected New Haven attorney, Jared Ingersoll, was named stamp distributor, a crowd dutifully gathered to demand that he resign and threatened to tear his house down if he refused. Ingersoll was clearly shaken by the threats, but he managed to stall the crowd with a legal technicality. He claimed he couldn't resign until the assembly took some sort of official position on the matter.

Not wishing to buckle to the mob's demands, the governor delayed calling a special session of the assembly for several weeks. Eventually, Ingersoll did resign, but even then the ceremony was anything but violent. Ingersoll read his letter of resignation and tossed his hat into the air in celebration, after which he and the leaders of the crowd went to a nearby tavern to have dinner. Those in authority who supported Great Britain's position had given way to the protests, but they had demonstrated as much control as possible by doing it slowly.

The Boles-Arnold incident, however, was an altogether more serious matter to New Haven's town elders. The old-guard citizens who controlled the appointment of the tax collector knew that if the Stamp Act was to have any chance of succeeding, informers were necessary. This was why the law provided anyone who reported a violation with substantial financial rewards for their information. In effect, Arnold, a newcomer, had threatened what little power the old families still had by running their valuable source of information out of town.

The fact that this had happened in a town and in a colony whose governing bodies were very supportive of British policy was what captured everyone's attention. It was considered an important enough event that newspapers in Pennsylvania, New York, and Massachusetts ran stories about it.

This merchant's open defiance of established authority, plus the bad press the episode received, was why old-guard members of the city government convened a grand jury, a secret meeting of individuals to determine whether a crime had been committed. Two grand jurors (both members of old families), Tilley Blakeslee and John Wise, had Benedict and nine others arrested on February 3 for disturbing the peace. Despite a spirited defense (by none other than Jared Ingersoll, the recently deposed Stamp Act commissioner), Arnold was found guilty and ordered to pay a fifty-shilling fine and to apologize for his actions.

This French engraving shows a mob, including a number of children, jeering at Boston tax collector John Malcolm, who is about to be tarred and feathered. THE LIBRARY OF CONGRESS

To explain their position, the old guard called a town meeting a few days after Arnold's arrest. They discussed the growing unrest in the community and voted to "mutually assist one another and particularly the civil authority" in eliminating "the growing disorder and violence and breaches of law" that threatened "the public peace and [were] even dangerous to civil society." In short, they wanted to support British policy, and to do that they had to keep the newcomers in their proper place.

Benedict could have paid his fine, apologized, and gone back to his business. But he felt that the court finding had been unjust, the result of the lopsided power of the old families. And while Benedict had an inbred respect for established authority, he was not about to submit to any sort of injustice.

Benedict paid his fine but refused to express any regret for what he had done. Instead, he held a nighttime gathering of his own, at which his friends gave rousing speeches defending his actions. Effigies of Blakeslee and Wise were paraded through the streets of New Haven by torchlight and finally tossed onto a huge bonfire. Many of those cheering the activities were unemployed workers who blamed the British—and those who supported British policies—for their economic troubles.

Several weeks later Benedict wrote an anonymous article for the *Connecticut Gazette*. In it he condemned Boles as an odious informer and blamed him—and anyone who in any way encouraged him—for the depression that was causing them all so much financial pain. "Every such information tends to suppress our trade," Benedict pointed out, "which is nearly ruined by the late detestable Stamp and other oppressive acts."

Benedict followed up this article with two others. In each he linked the economic good of the community to freedom from the arbitrary and illegal interference of Parliament and of the British government's supporters in the colonies. By attacking these two groups, Benedict was distancing himself from the very source of power and prestige he sought to join. He had, at the age of twenty-five, become a visible and fervent spokesman for radical change.

5

GOOD GOD ARE THE AMERICANS ALL ASLEEP?

Benedict wanted change in the relationship between the mother country and its colonies, but he did not want revolution. Not in 1766, at any rate. Like most Americans at the time, he was not yet seeking a complete break from Great Britain and its king. Even as he called the Stamp Act an illegal and immoral move by Parliament, he did so as a "freeborn Englishman."

This was more than just a catchy phrase for Benedict. His ancestors had come from England; he spoke English, wore English-style shoes and clothes, and read books printed in England. Much of his day-to-day living, such as the holidays he celebrated, the weights and measures he used, and the currency he exchanged, originated in England. In custom and culture, Benedict was English, and not about to reject his heritage wholesale.

As a practical man, Benedict felt that in order for the American colonies to survive and thrive, they needed access to British markets and also British naval protection for their trading ships. Besides, a complete break would cast American society into an uncertain future. Without English laws, would mob rule ensue? Would the larger colonies seize their smaller neighbors and impose even more oppressive laws than Great Britain had? These were very real concerns for people like Benedict Arnold and worrisome enough to make him a cautious protester.

The extent of Benedict's involvement in the Revolutionary movement immediately following the Boles incident is unclear. His long absences at sea most likely forced him into the role of interested observer rather than activist. He remained with the Freemasons, among whom talk of freedom from British interference was common, and he was probably a member of the local Sons of Liberty. At the time, many other Patriots were already fully committed to the cause of independence. In Boston, for instance, Paul Revere was an active member of at least five different Revolutionary organizations, and may have been a sometime member of eight others. As such, he acted as a vital conduit of information among all of them and helped organize and direct their resistance efforts. By comparison, Benedict was still on the sidelines.

Moreover, Benedict had other things to occupy his attention. His courtship of Peggy continued, and in early 1767, one year after his arrest in the Boles affair, the couple was married. Their first child, Benedict (VII), was born in February 1768, followed by Richard in 1769 and Henry in 1772.

From all appearances, Benedict and Peggy seem to have had a close, loving marriage, at least in the early years. A number of letters that he wrote to her while sailing in the Caribbean survive. They are filled with care and concern, telling her how much he missed her. "My dear girl," one begins, "you and you only can imagine how long the time seems since we parted and how impatient I am to see you and the dear little pledge [young Benedict] of our mutual love. God bless you both and send us a happy meeting soon."

In another he is candidly sentimental: "The most pleasing scenes are not agreeable when absent from you." And he closes another letter with: "May the best of Heaven's blessings attend you, and may we both be under the care of a kind Providence, and soon, very soon, have a happy meeting is a sincere prayer of your ever affectionate husband."

If there was a cloud in their relationship, it was that Peggy did not write to her traveling husband as much as he would have liked. His letters to her are filled with requests for some sort of word from her. "I have not had the pleasure to receive any letters from you," he wrote on one occasion, "though there has been several vessels from New Haven." A few days later he sent another, more distressed message: "I assure you I think it hard you have wrote me only once where there has been many opportunities [to send letters by outgoing ships]."

Some historians have suggested that Peggy's failure to write is a sign that theirs was a troubled, loveless marriage from the start. These writers apparently overlooked the fact that Peggy was a reluctant correspondent even before she married Benedict, as this passage from one of his 1766 letters demonstrates: "I have now been in the West Indies seven weeks and not heard one syllable from you since I left." What is more, Benedict never complained about the lack of correspondence without adding some word of endearment. After penning the above line, he quickly added, "Dear girl, it seems a whole age since I left you."

Where did the idea originate that Benedict and Peggy's marriage was an unhappy one? One possible source is the rumors that began circulating around 1770, suggesting that Benedict had contracted venereal disease while in the West Indies and had fought several duels with the men who had cooked up these stories.

The rumors of his infidelity and venereal disease seem to have been just that—vicious rumors perhaps started by someone once in his employ. The best evidence of this is that Benedict never exhibited any of the symptoms of disease and was never absent from his work. The standard cure at the time was known as "salivating," and required taking doses of mercury for twenty-five days, during which time the patient was bedridden and produced up to three pints of drool a day. In addition, the treatment was so harsh that it could take several months before the patient's body fully recovered.

Benedict, of course, was extremely upset by these rumors. Not only would they be highly distressing to Peggy, but they were a slight to his sense of personal honor. To counter them, Benedict had legal depositions taken from business associates in the Caribbean testifying to his good health, good character, and the good company he kept. He also filed a lawsuit against a Captain Fobes, a former employee, for defamation of character. By doing so, he brought the matter out into the open, a desperately risky undertaking unless he was above reproof and certain he would receive excellent character references.

There seems to be more substance to the suggestions that Benedict fought two pistol duels around this time. The first may have been related to the venereal disease rumors and involved a Mr. Brookman. Benedict escaped the duel unharmed; we have no record of what happened to Mr. Brookman. We do know that after the duel, Benedict sought out testimony from associates refuting a claim Brookman was spreading "about a whore I wanted to take from him." Again, it isn't likely he would have taken this action unless he was absolutely sure he would be vindicated.

The second duel was fought against a Captain Croskie, who felt insulted when Benedict failed to attend one of his social gatherings. When Benedict came by the next day to apologize and explain his absence, Captain Croskie called him "a damned Yankee, destitute of good manners or those of a gentleman." Benedict was incensed enough to fight a duel with the man, during which he wounded his adversary with his first shot. When Benedict insisted the duel proceed, Captain Croskie had second thoughts and apologized for his rude remark.

Some historians have interpreted Benedict's use of depositions, lawsuits, and dueling as proof that he was a man who would go to any length to win, even if it meant resorting to violence. However, according to the conventions of his day, the steps Benedict took to protect his reputation weren't extreme. Growing up in a family struggling to rebuild its standing in a community and then watching it all disappear may well have made Benedict acutely sensitive to any slight or challenge, and quick to defend his honor. But while dueling was frowned upon as a way to settle disputes, and in some areas was even outlawed at the end of the eighteenth century, it was still widely practiced, especially by young men like Benedict. Lawsuits were less common than they are today, but they were beginning to replace dueling as a way to seek justice in matters of honor.

What was it about Benedict and his interaction with others that prompted hostile responses? Again, there are no reliable records to explain why, for instance, someone invented and spread the nasty rumors about venereal disease. Youthful impatience, a quick temper, and a sea captain's sense of entitlement might annoy people of similar temperament and prompt them to retaliate (in effect, to take Benedict down a notch or two). Whatever the cause, it was a pattern repeated often throughout his life.

The other issue that some historians claim distracted Benedict and disrupted his marriage was a fanatical quest for money. True, he wanted to be wealthy. A secure financial base would help elevate the Arnold name to a position of importance and guard it from community ridicule. It is also true that Benedict had a wife and family, including his sister, Hannah, plus employees, to support.

An additional concern was the terrible economic situation in the colonies. Merchants had a very difficult time selling their goods after the French and Indian War ended and the economy went bad. Most of them had purchased goods from London on credit and now found it difficult to repay their loans. Literally hundreds of merchants faced bankruptcy, and the newspapers began listing more and more business failures.

Benedict was among the merchants whose sales dropped off in 1766. Because he'd run a tight, profitable business until then, he avoided immediate collapse by using past profits to pay down debts. Over the next year or so, however, he exhausted his cash reserves, and his debts mounted, reaching approximately £1,700 ($71,700) in 1767.

Up to this time, Benedict had been reluctant to press customers for payment, not wishing to offend them and have them take their business elsewhere. But as his London creditors increased pressure on him, Benedict was in turn forced to seek payments from his customers. Even so, he was almost always businesslike and polite in his letters. In one sent to Dr. William Jepson he tactfully explained that he was having "trouble collecting a little hard money, which I very much [lack], so that necessity obliges me to ask you for the money."

Benedict could have done what hundreds of other merchants were doing: He could have wiped out his debts by declaring himself bankrupt and closing his business. Instead, he took a sensible and honorable two-pronged approach to his financial woes. First, he had his lawyer work out with his London creditors a compromise payment plan that left them satisfied and left him in business. Next, to increase income, he broadened the range of goods he traded to include cattle and hardwoods for furniture makers, and widened his contacts until he and his ships were making stops all along the American coast and in Canada, as well as at British, French, Dutch, and Danish controlled islands in the Caribbean.

These were lengthy voyages, often taking him away from home for six months or longer, buying goods in one place to sell in another. These long

A photograph of Benedict's imposing New Haven home, taken in the 1890s, after years of neglect had caused the property to fall into disrepair.
THE LIBRARY OF CONGRESS

absences must have been very trying for Peggy, left behind in New Haven to care for their children and home, and to handle nagging creditors, with only Hannah to help her. And while Benedict acted as quickly as he could to prove the rumors false, the stories of his infidelity, venereal disease, and dueling must have been painful for Peggy and hard on the marriage.

The truth is that Benedict's intense focus on his business wasn't particularly unusual or a sign of fanatical greed. No one has called George Washington fanatically greedy, and yet he was, if anything, more obsessed with acquiring and holding on to wealth than Benedict Arnold was.

Washington grew up as a member of the wealthy Virginian aristocracy and inherited the 2,500-acre estate of Mount Vernon when his older brother Lawrence died of tuberculosis. He added to his land holdings by buying up neighboring properties as well as land in the west, and by marrying the wealthiest widow in Virginia, Martha Dandridge Custis, who had inherited an estate of over 18,000 acres.

Washington managed every tiny detail of his vast land holdings, riding from farm to farm, making decisions about crops, issuing work orders, and deciding how to discipline recalcitrant slaves. He worried about money constantly, and became incensed whenever he felt someone was cheating him. One time, Washington had a local iron maker indicted for fraud, believing (incorrectly, as it turned out) that the man had weighed the iron improperly. He accused a wine merchant of thievery for not filling one cask to the very top. And he was constantly quibbling with his London agents over the price they got for his crops of tobacco and wheat, often accusing them of cheating him.

In 1774 he hired a friend, Valentine Crawford, to manage his western properties and sent him the following pointed instructions. Remember, Washington wrote, because "you are now receiving my Money, your time is not your own; and that every day or hour misapplied, is a loss to me, do not therefore under a belief that, as friendship has long subsisted between us, many things may be overlooked in you."

There are many such incidents in George Washington's life. Yet histo-

rians either overlook his excesses or praise him as a careful, diligent businessman. Benedict Arnold, on the other hand, is criticized for avarice for much the same activity.

Through hard work and careful management, Benedict gradually paid off his debts and began again to save money. A sign of his increasing financial security was the stately new home he had built on three choice acres on Water Street, complete with an elaborate formal garden, stable, and coach house behind and a white picket fence in front. In addition, he built a large wharf to accommodate his sailing vessels. By the early 1770s Benedict was once again one of New Haven's wealthiest and most respected merchants. "There are few or no men here," wrote fellow businessman Charles Chauncey about Arnold, "that are thought more sufficient at present, as he has had great luck at sea of late."

The 1770s also saw a shift in Benedict's political attitude, from disgruntled British subject to radical American activist—a change that took place slowly and involved a number of issues.

From 1766 into the mid-1770s the British king and Parliament took an aggressive stance toward the colonies, passing a succession of repressive acts and laws. Their chief aim was to raise revenue in order to pay for the defense of North America, both on land and at sea. Each new law was met with protest from the colonies, and each was in turn repealed or modified.

Colonial protests intensified as the economic situation in America worsened. Instead of backing off to allow the colonial economy and bruised feelings to heal, Great Britain would always come back with a new set of rules. In 1767, just fifteen months after repealing the despised Stamp Act, Parliament put through the Townshend Duties, which placed import tariffs on British-made items such as glass, lead, paper, and tea. All of these duties were repealed in 1770—all except the three-pence-per-pound tax on tea.

Three years later king and Parliament reaffirmed their power to control the colonies by passing the Tea Act. Tea would be sent directly from India to America, thus eliminating costly stops in England, and to specifically chosen merchants. The merchants chosen for this lucrative trade were all royal favorites; those who had clashed openly with royal authority, such as Benedict Arnold, were routinely passed over.

More protests followed the Tea Act, including the Boston Tea Party, where feisty Bostonians dressed as Indians dumped a ship's cargo of tea into the harbor rather than allow it to be landed. This act of defiance infuriated the British government and prompted it to pass what came to be known collectively as the Coercive Acts. These measures closed down the port of Boston, suspended provincial and local government, shifted control of the courts to Great Britain, and gave the colonial governor what amounted to dictatorial powers.

For several reasons, Great Britain found it increasingly necessary to come back time and again to raise money and assert its power. In addition to its drained coffers because of the French and Indian War, its own economy as a whole began to falter when the country's largest and most powerful business, the East India Company, discovered itself near financial collapse (in part because the American colonies were so clever at smuggling in non-British tea). Great Britain desperately needed new rev-

A 1768 American print depicts British troops at Boston. The numerous tall church steeples were meant to suggest that the people of Boston were pious, law-abiding citizens.
COURTESY AMERICAN ANTIQUARIAN SOCIETY

enue. Besides, to back down might encourage other British holdings around the world to challenge governmental authority.

This cat-and-mouse game might have continued for many years if Britain hadn't decided to back up its laws by force. In the autumn of 1768 British troops landed in Boston to put down anti-British violence. Thirty-five hundred more troops arrived in 1770 under the command of General Thomas Gage.

Boston citizens viewed the soldiers as oppressors sent to break their spirit and steal their money. Before the occupying troops arrived, the rhetoric of dissent was often measured and amazingly polite. In protesting the Stamp Act in 1765, the Massachusetts Assembly sounded downright apologetic: "We look upon those Duties as a tax, and which we humbly apprehend ought not to be laid without the Representatives of the People affected by them." After British soldiers began patrolling the streets of

Boston, the tone changed. John Adams had been a cautious critic of the king and Parliament until he found Boston under military rule. "The people were told weekly that the ministry had formed a plan to enslave them," he remembered. "This perpetual incantation kept the people in continual alarm." Bostonians came to desire full independence from England much sooner than Americans in other regions, mainly because the British thumb came down upon Boston sooner and harder than elsewhere.

Where was Benedict in all this? When did he finally realize that there was no other course but to break from England once and for all? Without specific, reliable evidence, we can only speculate that like all merchants, he felt frustrated and betrayed by every new law, every new import tax the British laid on the colonies. And like the other merchants, he protested them and found ways to get around them. Years went by like this until it became apparent that neither the king nor Parliament was about to give up the quest for colonial money.

All along, the colonists' resistance to import duties and other costly laws was linked to a demand for the same rights granted every Englishman. "No taxation without representation" was not simply a refusal to pay import duties; it was an implicit promise that if those rights were granted, the colonies would fall back in line and behave.

A shift came in March 1770, when a handful of British troops in Boston who had been driven through the streets with stones and wooden clubs fired into the unruly mob. Five citizens died, and the incident immediately became known as the "Boston Massacre." For many the deaths were a clear signal. The British were not going to treat them like true British citizens; on the contrary, they were willing to kill their colonial "children" in order to maintain power over them.

Benedict was sailing in the West Indies when word of the massacre reached him. He was "very much shocked," he wrote to a friend, "[by] the accounts of the most cruel, wanton, and inhuman murders, committed in Boston by the soldiers." Then he revealed his state of mind in no uncertain terms. "Good God are the Americans all asleep and tamely giving up their liberties, or are they all turned philosophers, that they don't take immediate vengeance on such miscreants."

From this point on, Benedict was more fully engaged in the quest for independence. His name was mentioned frequently as a leader of New Haven's Sons of Liberty, and he was instrumental in organizing New Haven's militia company in 1774. A year after this, the sixty-five members of the militia voted Benedict their captain, a position he took very seriously. Later that same year, it was "Dr. Arnold and his mob" who confronted an outspoken supporter of the king, the Reverend Samuel Peters, and persuaded him to leave town.

Benedict Arnold's attitudes had changed over the years. He had evolved from a concerned observer of events into a full-fledged Revolutionary.

6

NONE BUT ALMIGHTY GOD SHALL PREVENT MY MARCHING

While Benedict was becoming more fully involved in the cause of independence, King George III of England was arriving at a point of no return. In September 1774 he told his chief minister, Lord Frederick North, that he and his government had compromised and coddled the Americans too much. "We must not retreat," he stated. Two months later he was even more emphatic: "The New England governments are in a state of rebellion. . . . Blows must decide whether they are to be subject to this country or independent."

King and Parliament then set about tightening the noose around the necks of the colonists. Massachusetts was declared to be in a state of rebellion, and martial law replaced the colonial government. Martial law allowed the king's troops to seize and execute rebel leaders without bothering to bring them to trial.

Pressure was also put on General Gage to provoke some sort of incident that would require military action. The belief was that some blood-

shed and destruction of property would send the rebellious upstarts running. As John Montagu, the Earl of Sandwich, boldly proclaimed to the
House of Lords, "The very sound of a cannon would carry them off."

Gage received his orders on April 14, 1775, and four days later he sent
out nearly 900 men to seize munitions in Concord, some sixteen miles
outside Boston. The action should have succeeded easily. At the time, the
British army was the most powerful, best-trained military force in the
world. And while every American town had its own militia unit, such
groups were no match for the British regulars.

The mission turned out to be anything but a cakewalk. Warned by a
series of riders, including Paul Revere and William Dawes, approximately
60 armed men assembled on the town green of Lexington, intent on
stopping the British advance. The British quickly swept aside this group,
killing eight Americans and wounding ten. But by the time they reached
Concord word had spread and several hundred Patriots were on hand to
greet them, with hundreds more on the way. The British soon found themselves outnumbered and surrounded and literally had to fight their way
back into Boston. In the end, the British suffered 273 killed and wounded
to only 95 for the amateur colonial fighters.

Benedict learned about the Battles of Lexington and Concord on
Friday, April 21, when a rider came to New Haven with the news. Immediately, Benedict had his small militia group organized and ready to march
to Massachusetts. Unfortunately, the majority of his men did not own
weapons, so Captain Arnold asked that they be given access to the town
powder house, a stone structure where muskets and powder were stored.

The town elders took a cautious position. Before sending off military
support for the colonists in neighboring Massachusetts (and possibly
drawing the wrath of British officials), they wanted to know exactly what
had provoked the fighting.

Benedict was not about to cool his heels and wait for a decision, not
when "our enemies [had] obliged [us] to have recourse to arms in defense
of our lives and liberties." He formed his men into a line facing the tavern

This 1832 engraving of the fight on Lexington Common was based on a similar sketch by Ralph Earl that was done shortly after the battle. It is considered a very accurate depiction of where the British and American units stood, and of the Common itself. Almost all of the Americans have their weapons shouldered, which implied that they were the innocent victims of aggressive British troops.

where town officials were meeting and demanded the keys to the powder house. They refused his request, adding that neither he nor the group had authorization to march off. It is reported that Benedict replied, "None but Almighty God shall prevent my marching," and then told the officials in the tavern that they had five minutes to hand over the keys or he would have his men kick in the door to the powder house and take what they wanted.

The town elders had no choice but to surrender the keys. Soon Benedict and his company were outfitted and marching toward Massachusetts, where they would join the thousands of other Patriots confining General Gage and his troops in Boston.

It was during this journey that Benedict met a fellow citizen of Connecticut, Colonel Samuel Holden Parsons, who was returning from the siege of Boston. Parsons told Benedict about the situation and said that the American forces were woefully short of cannons, powder, and other equipment. Benedict replied, according to Parsons, with "an account of the state of [Fort] Ticonderoga, and [reported] that a great number of brass cannons were there."

Fort Ticonderoga was one of a series of fortifications built by the French at the southern end of Lake Champlain to defend their Canadian holdings. The British seized these forts during the French and Indian War, but never repaired the damage caused by cannon fire and the area's severe winter weather. Benedict had visited Ticonderoga several times during trading voyages to the north and had noted that it contained a large number of cannons and few British defenders (the rest having been relocated to Boston). Benedict felt that a few hundred men could easily overrun the handful of guards still there.

After this brief encounter with Parsons, Benedict hurried his men to Cambridge, where he got them settled in the recently commandeered mansion of the royal governor, Andrew Oliver. All the time he was thinking of Fort Ticonderoga sitting nearly defenseless on the shore of Lake Champlain and what it would take to capture it.

Meanwhile, Parsons continued on to Hartford, where he mentioned Ticonderoga to a group of leading citizens and suggested it should be seized. Without any official authority, they agreed. They promised to pay for the mission and appointed Captain Edward Mott to lead it. In addition, they sent word to a popular leader in Vermont, Ethan Allen, suggesting that he and his independent militia band, called the Green Mountain Boys, enlist in their effort.

Ethan Allen was a big, blustering man, willing to use intimidation, violence, and arson to get his way. Like hundreds of others, he'd settled in the Green Mountain region of Vermont after buying a cheap land grant from New Hampshire governor Benning Wentworth. These New Hampshire grants were cheap because they were fraudulent; the British government had actually given the land to New York. But when new settlers arrived with legitimate land Grants from New York, and even when New York officials came to evict him and other squatters, Ethan Allen refused

to leave his farm. Instead, Allen organized his neighbors into an unauthorized militia that eventually numbered some two hundred individuals. Their aim was to drive off anyone who dared trespass on "their" land. As one New Yorker complained, the area had become "a refuge for the vagabonds and banditti of the continent."

Mott had about sixty men with him (fifty of whom were from western Massachusetts under the command of Colonel James Easton and Lieutenant Colonel John Brown) when he joined forces with Allen and the Green Mountain Boys. Despite being appointed the commander, Mott turned over control of the invasion force to "Colonel" Allen, because the Green Mountain Boys said they wouldn't serve under anyone else.

Meanwhile, Benedict Arnold was organizing his own strike force. On reaching Cambridge, Arnold spoke with noted Boston Patriot (and fellow Mason) Dr. Joseph Warren and the Massachusetts Committee of Safety, the group responsible for organizing the defense of the colony. The Committee named Benedict a colonel and placed him in charge of raising troops to capture Ticonderoga. To raise these troops, Benedict dispatched his captains to visit every major town in Massachusetts, while he set off on his own for Lake Champlain.

What followed when he reached Castleton, some twelve miles from Ticonderoga, and bumped into Ethan Allen's men was sadly predictable. Allen was at a forward position when Benedict claimed command of the entire operation and waved around his Massachusetts commission as proof. Allen's followers in Castleton scoffed at Arnold's demand and wondered if he had any troops to back up his claim.

Benedict confronted Allen at Shoreham the next day. Naturally enough, Allen refused to give up command of his 260 men or to call off his attack on the fort. But he did not dismiss Benedict completely, despite the fact that Benedict had absolutely no troops of his own. Allen knew perfectly well that Arnold's authorization was far more legitimate than his own. Besides, he felt it might be wise to curry favor with the Massachusetts legislators for himself and the New Hampshire Grants. So instead of sending Benedict packing, he offered a shared command. Benedict bristled at this notion, but he finally agreed. Like the New Haven town elders who had given in to his demand for arms, Benedict had no choice.

The actual battle for Fort Ticonderoga was anticlimactic, to say the least. When Arnold, Allen, and the Green Mountain Boys attacked at four A.M. on May 10, 1775, only one sentry was awake and guarding the fort. This man saw the Americans swarming toward him, screamed for help, then turned and ran into the fort. A few minutes later Arnold and

Allen encountered Lieutenant Jocelyn Feltham at a second-floor doorway with his breeches in his hands. According to Feltham, Arnold's request for the surrender of the fort was delivered "in a genteel manner but without success."

When Allen realized Benedict wasn't talking to the commander of the fort, he shouted, "Come out of there, you damned old rat," and threatened to kill everyone in the fort if it wasn't surrendered immediately. Feltham stalled Arnold and Allen until a fully dressed Captain William Delaplace appeared and officially turned the fort and his forty-four soldiers over to the Americans.

The entire fight might have lasted ten minutes at most; the celebratory party that followed went on for several days. Allen encouraged his Boys to ransack the fort and stood by when they discovered a large supply of liquor and proceeded to become roaring drunk. Food, silver forks and spoons, clothing, and anything else that seemed valuable were appropriated by the Boys.

Ethan Allen did have the presence of mind to have the prisoners moved to Connecticut for detention and even sent a force of fifty men to capture another British fort at Crown Point (this one with only nine defenders). He then got as drunk as his men.

Benedict Arnold was appalled by this lack of proper military discipline. He complained loudly to Allen and to the Massachusetts Committee of Safety about Allen's "wild people," demanding that the drinking and plundering be stopped. Allen had had enough of his co-commander by this time and publicly rebuked Arnold, asserting that he (Allen) was taking back "the entire command." For several days Benedict tried his best to regain control of the situation but felt as if he'd been demoted to "a private person often insulted by [Allen] and his officers." Many of the Green Mountain Boys joined their commander in openly ridiculing Arnold. A few even threatened his life and took shots at him.

Arnold was not about to be driven off by a bunch of louts. He intended to stay in order to secure the seized cannons and arrange to have them taken to Boston. He also meant to assume sole command, and impose military discipline, at some point in the future.

That time came sooner than Arnold expected. In the days to follow, increasing numbers of Allen's Boys began drifting home, some claiming they had planting to do. At the same time, Arnold's recruits began showing up at the fort. By Sunday, May 14, Benedict had more volunteers than Allen at Ticonderoga, and he officially took complete command of the operations on Lake Champlain. Relieved of command, Allen was now the one to brood away the days in his tent.

Unlike Allen, Benedict Arnold did not allow himself or his men any time to celebrate or even rest. He immediately formulated a plan to invade Canada and attack a third British fort on the Richelieu River at St. Johns. Benedict knew from his Montreal merchant friends that there were only a handful of soldiers at the fort and that it contained additional military supplies. He sensed, too, that time was running out. Once word of the attacks on Ticonderoga and Crown Point reached the British in Canada, they would send down a large body of soldiers to secure Lake Champlain.

On May 16 Arnold and his small force set sail in a schooner recently seized from a wealthy Loyalist landholder and two bateaux—wide, flat-bottomed boats that had to be rowed or poled. Two days later Arnold's raiders surprised the thirteen men guarding the decaying fort. The defenders had heard of the capture of Ticonderoga and Crown Point, but they had such disdain for the amateur American forces that they hadn't bothered to tighten their own security.

In addition to the military supplies at the fort, Benedict's men took possession of a British sloop and five additional bateaux. To deprive the British of possible building materials, Benedict made certain that any vessels not fit for use were burned before he and his men retreated to the safety of Lake Champlain. Their haste to leave Canada was fueled by word that a relief force of redcoats was within ten miles of St. Johns and moving fast.

The capture of the three forts had a number of long-term results. Of the 201 artillery pieces seized at Ticonderoga, Crown Point, and St. Johns, Arnold managed to get 57 across the Berkshire Mountains and to George Washington in Boston. Once these guns were in position overlooking Boston, the British decided to evacuate the city. In March 1776 they retreated by ship to the safety of Nova Scotia, Canada.

A far more profound effect was felt in England. When word of Arnold's Canadian invasion reached King George and Parliament, they were flabbergasted. The Battles of Lexington and Concord and the subsequent siege of Boston could be viewed as the angry response of colonists who felt themselves attacked. But to take three British forts without provocation— one actually requiring the invasion of another country—suggested that the rebellious colonists intended total warfare. From this point on, the British focused less on negotiations and more on preparations for war.

As he and his men sailed from St. Johns with the captured ships and military supplies, Benedict knew that at least one other goal had been accomplished. The woods that surrounded Lake Champlain were so wild and tangled that no army, not even the vaunted British army, could march down through them and control the region. To take control, they would need at least one large vessel capable of carrying several cannons.

Since Arnold had the only large sailing vessels on the lake, the enemy would have to build new ones. This, he knew, would take months, by which time colder weather would make maneuvering on Lake Champlain impossible. Benedict was foresighted enough to understand that the raid on St. Johns had bought nine or ten months' breathing space in which to prepare for the British counterattack.

On the way home Arnold's men had an unexpected encounter. There, rowing toward them, were four bateaux loaded with Ethan Allen and his remaining Green Mountain Boys. They had been paddling furiously for nearly two days, hoping to catch up to Arnold's men and join in the action (and the pillaging they assumed would happen after a victory).

Considering the way he'd been treated, it would have been understandable if Benedict had sailed past Allen and left him to his fate. Instead, he graciously stopped to tell Allen about the advancing British troops and advise him to turn around. When Allen and his men decided to continue, Benedict even gave them fresh supplies.

Allen's expedition proved to be just as ineffectual as Benedict had anticipated. When Allen and his men arrived, Allen sent out scouts, who returned to tell him that a column of 200 redcoats was about to enter St. Johns. Instead of doing the wise thing and retreating, Allen ordered his men across the Richelieu River, where they set up camp and went to sleep. The next morning they received a rude wake-up call from the British in the form of cannon fire. Allen and his men staggered to their bateaux and somehow managed to escape, leaving behind most of their equipment and three men.

Allen never forgave Benedict for imposing on his command and even managed to lay the blame on Benedict for his, Allen's, near capture. He claimed that Arnold hadn't stressed the danger strongly enough, implying that Arnold had wanted him either killed or captured. Backing up Allen were his friends and fellow officers Edward Mott, James Easton, and John Brown.

Benedict Arnold had left his family and business to fight the British; he had no idea that his most vicious enemies were actually on the American side.

7

I HAVE RESIGNED MY COMMISSION

*I*n the weeks following the raid on St. Johns, Benedict kept himself and his troops busy. He oversaw the removal of the cannons to Boston, began repairing the barracks at Crown Point, and started construction of additional bateaux. He even went on a scouting mission after he learned from Montreal friends that Canadian governor Sir Guy Carleton was trying to get the locals there and the Caughnawaga Indians to help defend the city against a rebel attack. To Arnold's delight, he discovered little enthusiasm for the British among the mostly French citizens.

His contacts in Canada had told him something else as well. British forces in Canada were stretched thin and scattered all over the country. In other words, Canada was ripe for total invasion.

Benedict wasted no time at all. He put together a proposal to invade Canada and sent it off to the Second Continental Congress in Philadelphia. His plan was bold: American forces would seize Montreal first, then capture the forts at Chambly and St. Johns, ending with the taking of

Quebec, the capital of the country. He called for swift action and suggested that "on our arrival at [Montreal, the gates] will be opened by our friends there, in consequence of a plan for that purpose already entered into by them."

This action would require approximately 2,000 men, though Benedict stressed there should be "no Green Mountain Boys." He also proposed that he would be available to lead the expedition. This done, Arnold returned to readying Crown Point for the inevitable British attack.

Meanwhile, over in Massachusetts, regionalism, politics, and old-fashioned gossip were also at work.

Shortly after the victory at Ticonderoga, Ethan Allen prepared two military reports about the assault. In the first, which went to the Albany Committee of Correspondence, Allen boasted, "I took the fortress of Ticonderoga." He mentioned only in passing that "Colonel Arnold entered the fortress with me side by side." His second report went to the Massachusetts Provincial Congress and didn't mention Benedict at all. Allen claimed the victory for himself, adding that the Green Mountain Boys "behaved with . . . resistless fury." He also praised his second in command, James Easton, as well as John Brown.

Instead of sending his report by messenger, Allen had Easton deliver it to the Provincial Congress in person. Easton was the perfect choice. Shortly after the raid, Easton had approached Arnold and asked for a lieutenant colonel's commission in Benedict's regiment. Arnold turned him down, in part because he suspected Easton of plotting with Allen against him, and also because he felt Easton had acted in a cowardly fashion by hanging back during the attack. Easton could thus comment favorably on Allen's command and criticize Arnold at the same time.

Easton also delivered Edward Mott's report on the engagement, in which Mott had purposefully twisted the facts. Arnold, Mott claimed, had appeared only at the very last moment and taken command in a way that caused "mutiny among the soldiers which . . . nearly frustrated our whole design." It was only the calm intervention of both Allen and Easton, Mott insisted, that stopped the men from marching home. Mott also failed to mention that Benedict had taken part in the fight for Ticonderoga.

Benedict wrote his own report of Ticonderoga without knowing what Allen and Mott were up to. His report held to the facts of the situation, though he did claim to have been "the first person who entered and took possession of the fort." He then related how Mott had stripped him of command because he had tried to stop the "anarchy" and "plundering and destroying [of] private property" by Allen and his men after the British force had surrendered.

Arnold went on to say he would be happy to resign his command as long as it was done "honorably" so that "a proper person might be appointed" at Ticonderoga. Once again, Benedict demonstrated his heightened sense of honor and his eagerness to protect his good name from slander.

Benedict was a political amateur, at least when compared with Allen and his friends. He sent his report by regular messenger, which meant he had no one in Massachusetts to speak for him in person. And he followed strict military procedure by sending his report to the Committee of Safety, the group that had commissioned him in the first place. The Committee was a small part of the larger Provincial Congress. The Allen and Mott reports would be heard by the entire group, Benedict's by a select few.

This first round went to Allen. Easton's condemnation of Arnold as a troublemaker upset a great many delegates, some of whom wondered why his commission hadn't gone to an able Massachusetts Patriot instead of an outsider from Connecticut. The Massachusetts Provincial Congress voted to let Allen have sole command of Ticonderoga; it directed Benedict to concentrate his energies on getting the cannons to Boston. Benedict left no written record of his feelings, but we can assume he wasn't happy with the Provincial Congress's decision.

While this was taking place in Massachusetts, the Second Continental Congress in Philadelphia had a mixed response to the raids on Lake Champlain. A majority of the delegates, especially those from New York,

An etching of Benedict in civilian clothes, based on a drawing by Swiss artist Pierre Eugene Du Simitiere.
THE NEW YORK PUBLIC LIBRARY

New Jersey, and Pennsylvania, were still eager to resolve the differences with Great Britain. These were men of property who feared that without the stabilizing influence of the British military, a complete breakdown of social order was inevitable. In addition, they weren't at all certain that their ragtag American soldiers could stop the much-vaunted British army.

Most New England delegates, on the other hand, thought reconciliation with Britain was out of the question, especially after the unprovoked attacks on Lexington and Concord. A few even suggested that it was time to declare complete independence from England. The New England group wanted to send Allen and Arnold an official congratulatory message from Congress, but they were in the minority, and their suggestion was voted down.

When the more moderate delegates heard that Arnold had invaded Canada, they were outraged. They reasoned that if an agreement was ever going to be worked out between England and America, they would have to rein in such aggressive acts of rebellion. Instead of sending Allen and Arnold accolades, they voted to abandon the Champlain region entirely as a sign of their desire to settle the dispute peacefully.

Arnold reacted to the news by firing off a strongly worded letter to Congress in which he expressed dismay over the decision to abandon Ticonderoga. It was, he asserted, "the key of this extensive country, and if abandoned, leaves a very extensive frontier open to the ravages of the enemy." He mentioned that word had reached him that British troops were advancing on his position and suggested that the military importance of the region far outweighed any political problems that might result from holding on to it.

Ironically, he was backed in this view by the Massachusetts Provincial Congress. It sent its own separate note to the Continental Congress, stressing that holding the Champlain region insured an early alert for New England and New York against "all movements from Canada, . . . whether by scalping parties or large bodies [of troops]." The forts could also be used "if it should become necessary and just that the United Colonies should annoy the inhabitants of Canada."

Based largely on Arnold's letter, the Continental Congress reversed its decision regarding Ticonderoga. They also called on Connecticut to assemble "a strong reinforcement" and urged the colony's recently elected governor, Jonathan Trumbull, to "appoint a person, in whom he can confide, to command the forces at Crown Point and Ticonderoga."

Trumbull did not even consider giving the command to Arnold. He'd heard about Benedict's differences with Allen and Mott, and besides, Benedict lacked an influential sponsor in the Provincial Congress to back his candidacy. Trumbull chose a politically well-connected friend, Benjamin Hinman, to command the 1,000 Connecticut troops about to depart for Ticonderoga.

This was followed by yet another setback for Benedict. In June the Continental Congress reversed itself again and voted to launch an invasion of Canada. The Congress, though, had no interest in giving Benedict the command; they had heard from John Brown that Benedict was rash and a troublemaker. Instead, they appointed Major General Philip Schuyler, because he had experience in the French and Indian War and because he was a wealthy New York landholder and merchant.

More trouble for Benedict was stirred up by the Massachusetts Provincial Congress. Worried about the financial burden of maintaining Arnold's regiment on Lake Champlain, it sent a three-man delegation to observe him and his men firsthand. The delegation, headed by Walter Spooner, was instructed to determine "in what manner . . . Colonel Arnold has executed his . . . commission and instructions." They took this measure even though they had praised Arnold just weeks before, saying they had "the greatest confidence in your fidelity, knowledge, courage, and good conduct."

Benedict could have stayed on to lead his troops under the command of Benjamin Hinman, but this he found difficult to do. Both he and Hinman held the rank of colonel, but Benedict had been commissioned before Hinman and was thus considered higher ranking by the military. To accept Hinman as his superior officer might easily be interpreted as "a most disgraceful reflection on him and the body of troops he commands."

After thinking over the situation for a short time, Benedict "declared he would not be second in command to any person whatsoever . . . [and] resigned his post." He believed that his command in the Champlain region had been above reproach—that, in fact, he deserved praise and possibly advancement, but certainly not what he viewed as arbitrary demotion. "I have resigned my commission," he would explain, "not being able to hold it longer with honor."

Benedict had no intention of abandoning the American cause. He decided to journey to Albany, where Schuyler was organizing his invasion force, hoping to meet and gain favor with him. He left Crown Point on July 4, 1775, after receiving yet another bruising insult. The Spooner committee that had come to investigate Benedict appointed James Easton to lead Benedict's troops, with John Brown as second in command.

When he reached Albany, he was greeted by tragic news. His wife, Peggy, had died two weeks before of an unnamed fever. Three days after her death, his father-in-law, Samuel Mansfield, died as well. In a remarkably brief time two of the pillars of his life—his family and his honor—had suffered great harm. The question now was: Could Benedict Arnold come back once again?

8

OUR GALLANT COLONEL

After meeting briefly with General Philip Schuyler, Benedict returned to New Haven to be with his three sons and his sister, Hannah. He had often told Peggy that New Haven was his "safe, happy asylum" where "mutual love and friendship doubled our joys." But now everything was different. "How is the scene changed," he lamented to Hannah. "Every recollection of past happiness heightens my present grief."

Benedict did not wallow in his sorrow, however. He was a man of action and seemed to deal with distressing emotions by taking positive steps to correct—or at least block from his thoughts—whatever the problem might be. Besides, he had witnessed in his father what happened to an individual who allowed emotions to control his fate. He decided that the best way to overcome his personal sorrow was in "consideration of the public" cause.

As a first step he enlisted Hannah's help. He turned over the care of his children to her, and she promised to do her very best as surrogate mother.

Silas Deane was a fellow Connecticut merchant who championed Benedict's military career in the Continental Congress.

She also assumed full control of his numerous business dealings. Then Benedict headed for Massachusetts, where he had to settle his financial accounts with the Provincial Congress. He also hoped to meet with the commander of the American forces, George Washington.

Benedict had no idea that even as he traveled, his fortunes were beginning to change. Schuyler had been highly impressed by his meeting with Benedict and the verbal report he'd given on conditions at Ticonderoga and Crown Point. In addition, Schuyler had read about the young officer's command of the Champlain forces and how, despite a lack of money and supplies, he'd begun readying for a British counterattack. In comparison, the man who had replaced Arnold, Benjamin Hinman, was sending Schuyler one dispatch after another whining about the lack of money, ammunition, and other supplies, especially the lack of "rum and . . . molasses for beer." One unsettling message ended with Hinman confessing, "I find myself unable to steer in this stormy situation."

Schuyler sent off his own message to an important Connecticut congressional delegate, Silas Deane, asking, "Could you not get Arnold appointed Deputy Adjutant General in this department?" In this job Benedict would organize the day-to-day operations of Schuyler's Northern Army, recording and transmitting all orders, instructions, and assignments.

Schuyler could not propose Benedict's appointment himself. Representatives in Congress were extremely wary of the military and balked at any intrusion by senior officers in their affairs, one of which was the appointment of all high-ranking officers. They had witnessed the seizure of the Massachusetts government by the king's military representative and didn't want the same to happen to the fledgling American government. The appointment would never materialize, but Benedict had nonetheless found two powerful patrons in Schuyler and Deane.

Benedict's dealings with the Massachusetts Provincial Congress turned out to be a frustrating and insulting exercise. A committee of five, headed by Dr. Benjamin Church, was appointed to review Benedict's accounts and recommend a final settlement. Because the wording of the summons to appear suggested that Benedict owed the Provincial Congress money remaining from the £100 ($6,750) advanced him, Benedict sensed that the meeting would not be pleasant. So Benedict wrote out a detailed accounting of the money he had spent above and beyond

Major General Philip Schuyler, the commander of the Northern Army, was one of the first high-ranking officers to recognize Benedict's military talents.
THE LIBRARY OF CONGRESS

the tiny amount he'd been issued to keep his troops supplied. Not including his pay, he felt he was owed nearly £400 ($27,000).

The committee's function was to keep tight control of the cost of running a war, but the degree to which they quibbled with Arnold suggests another agenda. Church and the others on the committee questioned every one of Benedict's listed expenses and suggested several times that he was padding his account. They disallowed the £38 paid a wheelwright to build gun carriages to transport the captured cannons. They claimed that troops available at Ticonderoga should have done the work, even though none of these men had the necessary skills. They also refused to believe that Benedict had paid the sailing crews £100. Not only did they reject this claim, they sent an additional £100 to the very surprised sailors.

At one point the committee insisted Benedict would need to provide more convincing evidence if he expected to be reimbursed for the purchase of oxen, cows, sheep, and horses. When Benedict asked how he could accomplish this, the committee suggested he travel to Ticonderoga and ask James Easton for help. Benedict knew that Church and the others were taunting him because he had challenged the Spooner committee and humiliated Easton and called him a coward. Evidently, the arguments grew quite heated, mainly because Benedict was not shy about challenging their accusations and slurs. After nearly three weeks of haggling and insults, the committee rejected half of Arnold's claims for expenses.

Benedict's reaction to this was mild indeed. According to Silas Deane, Benedict was frustrated and angry at how he had been treated. But he did not issue any public statements of complaint, and instead he accepted the settlement quietly. It's very likely that Deane, who was in Cambridge inspecting the American troops, advised Benedict to hold his tongue. Deane did write to Philip Schuyler about how Benedict had been handled, saying "he has deserved much and received little, or less than nothing." He also suggested that Arnold submit his unpaid expenses to the Continental Congress, which after prodding from Deane finally agreed to consider reimbursing him.

Benedict prepared for his meeting with George Washington, and it went extremely well. The commander of the American forces was impressed by the young officer's energy and drive, his quick mind and attention to detail. In a letter to his cousin Lund Washington, the commander had called the New England officers in camp "the most indifferent kind of people I ever saw." No one would ever call Benedict mediocre in any respect.

Washington asked Arnold about the Champlain region and about the readiness of British forces in Canada. Benedict had been there as a trader and had received recent reports from Canadian friends who were sympathetic to the American cause. Washington was particularly grateful for Benedict's account of the remaining military supplies at Ticonderoga and Crown Point. Washington's own troops at Boston were down to nine rounds of powder and ball per man, so he immediately sent off a request to Ticonderoga for lead.

The two men also discussed the letter Benedict had sent Congress in

June about an invasion of Canada. It was during this talk that Benedict suggested that a second diversionary force might strike at Quebec by way of the Maine wilderness, thus compelling the British to divide their troops.

Washington liked the idea of such a two-pronged attack. He dispatched a rider with a letter for Schuyler asking what he thought about it and suggesting Arnold as commander of the second strike force. Schuyler was delighted by the news and with the choice of Benedict as commander, though he wisely suggested that Washington "be particular in your orders . . . that there may be no clashing should we join [forces]." As highly as Schuyler regarded Benedict, he wanted the command issue to be clear and in writing to avoid what had happened on Lake Champlain.

Schuyler's reply reached Washington on September 2. Shortly thereafter, Benedict received his commission as full colonel in the newly organized army, the Continental Line. Even before the official orders were drawn up, Benedict was at work pulling together his command. With the help of Adjutant General Horatio Gates and several other officers, he interviewed nearly 4,000 candidates searching for tall, physically fit men who could endure a grueling 350-mile march. He selected 786 soldiers, who were later joined by about 300 additional woodsmen from Virginia and Pennsylvania.

He also arranged to have nine ships available to transport his troops from Newburyport in Massachusetts to the Kennebec River in Maine. Two hundred bateaux had to be constructed for the water segment of the inland journey, and provisions gathered (forty-five days' worth of food per man). Native American scouts and backwoodsmen had to be interviewed about the terrain they would be covering, and officers had to be briefed.

Speed was essential. Washington, Schuyler, and Arnold knew it was imperative to capture either Montreal or Quebec, and ideally both, before winter. The majority of British troops in America were still bottled up in Boston; this meant that additional reinforcements wouldn't arrive from England until the spring of 1776. The Americans had until then to secure their hold on Canada and prepare to defend it.

Amazingly, Arnold had all his men marching out of Cambridge between September 11 and 13 and sailing to the Kennebec River on September 19. When he arrived at Gardinerston, Maine, Arnold discovered that the two hundred bateaux had been slapped together from green pine, which would begin to warp and leak once in the water. What's more, several of the craft were too small. Arnold insisted that twenty additional bateaux be made within three days. On September 23 the expedition was officially launched when two scouting parties were sent out to chart the initial phase of the march.

Arnold divided up his regiment into four divisions of roughly 250 men, each with its own commander. This arrangement would allow space between divisions and reduce backups at the many places where the bateaux had to be taken out of the water and carried, or portaged, upriver.

The first division to embark was the riflemen under the command of Daniel Morgan. These big backwoodsmen wore buckskin instead of military attire and carried long Pennsylvania rifles and scalping knives. The guns had already caused a stir among the British, because they were capable of hitting a man in the head from nearly half a mile away. One disgusted officer referred to them as "cursed twisted guns the worst widow-and orphan-makers in the world."

The remaining divisions followed, each leaving a day after the previous one. Going upriver, against the flow of the water, would be hard enough, but recent rains had created fast-moving, powerful currents. When the men came to the first series of rapids, they were confronted by eight miles of exposed rocks and surging water.

The men were eager volunteers, but most were not experienced woodsmen. Poling the heavy bateaux against the force of the water was grueling work; in places where the bottom scraped against rocks, the men had to leap out and haul their boats along with ropes. Frequently, they came to waterfalls or spots where the water was so shallow that the bateaux had to be carried to the next section of deep water. The procedure was the same at each such portage. The four-hundred-pound bateaux had to be emptied and hoisted onto the shoulders of four men. Groaning under the wet weight of the boats, the wood digging into their shoulders, the men struggled uphill along the thickly wooded dirt trails cut by the

Virginia's Daniel Morgan was an easy-going, skilled frontiersman who proved a valuable ally of Benedict's during the march to Quebec and later at the Battles of Saratoga.
THE LIBRARY OF CONGRESS

advance scouts. Teams of men trailed along with barrels and packages of provisions, plus rifles and ammunition.

Other things besides the terrain and inexperienced troops slowed the march. As feared, the poorly constructed bateaux began to warp and split along the seams. The barrels, also made of green wood, leaked brine meant to preserve salted meat. Much of the salt beef and cod, cornmeal, and flour spoiled and had to be thrown away.

Benedict was worried by the slow progress—they had covered only fifty miles in the first three days—and wrote to George Washington to explain the situation. "We have had a very fatiguing time," his report began. "The men in general, not understanding bateaux, have been obliged to wade and haul them for more than half way up the river." In a postscript he added, "You would have taken the men for amphibious animals, as they were [a] great part of the time under water. . . . The officers, volunteers and privates have in general acted with the greatest spirit and industry."

Which was true. The men had chosen to be there and knew it was going to be an arduous, even dangerous, journey before they left. The best way to get through the long, hard days was to maintain a sense of shared hardship, adventure, and excitement. During one twelve-mile portage at the Great Carrying Place, the men found themselves bogged down in mud. "We were half [a] leg deep in mud," wrote rifleman George Morison in the lead division, "stumbling over fallen logs, one leg sinking deeper in the mire than the other. . . . Down goes a boat and the carriers with it. A hearty laugh prevails."

Another important inspiration was Benedict Arnold. He seemed to be everywhere along the line of march. He rose before his troops each morning and helped scout advance positions and portage routes. He traveled downriver to encourage the weary or to solve problems. At one point scores of men—possibly as many as a hundred—fell ill from drinking tainted water, and Arnold was there to supervise setting up a hospital. Several days later a detachment of men wandered up the wrong branch of a stream and became lost. Benedict led the force to rescue the wet, bedraggled group.

Many commanders would have stayed at the rear of their troops, following along once a proper trail had been located and cut. But Benedict was always there with his men as they broke the trail, and they loved him for it. And no matter how bad the situation, Benedict always maintained a confident, encouraging attitude.

Still, forces were at work to further discourage and thwart the expedition. Cold weather arrived in early October, and snow began falling a

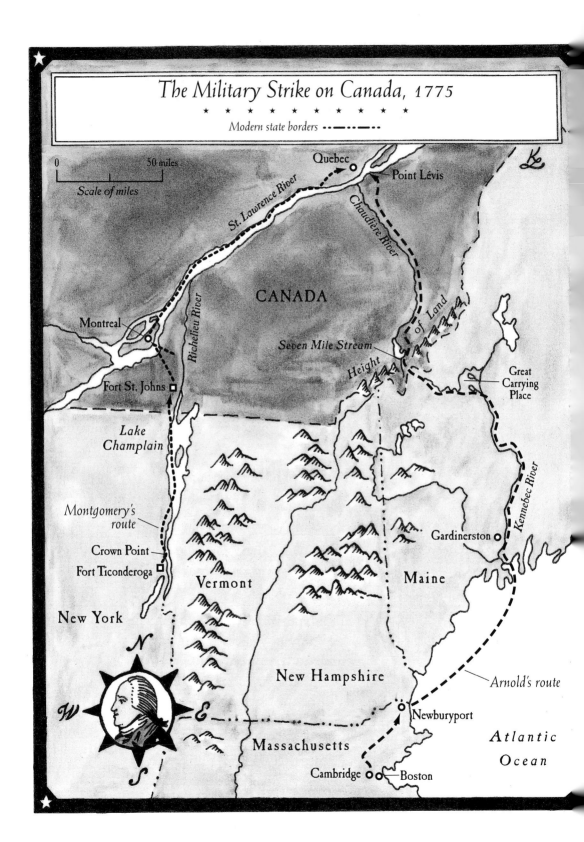

The Military Strike on Canada, 1775

★ ★ ★ ★ ★ ★ ★ ★ ★

Modern state borders ·–·–·–·–·

0   50 miles

Scale of miles

Quebec

Point Lévis

St. Lawrence River

Chaudière River

CANADA

Montreal

Richelieu River

of Land

Seven Mile Stream

Fort St. Johns

Height

Great
Carrying
Place

Lake
Champlain

Kennebec River

Montgomery's
route

Crown Point

Fort Ticonderoga

Vermont

Maine

Gardinerston

New York

N

New Hampshire

Arnold's route

W   E

Newburyport

S

Atlantic
Ocean

Massachusetts

Cambridge   Boston

week later. One shivering soldier recalled, "Our fatigue seemed daily to increase, but what we most dreaded was the frost and cold from which we began to suffer considerably." Benedict and his officers also began to notice something else disturbing. The physical features of the landscape they were struggling through often did not match what was on their maps.

The entire expedition had been planned around the 1760 journal and map of a British military engineer, Lieutenant John Montresor, who had made two trips from Quebec through the wilderness to the Maine coast. Before setting off up the Kennebec, Benedict had asked Samuel Goodrich, a surveyor from Gardinerston, if the journal and map could be made into a series of maps showing the precise route, plus charts indicating the depth and speed of the water. It turned out that Goodrich was a Loyalist. The surveyor made the maps as ordered, carefully showing incorrect routes and distances. After many missteps and costly delays, the deception was discovered and the maps discarded.

This was bad enough, but an even more devastating betrayal came from within Benedict's own troops. The freezing bad weather and snow persisted throughout October, and food supplies began to run desperately low. The second division had so little food that its commander had put his men on half rations of pork and flour. Then a storm blew in, flooding the river and damaging what few provisions were left. Dr. Isaac Senter noted that some men were so desperate to fill their bellies that they'd taken to eating candles. "Our provisions almost exhausted," Benedict wrote in his military diary, "we have but a melancholy prospect before us."

Some leaders would have reasoned that they had done their best against impossible odds and given up, but not Arnold. He organized two groups of men. One would head downstream to the fourth division, which had most of the available food. They would bring forward two weeks' worth of provisions and order all fit men to advance as quickly as possible. The other group, which Benedict planned to lead himself, would plunge ahead and locate the closest French settlement. They would purchase whatever supplies they could and then rush them back to the starving sol-

diers. "Our gallant colonel," George Morison wrote, "after admonishing us to persevere as we hitherto had done, set out with a guide for the inhabitants in order to hasten the return of provisions."

Benedict did not know it at the time, but two divisions were squabbling over the remaining provisions. Because of widespread illness among his men, the second division, under Colonel Christopher Greene, had dropped back and asked Colonel Roger Enos, leader of the fourth division, for supplies. Rather than sending food, Enos arrived with his officers for an unscheduled and unauthorized meeting. To Greene's dismay, Enos proposed that they ignore Arnold's orders to send forward fresh soldiers and supplies; instead, Enos suggested that both divisions retreat to Cambridge with all the food in their possession.

Greene and his officers voted to move forward as ordered, but Enos and his officers refused. Following a heated argument, Enos agreed to turn over some supplies before abandoning the march. The next day, when Greene's men went to collect food, they were given a paltry two and a half barrels of flour. After this, Enos and his division scurried back to safety, taking with them most of the regiment's provisions and three hundred healthy men.

Greene's men discovered one good thing about being abandoned with so little food. "We were sure to die if we attempted to return back," Captain Henry Dearborn wrote in his journal, "and we could be in no worse situation if we proceeded on our route." So onward the sick and weary men went, though first they mustered enough strength to say a prayer. It was, Dearborn recalled, "a general prayer, that Colonel Enos and all his men, might die by the way, or meet with some disaster, equal to the cowardly, dastardly, and unfriendly spirit [they had shown] in returning back without orders." Enos's actions, examined from any angle, were nothing short of treasonous, and the moment Enos arrived in camp, George Washington had him placed under arrest to await trial.

Heavy snow fell on October 25, accompanied by high winds. Arnold and his advance party were nearing the Height of Land, a mountainous Appalachian region that acted as a natural border between Maine and Canada. After a slippery two-day climb over icy boulders and down twisting, narrow trails, they reached Seven Mile Stream, a crooked, log-strewn route that passed through several dead-end bogs.

Benedict pushed his men hard, knowing that lives were at stake. One day they covered an incredible forty miles of rough terrain. Several days later, while on the Chaudière River, they had two bateaux shattered to pieces in a long set of rapids and very nearly went over a waterfall. On October 30 they reached the first settlement on the river; by the next

morning they were already moving provisions, including cattle, back to the starving men.

The division closest to them, the one under Daniel Morgan, had managed to survive the shortages. Morgan had put his men on half rations and had hunting parties out searching for game. The two divisions trailing Morgan, however, were suffering terribly. Private Simon Fobes noted that his fellow Patriots "were obliged, in order to sustain life, to eat their dogs, cartridge boxes, old shoes, and clothes."

Because the troops were starving, the idea of an orderly march was abandoned and every man was told "to do for himself as well as he could." Men began dying, but there was no time to bury them. Instead, leaves were tossed over the bodies, a few prayers mumbled, and on the survivors went. George Morison considered himself one of the stronger men, and yet he "staggered about like a drunken man."

On the morning of November 2, Private Caleb Haskell remembered, the men were "very much discouraged, having . . . no prospect of anything" to sustain them. Then, as Mattias Ogden recalled, some of the men in the lead thought they were seeing a mirage. It was "the finest sight my eyes ever beheld." Cattle were being driven toward them, and a number of birch-bark canoes appeared loaded with grain, mutton, tobacco, and other supplies. Benedict Arnold had gotten food to them in time to save hundreds of lives.

Benedict demanded a great deal of his soldiers, but he genuinely cared for them and often used his own money to provide them with the supplies that Congress did not. Many officers routinely paid for food or medicine for their men, with wealthier individuals, such as Benedict, spending more to keep troops marching and fighting. After Private John Joseph Henry collapsed with a fever, Benedict noticed him slumped at the side of a path. Henry was startled that his commander "knew my name and character, and good-naturedly inquired after my health." When Benedict learned how sick Henry was, he "ran down to the river side, and hailed the owner of the house which stood across the water." Benedict made arrangements for Henry's care and even gave him two silver dollars to pay for food and lodging. His small acts of compassion were noticed and appreciated by his men and made them willing to follow him into any situation.

Forty to fifty men died because of Enos's treachery, and their bodies were left to rot along the trail. Having made it back in time to save 650 of his men, Benedict allowed them just two days' rest before turning north again. His assignment was to attack and capture Quebec. He'd been given direct orders by George Washington, and Benedict was honor bound to obey those orders, no matter what the consequences.

9

THE FORLORN HOPE

*H*aving rescued his troops from starvation, Benedict urged them on toward the St. Lawrence River and their objective. On November 9, as they reached the southern bank of the river at Pointe Lévis, a swirling snow whipped their faces. Across the river and barely visible was a daunting three-hundred-foot-high cliff, with the walled city of Quebec on top.

Benedict would have organized an attack at that instant, but the wind was too strong and the waves too choppy for a safe water crossing. Besides, there were no boats to be seen on his side of the river.

The highest-ranking British official in Quebec at the time, Lieutenant Governor Hector Cramahe, had intercepted two of Arnold's letters to merchant friends in the city. The letters promised a rebel attack in the very near future and asked for any information that would aid Arnold's battle strategy. Cramahe had no military background, but he knew enough to take what steps he could to defend the city. He kept close watch on (and sometimes imprisoned) any merchants who might act as spies, had his 170

A view of Quebec from the south shore of the St. Lawrence River.
Benedict first saw Quebec from Point Levis, which is the tiny spit of land
just across from the city. COURTESY AMERICAN ANTIQUARIAN SOCIETY

troops, plus citizen-soldiers, on constant alert, and ordered the removal of all boats from the southern side of the river.

Luck was also with Cramahe. Just days before, the British frigate *Lizard* had arrived carrying arms, ammunition, and cash for the city's defense. Her twenty-six guns, added to the sixteen on a smaller ship already in port, would make any river crossing from the south a dangerous adventure.

In addition, one of Benedict's Native American couriers had been captured on the St. Lawrence River with a letter that suggested Arnold was poised to attack Quebec. A British officer, Lieutenant Colonel Allan Maclean, was then bringing a sizeable relief detachment from St. Johns to Quebec. When he learned that the Americans were about to attack, he pushed his troops on despite the cold and terrible weather.

It's very likely that if Benedict had been able to launch an attack a day or two after his arrival, Cramahe would have surrendered the city without much resistance. Not only did Cramahe lack the necessary military experience to mount a coordinated defense of the city, but the men he had were untrained and lacked discipline. Unfortunately, the stormy weather persisted, and Benedict was unable to take advantage of these weaknesses.

While Benedict waited for the weather to break, he had his men prepare for the upcoming battle. They scoured the riverbank for boats that might have escaped British eyes, eventually finding twenty boats, plus a dozen canoes. They made scaling ladders to climb the thirty-foot-high city walls and pikes to drive back any defenders. Finally, Benedict organized the men into attack units.

As Benedict was preparing for battle, events were taking place that, had he known, might have spurred the young commander to chance an attack regardless of the risk. Philip Schuyler, too, had experienced serious problems getting his main invasion force to Canada. His troops were mostly raw, untrained recruits, and they'd become ensnared in a lengthy siege at St. Johns. Schuyler himself had fallen ill with a ferocious case of gout, which forced him to return to Albany and turn his command over to Brigadier General Richard Montgomery.

After forty-two days the British finally surrendered the fort at St. Johns. Now nothing stood between the rebels and Montreal except 20 miles of forest. When word of St. Johns's fall reached Montreal, the governor of Canada, Guy Carleton, knew there was no way his

Brigadier General Richard Montgomery took command of American forces at Montreal after a painful attack of gout forced Philip Schuyler to return home.

small detachment (which numbered under 200) could resist 2,000 American invaders. On November 11 Carleton and his troops fled Montreal for Quebec.

Benedict had no idea that both Maclean and Carleton were rushing to Quebec. Had he known, he might have urged an immediate attack and taken Quebec, trapping Carleton between two American forces and securing all of Canada for America. Instead, he continued preparations, all the time hoping that the wretched weather would break. While he waited, Maclean and his relief column slipped into Quebec undetected on November 12.

The governor of Canada, Guy Carleton, proved to be a shrewd and formidable opponent of Montgomery and Arnold.
THE LIBRARY OF CONGRESS

Later that same night an impatient Benedict called his officers together. He ordered them to ready the troops to cross the river under cover of darkness sometime in the next forty-eight hours. However, the balance of power had shifted. He had approximately 600 healthy men available for the attack, while Cramahe and Maclean had more than 1,100 ready to defend the city.

At nine P.M. the following day, November 13, the first wave of Benedict's troops pushed off from the southern shoreline, their canoes and boats pointed toward Wolfe's Cove. Benedict had chosen to follow the route used by General James Wolfe in 1759, when he conquered the city in the French and Indian War. From Wolfe's Cove Benedict's men would scramble up the steep embankment and onto the Plains of Abraham, just west of the Upper Town.

On November 14 Benedict had his men march to within three hundred yards of the walls of the Upper Town. There they gave a series of loud cheers in the name of the Revolution and liberty and let loose sporadic musket fire at those on the walls. Benedict hoped that this show of strength would convince Cramahe to surrender, and indeed the lieutenant governor was nervous enough to consider the possibility. But the veteran Maclean laughed off the American performance and fired several rounds of artillery until the rebels withdrew from the field. Maclean knew his his-

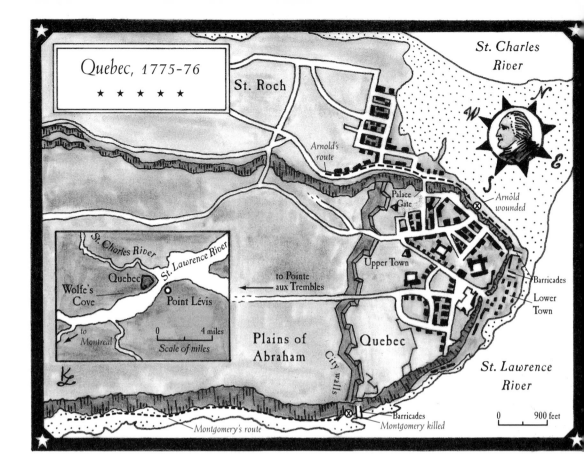

Quebec, 1775–76

★ ★ ★ ★ ★

St. Charles River

St. Roch

Arnold's route

Palace Gate

Arnold wounded

Upper Town

St. Charles River

St. Lawrence River

Quebec

Wolfe's Cove

Point Lévis

to Montreal

0   4 miles
Scale of miles

to Pointe aux Trembles

Barricades

Lower Town

Plains of Abraham

City walls

Quebec

St. Lawrence River

Barricades
Montgomery killed

Montgomery's route

0   900 feet

tory as well as Benedict. He had no intention of making the same mistake French Canadian governor Montcalm had made in 1759, when he had marched his troops out to meet Wolfe's challenge and had been soundly defeated.

For the next five days Benedict challenged and taunted Cramahe to come out and fight, at one time sending him a written message saying the cannon fire was "contrary to humanity and the laws of nations" and unbecoming of Cramahe's "honor and valor." Maclean knew better than to be provoked by such bombast. He had plenty of food and ammunition (thanks to the timely arrival of the *Lizard*), and enough soldiers to defend the sprawling city walls. If the rebels wanted the city, they would have to fight and die for it.

Then on November 18 Benedict had some unsettling news. He learned that Maclean was already inside Quebec and that Carleton was on the way with additional soldiers. He also received a depressing report on his weapons inventory. He already knew that they had only a few pieces of light artillery and no bayonets. The new report told him that many of the men's muskets had been ruined or lost during the long march through the wilderness, and that each man had on average only five rounds of ammunition.

After consulting with his senior officers, Benedict did what he thought was most prudent for his troops and the American cause. He withdrew twenty miles to the hillside village of Pointe aux Trembles (today called Neuville). There he would wait for Montgomery's arrival and allow his exhausted troops to rest and locate supplies. Despite his unpleasant run-in with the Massachusetts Provincial Congress over expenses, he still had all costs over and above the regimental cash charged to his own personal accounts with local merchants. He did this, he said, out of compassion for his "brave men . . . who were in want of everything but stout hearts."

The storm that had delayed and frustrated Benedict had done the same to Guy Carleton. His fleet was bobbing helplessly in the water on November 15 when Benedict's old regiment from Ticonderoga, under the command of Colonel James Easton and Major John Brown, attacked and appeared to have the British bottled up. But Guy Carleton was every bit as resourceful and tenacious as Benedict and refused to believe he was trapped. The next night the governor—dressed as a common citizen, complete with wool cap—slipped over the side of his flagship and into a whaleboat. The crew used their hands to paddle the boat as quietly as possible and slipped past the American blockade. Carleton made it to Quebec on November 19 and took charge of the city's defense.

Carleton was not just another British bureaucrat. He had served under James Wolfe when Quebec was taken from the French in 1759, receiving a head wound during the climactic battle and achieving the rank of major general. As Benedict had done, Carleton immediately asked for a report on available troops and supplies. He had approximately 1,800 men under arms, though half of them were untrained local inhabitants, plus enough provisions to survive an eight-month siege. There were some shortages, he discovered, chiefly of firewood, oats, and hay.

Carleton was typically decisive and stern. According to his orders, every piece of available wood inside the town (chairs, tables, cabinets, and even brooms) was to be used for fuel, while any horses, cattle, and other animals that starved to death were to be tossed over the walls before they rotted. Carleton, his soldiers, and all the citizens were going to stay put for the winter and wait for reinforcements to come in the spring.

After taking Montreal, Montgomery hastened to reorganize his exhausted troops and get a strong force to Quebec. On November 28 he set sail with 300 men, picking up 360 additional men along the way. When he met up with Benedict on December 1, American troop strength stood at 1,325 (700 fewer than Benedict had suggested for taking Quebec).

With Benedict's help, Montgomery began to plan and prepare for an attack. One step in these preparations was to lay siege to the town, chiefly by harassing the inhabitants with artillery and sniper fire. The aim was to keep citizens and soldiers on edge and nervous, wearing them down physically and emotionally and possibly convincing them to surrender.

Rebel cannon fire turned out to be sadly ineffective. The few pieces of artillery they had were of small caliber and barely chipped away at the ten-foot-thick walls. "Their shot had no more effect upon our walls," recalled Customs Collector Thomas Ainslie, "than peas would have against a plank."

Daniel Morgan's sharpshooters had a much more devastating effect, picking off several British sentries and prompting a worried Ainslie to call them "worse than savages." Continued sniping might have worn away at the spirit of resistance, but both Montgomery and Benedict knew that time was quickly running out for the Americans. Diseases such as smallpox and dysentery were beginning to diminish troop strength, as were desertions. Even more problematic, many enlistments would run out come January 1, and these men would probably head home despite the harm this might do to the assault and the Revolution.

Montgomery's original plan called for the main body of rebels to attack the Upper Town on the first overcast night in December. A night sky without stars or the moon would allow his army to move about in the dark undetected. After two rebel soldiers deserted, Montgomery decided to focus on a different area. The new plan called for Montgomery and Benedict to attack the Lower Town from two different directions. Once they had possession of the Lower Town, they would join forces and storm the Upper Town. As a way to confuse and divert British forces, two other smaller groups of men would strike at different gates into the town. Once the details had been settled, Benedict and the rest of the army waited for a cloudy night.

Carleton also waited. He'd been alerted to the rebel preparations and, knowing enlistments were about to expire, assumed any assault would be made before the end of the year. From Christmas on, he slept in his uniform, and when a snowstorm struck at sunset on Saturday, December 30, he sensed the attack was imminent.

After midnight, in the early hours of December 31, the American troops moved out into the raging storm. By four A.M. Benedict had his 600 soldiers in position at St. Roch, waiting for the signal to move forward.

Benedict had asked for 25 volunteers—whom he dubbed the "Forlorn Hope" because of the great odds they faced—to follow him to the first barricade. They were to act as an advance party, clearing out any defenders who might be stationed outside the walls and making a trail through the deep snow for the rest of the men to follow.

Benedict was not the sort of officer to hang back at a safe distance while his men went into a dangerous situation. Even when he rose in rank to general, he always took the field with them, in part because he needed to see the developing battle firsthand but also to inspire them. On this stormy night it was Benedict who was out front breaking the trail. He made it through the Palace Gate and paused when he heard a jumble of sounds through the howling wind—the booming of a cannon, the clang of warning bells, the frenzied barking of dogs. That would be one of the diversionary forces striking.

British soldiers withstanding the charge of Benedict's men at the second barricade.
THE LIBRARY OF CONGRESS

Several hundred feet farther on, he drew near the first of two barricades. He stopped to allow the men of the "Forlorn Hope" to assemble and ordered that their small cannon be brought forward. The cannon would fire a six-pound ball at the wooden barrier, punching a hole in it big enough to get several men through.

While they were waiting for the cannon to be positioned, the snow slashing at their faces, the barricade erupted with a blaze of musket fire. One ball sliced into Benedict's left leg. The physician who removed the ball described later what he thought had happened. A musket ball had struck "a cannon, rock, stone or the like" and splintered into several jagged pieces, the biggest one entering "the outer side of the leg, about midway" between the knee and ankle, before angling down and lodging "at the rise of the tendon Achilles." The pain was excruciating, and when Benedict tried to put weight on his left foot, he nearly fell over. Blood began to fill his boot, and a searing pain spread from his leg to his torso. He was fighting to stay conscious, but even so, as Private Henry recollected, Benedict "called to the troops in a cheering voice . . . urging us forward."

Daniel Morgan appeared at Benedict's side to tell him the rest of the artillery was stuck in the deep snow and then noticed his colonel's shattered leg. Benedict protested that he wanted to continue leading the charge, but he was already in shock and unable to stand without support. Morgan ordered one of his riflemen and the regimental chaplain to carry Benedict back to the field hospital for treatment.

Then Morgan resumed the attack, easily breaking through the first barrier. He was halted temporarily at the second barrier, when a cannon blast caused him to topple off a ladder and hit the ground so hard that he lost consciousness. But a few moments later he was up the ladder again, this time literally tossing himself over the top of the barricade and onto a platform that held two cannons. His men followed him over, and the defenders surrendered instantly.

Morgan was all for taking Benedict's detachment into the Upper Town, but his officers refused. Their orders were to wait for Montgomery, they insisted. Besides, they had over two hundred prisoners who might overcome their guards and block their retreat. Much against his will, Morgan agreed to wait.

Montgomery, meanwhile, had also gotten through his first barricade and cautiously approached the second. No defenders seemed to be around, so Montgomery sawed through the log posts of the second barrier, climbed through the opening, and approached a two-story-tall log building just beyond. A few men inside the house had panicked when the Americans first appeared but had decided to put up a token defense before retreating.

Montgomery inched up to the building and raised his sword to call for a charge, when suddenly wooden trapdoors were flung open and four cannons fired simultaneously. Flying pieces of metal took off Montgomery's head, killing him instantly, along with two other officers and six men as well. Those who survived the blast fled the barricade and the walled town.

Governor Carleton had responded to the onslaught like the veteran soldier he was. When he learned where the main attacks were taking place, he dispatched two forces to circle behind the rebels and close off their escape routes. Because Montgomery's forces had already fled the city, this meant that Benedict's troops under Morgan were outnumbered and trapped in the narrow streets of the Lower Town by two columns of soldiers. Legend has it that Morgan vowed he would never surrender his sword to the British and slashed away at the enemy until a minister approached him. He could surrender his sword to him, the preacher suggested, thereby saving his honor and his life. Reluctantly, Morgan agreed.

When Benedict learned of the outcome, the magnitude of the defeat shocked him: fifty-one Patriots killed, thirty-six wounded, with two thirds of his column captured. Carleton had only seven men killed and eleven wounded. Lying in his hospital bed, his leg throbbing with pain, Benedict was heartsick over the drubbing the American attack force had taken and the precarious position they found themselves in. A less dedicated commander might have pulled his men back to a safer location, or even withdrawn entirely from Quebec and hightailed it to the safety of Montreal. Benedict did neither. He had promised Washington and Schuyler that he would take Quebec, and he had no intention of going back on his word. Nor would he abandon the brave men being held captive in the walled city. Instead, from his sickbed he ordered a defensive line established near the hospital and laid siege to Quebec.

This was sheer bravado, of course. What with those captured, wounded, or ill, plus dozens of others leaving camp as their enlistments ran out, Benedict had only a few hundred healthy men left under his command. Carleton could have swept them away with ease, but he was nervous enough to hesitate. In the days ahead, Benedict kept repositioning the few troops he had, so that Carleton was never sure of how many men he really faced. "Had the enemy improved their advantage," Benedict

wrote to Washington two weeks later, "our affairs here must have been entirely ruined."

His doctor advised Benedict that it would take two months of quiet bed rest for his leg to properly heal. Even in pain and bedridden, Benedict was planning his next attack. He wrote to Washington and Congress, asking for 3,000 men for a proper siege, 5,000 if another assault was to be attempted. He knew full well that he would be lucky to get a fraction of those numbers, so he stepped up the recruitment of French Canadians eager to shake off the British. He also asked Congress for "an experienced general" to take charge of the Quebec campaign and suggested Major General Charles Lee for the task. Lee had been a British officer during the French and Indian War and was considered by many as the most gifted general in the army. Benedict was certain that Lee was an aggressive enough soldier to carry out his plan to take the walled city.

In letters he pleaded with the new commander at Montreal, Brigadier General David Wooster, for aid. "For God's sake," he urged, "order as many men down as you can possibly spare, consistent with the safety of Montreal, and all the mortars, howitzers and shells that you can possibly bring." Some of this message's urgency came from his frustration with being wounded and from the lack of support he had received from Congress. But it also reflected his clear-eyed appraisal of the military situation. He knew there was no time to delay and rest. Quebec had to be taken by mid-March at the latest so they could prepare to defend it against the expected British reinforcements that would certainly arrive by late April or early May.

For once, Congress responded quickly, ordering an additional 6,500 men to be recruited and sent to Canada. This was a positive step, but Benedict knew it would be weeks, if not months, before the entire number was assembled and properly trained. Unfortunately, Congress did not send money to pay the soldiers and did not appoint a new commander.

Benedict still felt the need for a more experienced commander to take charge of the Quebec forces, so he asked that Wooster take personal command at Quebec. Assuming Wooster would respond quickly, Benedict set about drawing up detailed plans for another assault. A key feature of this new attack would be the elimination of the six British warships in the harbor (four more had arrived at the close of November). This would be accomplished in the spring by sailing two burning ships loaded with explosives into the middle of the anchored vessels, blowing them and their crews out of the water. Benedict volunteered to use one of his own ships, the *Peggy*, that happened to have been stranded in Quebec when hostilities began.

Benedict kept his ragtag little army together through a bitter, snow-filled winter, using his own money to buy food and clothing for them. He had them harassing the town to keep Carleton and his troops on edge; he kept drilling them so they would be ready when his hoped-for attack took place. At the end of January he began hobbling painfully around the rooms of the hospital. "I have no thoughts of leaving this proud town until I first enter it in triumph," he wrote to Wooster. "I know no fear."

Wooster's responses to Benedict's pleas were slow in coming and vague in nature. He sent along a small contingent of men toward the end of January but did not accompany them himself. As the cold winter days dragged along, Benedict had the feeling that a prime opportunity was about to slip from their grasp.

When early spring arrived, more and more reinforcements from the New England colonies began drifting into camp. As March came to a close, the number of soldiers under Benedict had reached 2,505. This was only half the number Benedict felt was necessary for a successful assault (and at least 786 of these were ill with smallpox). Yet Wooster still did not appear. Benedict did his best to organize and prepare these new recruits for battle, but he was already losing hope that anything could be done in time. Finally, on April 1, Wooster showed up in camp and assumed command.

Brigadier General David Wooster was many years past his prime as a military man, gruff, short-tempered, and prone to drink. He had been lavish with praise for Benedict during the winter, but now as he inspected the rebel lines and artillery placements, he did nothing but criticize what he saw. After the inspection Wooster pointedly ignored Benedict and did not even ask what Benedict's plan of attack was. It's entirely possible that Wooster decided to snub Benedict after hearing that Benedict's first choice for commander had been Lee and not him.

Benedict slipped quietly out of camp on April 12. "Had I been able to take an active part," he wrote Philip Schuyler, "I should by no means have left the camp, but as General Wooster did not think proper to consult me in any of his matters, I was convinced I should be of more service [in Montreal] than in camp." He had absolutely no faith that Wooster would succeed in taking Quebec, and yet he did not challenge the man directly or complain. He had promised George Washington that he wouldn't argue with officers of higher rank, and he was determined to honor his word.

Even so, his fortunes were on the rise. His march to Quebec, his wounding during a gallant assault, his continued siege of the walled city despite impossible odds, had members of Congress calling him a "genius" and a "brave friend." George Washington proclaimed, "The merit of this gentleman is certainly great [and] I heartily wish that fortune may distinguish him as one of her favorites." As a reward, Congress elevated him from colonel to brigadier general.

Benedict had gone to Canada looking for military glory and come away a hero. Despite this acknowledgment of his military skill, despite the luster this added to the Arnold name, he rode to Montreal with a new and depressing thought on his mind: retreat.

10

HE WILL TURN OUT A GREAT MAN

etreat was not a concept that came easily to Benedict Arnold. Once committed to a plan, he would pursue his goal with unrelenting and, some would say, stubborn energy.

But he also had a very rational, realistic side. It was obvious to him that there were not enough troops at Quebec to successfully capture the town, and that Wooster didn't have the inner fortitude to either organize an assault or overcome the obstacles facing him. Withdrawal from Quebec and probably from Canada was inevitable.

Still, Benedict went out of his way to avoid faulting Wooster in any of his official reports. He respected the older man's previous military service, and he did not want to criticize a senior officer. Wooster was also the leader of the New Haven Masonic Lodge, and Benedict certainly didn't want to fix blame on a fellow Mason. But in a letter to Schuyler he expressed the real source of his frustrations. "I cannot help lamenting that more effectual measures have not been adopted to secure this country

Another English portrait of Arnold, this time wearing his brigadier general's uniform.
THE LIBRARY OF CONGRESS

[Canada] in our interest," he confided to Schuyler. While he did not name the culprit in this letter, Schuyler knew he was referring to Congress and the inadequate way it had been providing men and supplies for the army.

Fearing that its own military might set up a dictatorship if it wasn't constantly watched, Congress had held on to as much control of military affairs as possible, from the appointment of officers to the length and number of enlistments to the actual appropriation and spending of money. There were good reasons for such extreme caution; Britain's own history was filled with instances when the military had backed one or another individual and used force to keep him in power. While Benedict was aware of this background, he also knew as a businessman and as a field officer that this sort of constant scrutiny was often inefficient. In his opinion, those fighting the battles should have at their instant disposal the men, money, and arms needed to defeat the enemy. Instead, an elaborate and time-consuming system had been put in place by Congress to insure that nonmilitary people maintained control. If Benedict needed additional supplies or men, he had to submit requests to his immediate commander, who then submitted them to Congress, who then had to submit them to the individual states where the soldiers would be coming from; the state representatives, far removed from the action, would then study and debate the requests. This lengthy chain of examination caused dangerous delays and often led to shortsighted decisions based on local needs. It was not at all unusual, for instance, for a state to be asked to raise 1,000 troops for the Continental Army but then to withhold one quarter or more of those men for home defense.

Benedict Arnold was not the only officer to feel that Congress and its self-protective rules were hindering the Revolution. George Washington chafed under, and often fumed with anger about, the constraints imposed on him. He managed to avoid confronting Congress head-on and alienating it; instead, he used his connections in Congress to get most of what he needed. Benedict, on the other hand, lacked Washington's iron self-control and political contacts, and what he viewed as congressional neglect and incompetence ate away at him.

A glimmer of hope came his way at the end of April, when a three-man congressional commission, headed by a very spry seventy-year-old Benjamin Franklin, arrived. The commissioners' task was to assess the Canadian campaign and send recommendations to Congress. If they saw a need, they were also empowered to issue direct orders to the officers in charge to effect immediate results.

Far from being the overbearing, quarrelsome bully he is often portrayed as, Benedict received the commission gracefully and explained the military situation and needs in a straightforward, convincing way.

The commission agreed completely with Benedict's suggestions that various American positions be strengthened in the hope of holding Montreal and preventing a British invasion down Lake Champlain. One member, Charles Carroll, was so impressed by Benedict's military skills that he wrote: "An officer bred up at [the French king's palace of] Versailles could not have behaved with more delicacy, ease, and good breeding." He added, "Believe me, if this war continues, and Arnold should not be [killed] pretty early, he will turn out a great man. He has great vivacity, perseverance, resources, intrepidity, and a cool judgment."

The commission's resolve to hold on to Montreal evaporated seven days later when the first part of the British relief force landed at Quebec. Acting with unusual speed, Britain had assembled an army of over 8,000 men—British soldiers and hired soldiers from Germany, known as Hessians—and sailed through a particularly stormy winter in the North Atlantic. The commander of this massive force was the young, dashing Major General John Burgoyne. Governor Carleton was the ranking officer, however, and he took charge of the men and began marching up the St. Lawrence. His objective: to sweep the annoying rebels out of Canada.

Benedict's predictions about Wooster and the American forces at Quebec proved to be sadly correct. The rebel army fell back in "the most irregular, *belter skelter* manner," as an army physician noted. In fairness to Wooster it should be noted that a third to one half of his men were still unable to take the field, either because they lacked ammunition and food or because they were ill with smallpox. Even so, he was relieved of his command.

After a relief force arrived from Albany, led by Major General John Thomas, the American forces continued to retreat in disarray. Thomas attempted to slow the British, and even exploded Benedict's powder-packed ship in a futile attempt to destroy British warships. Nothing worked, and a halfhearted battle at Deschambault ended with his losing 600 men, killed or captured.

Benedict was under no real obligation to supply direct aid to the retreating American forces. He could have sat in Montreal, strengthening fortifications in preparation for the British onslaught or planning his own retreat. But the more he learned about the rout downriver, the more convinced he became that a stand had to be made, if for no other reason than to give rebel troops breathing space to organize a proper retreat.

Benedict was granted permission by Franklin's congressional commission to rush a force down the St. Lawrence River. They intercepted Thomas at Sorel, some one hundred miles from Quebec. "Most of our troops . . . are naked," Benedict reported. Many of these men literally stumbled into town, weakened by days of forced marching, lack of food, and the effects of smallpox.

While at Sorel, Benedict heard more disturbing news. Approximately 300 British regulars, Canadian volunteers, and Native Americans were marching on the fort at the Cedars, after which it was assumed they would

strike at Montreal. A second dispatch had even worse news: The commander of the American forces at the Cedars had panicked and abandoned his men, and they had been captured.

Benedict's reaction was immediate and decisive. He rounded up 150 soldiers and headed south to Lachine to engage the enemy. Along the way he recruited volunteers, so by the time he arrived, his troop strength had risen to 450.

Benedict wanted to launch a surprise attack on the British, but his officers refused, saying they preferred to wait for the enemy behind the protection of their fortifications. While Benedict could have overruled them and ordered the charge, he didn't. He needed his officers and the men they commanded united and with him when the time to fight did come, so he did not argue with them or try to force his opinion on them. However, the British never attacked. They had received wildly inflated reports of the strength of Benedict's troops coming toward them and had fled the scene during the night.

Benedict rallied his men and chased after the fleeing British troops, who were slowed by having to guard so many prisoners. When the enemy made camp at Fort Anne, Benedict once again urged an attack, and once again his officers declined. One officer in particular, Colonel Moses Hazen, criticized Benedict's plan as foolishly reckless, predicting it would surely result in the massacre of the prisoners. After four companies of soldiers from Pennsylvania sided with Hazen, all the frustrations of the campaign must have come to the surface for the young American commander. Tempers flared, and both men employed what another officer described quaintly as "some reproachful language." The officers still refused to attack, and Hazen, feeling that he had been maliciously insulted, became another one of Benedict's enemies.

Still, Benedict had no intention of withdrawing without a fight. Fortunately, the British force at Fort Anne decided it did not want to take on the Americans trailing it. So their commander, Captain George Forster, offered a prisoner exchange and suggested a six-day ceasefire, during which time he planned to pull back to a safer position and wait for reinforcements. Benedict accepted the proposal, then rode hard to Sorel, hoping that enough troops—and officers willing to take action—had arrived by then.

What he learned must have been extremely dispiriting. According to Franklin's commission, the soldiers straggling in lacked "most necessary articles—meat, bread, tents, shoes, stockings, shirts, etc." The army was "broken and disheartened, half of it under [smallpox] inoculation or under other diseases, soldiers without pay, without discipline, and altogether reduced to live hand to mouth." Canada was lost, and Benedict knew it. "I wish with all my heart we were out of the country," he wrote to the commission on June 2, then added, "We had much better begin anew, and set out right and methodically."

On the same day Benedict wrote this, Major General John Sullivan ar-

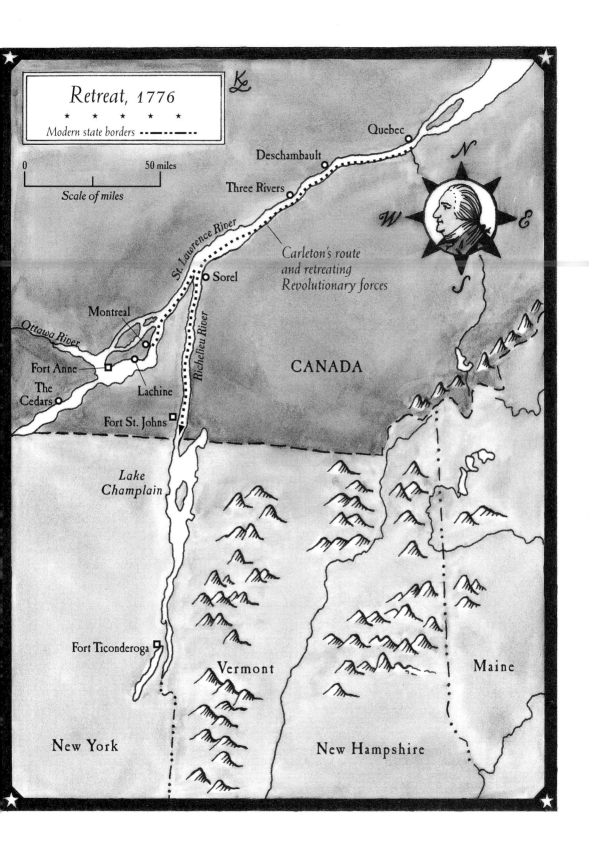

Retreat, 1776

★ ★ ★ ★ ★

Modern state borders ▪—▪—▪—▪

0   50 miles

Scale of miles

Quebec

Deschambault

Three Rivers

St. Lawrence River

N

W   E

S

*Carleton's route
and retreating
Revolutionary forces*

Sorel

Richelieu River

Montreal

Ottawa River

CANADA

Fort Anne

The
Cedars

Lachine

Fort St. Johns

Lake
Champlain

Fort Ticonderoga

Vermont

Maine

New York

New Hampshire

rived to take command of the Canadian expedition. Sullivan was vain and headstrong and was sure that all the Continental troops in Canada needed was his stern leadership. Despite Benedict's warnings, Sullivan launched a counterstrike at Three Rivers (Trois Rivières) and saw 200 of his men killed and another 200 captured. "There will be more honor in making a safe retreat than hazarding a battle against such superiority," Benedict advised Sullivan when they met again after the crushing defeat at Three Rivers. Humiliated, Sullivan agreed to a full retreat of Revolutionary forces.

By agreement Sullivan took most of the remaining soldiers, plus artillery and other supplies, up the Richelieu River and back to Fort Ticonderoga. Benedict lingered behind with a small detachment to burn anything that might be of use to the British. At St. Johns Benedict shot his horse and ordered his aide, Lieutenant Colonel James Wilkinson, to do the same. Then Benedict launched the boat that would take him to Lake Champlain and hopped aboard, the very last American to escape as British troops poured into town.

In the days and weeks following the retreat, a personal and political war began to take shape. Sullivan prepared a lengthy report for General Schuyler, in which he tried to throw off any blame for what had happened in Canada. "The grand post was lost before my arrival, and put beyond my power to regain," he wrote his commander. He never named Benedict, but his meaning couldn't be missed. In addition, Sullivan claimed "no merit, except in making a safe and regular retreat," failing entirely to say that it was Benedict who had planned the army's withdrawal and carried out the most dangerous part of it.

Meanwhile, Moses Hazen, James Easton, and John Brown all left the area of battle and hurried to Philadelphia, where Congress met. There they lobbied for investigations and court-martial hearings into Benedict's conduct and their own. Benedict was 250 miles away on Lake Champlain, preparing for the British invasion, and could not appear to defend himself, so the three men pleaded their cases while vilifying him unmercifully. They criticized his command decisions and his abrupt manner of issuing orders, and even suggested—contrary to fact—that he had stolen supplies and resold them at a handsome profit. Among the character witnesses to back these false claims was at least one relative of Ethan Allen.

The judges in all three proceedings were New England men who'd heard stories about Benedict from Ethan Allen and were not favorably disposed toward him. In one case a junior officer who testified against Hazen had all his testimony summarily thrown out. Even though the judges had been prejudiced, the verdicts were still a shock to observers. Hazen, Easton, and Brown were either acquitted of the charges against them or received promotions in rank and back pay.

Benedict was outraged by what Congress had done. Not only did he consider the verdicts travesties of justice, each one was an implicit condemnation of his command and, worse, a slap at his good name.

He did have some supporters. Lieutenant Colonel James Wilkinson saw rank jealousy of Benedict on the part of the judges. "Is it for men, who can't boast more than an easy enjoyment of the Continental provision," Wilkinson wrote immediately after the hearings, "to blast the reputation of [Arnold], who having encountered the greatest perils . . . fought and bled in a cause which they have only encumbered?" General Gates was even blunter in his criticism of the congressional hearings. "I am astonished at the calumnies that go to Congress against General Arnold," he told General Schuyler, "and more astonished they should be one moment attended to." He closed with this thought: "To be a man of honor, and in an exalted station, will ever excite the envy in the mean and undeserving."

All charges of wrongdoing against Benedict were eventually dismissed, and Gates elevated him to commander of the Patriot fleet on Lake Champlain. Still, his sense of betrayal and bruised honor persisted. "I cannot but think it extremely cruel," he wrote to Gates, "when I have sacrificed my ease, health, and a great part of my private property, in the cause of my country, to be calumniated as a robber and thief—at a time, too, when I have it not in my power to be heard in my own defense."

11

THE GALLANT DEFENSE

hile others were in Philadelphia plotting against Benedict (and doing little of real value to help the Revolution), he was on Lake Champlain preparing for battle. He knew perfectly well that the survival of the American Revolution was at stake.

The 11,000 troops under British general Sir William Howe had withdrawn from Boston in March 1776, largely because the big guns Benedict had sent from Ticonderoga had convinced them they would be obliterated if they stayed. When they sailed off, it was assumed they would eventually head for New York, the largest port in America and still in Loyalist hands. Military logic also suggested that the British forces in Canada would march south, take Albany, and then continue down the Hudson to join the British forces in New York. Such a pincer move would divide the area of rebellion in half and allow the British to disrupt the shipment of military supplies and reinforcements between the southern and northern colonies.

When Gates penned his official orders making Benedict commander of the Champlain fleet, he told him expressly that they were now fighting a defensive war. "No wanton risk or unnecessary display of the power of the fleet is at any time to influence your conduct," the orders stated, adding that no American ship should sail beyond Isle aux Têtes, which was just above the New York–Canadian border. Gates didn't want to lose any vessels in a risky attack on the more experienced British fleet.

The idea that there was an American "fleet" was a sad joke. Benedict felt he needed at least thirty ships to adequately defend the lake, but at no time did he have more than seventeen (of which nine were flat-bottomed, single-masted craft, called gundalows, which were extremely hard to maneuver). The lack of ships, however, wasn't Benedict's biggest problem. His supply of powder and ball was so low that one lengthy battle would exhaust his arsenal completely. Worse still, he had few trained shipwrights to build additional ships or repair those he had, and virtually none of his 670 men were experienced seamen.

Against him the British were amassing a fleet of thirty vessels, each well armed and supplied, and manned by almost 1,700 battle-hardened sailors eager to take on the impudent rebels. Even Benedict, who never backed away from a fight, knew that once Carleton transported his fleet over the ten miles of shallow rapids of the Richelieu River, he would be free to blast the puny American fleet from the lake.

To prepare for the British attack, Benedict kept crews working long into the night building and repairing boats. He drilled his men on handling the vessels on the choppy lake waters and on the tricky business of loading, aiming, and firing cannons from a moving deck. Benedict's energy and spirit were felt everywhere, as he limped about on his still-painful leg to supervise and instruct his troops.

Despite his outward display of optimism, he must often have despaired of ever being able to mount a creditable defense. In early August, for instance, the gundalow *Providence* was practicing firing its cannons when greenhorn Solomon Dyer rammed powder down the barrel of a recently fired gun. Dyer had failed to sponge out the barrel properly, so it was still white-hot, and the fresh powder exploded the instant it came in contact with the interior. The young man, who was "standing before the mouth of the cannon," had his hands blown off and "the sponge rod . . . went through the left part of his body at the root of his arm [and] blew him overboard." Despite this catastrophe and many other difficulties, Benedict went out of his way to encourage his officers and men. He even went so far as to boast that once he had adequately trained his men, he would attack St. Johns.

A number of officers, especially those who supported Moses Hazen, immediately condemned this idea. Here was another instance, they complained to friends in Congress, where Benedict Arnold was going to put their lives in jeopardy for his own glory. What none of them realized was that Benedict's bluster was part of an elaborate plan.

The British troops were still under Guy Carleton's command. Carleton, while a competent military leader, had shown himself to be a surprisingly cautious commander at Quebec. He had stayed safely behind the city's walls through the winter and early spring even though his forces outnumbered Benedict's. Even after thousands of British reinforcements arrived, Carleton had moved slowly and deliberately.

Benedict sensed he could play on his opponent's overly cautious nature. With Gates's approval, Benedict maintained an openly aggressive tone while going through camp, assuming spies would take word back to Carleton. If Carleton believed the rebels were putting together a fleet strong enough to initiate an attack, he might delay his own assault until he had brought his forces up to maximum strength. A delay of a few weeks might allow the winter weather to close in and stall Carleton until spring—during which time American reinforcements could be brought in to defend Ticonderoga and cities to the south.

Benedict knew that strong talk would hold back a veteran like Carleton for only so long. To convince the British commander that he would face strong opposition, Benedict decided to make a show of naval force. He prepared to sail his fleet up the lake at the end of August.

While preparations were being made and even after he sailed, Benedict bombarded his sympathetic superior, Horatio Gates, with requests for supplies and experienced men. Gates replied to each requisition as patiently as he could, telling his anxious young commander that he would send along everything requested just as soon as Congress sent it to him.

Benedict had already felt Congress's neglect as commander in Quebec and its disdain for him in exonerating Hazen, Easton, and Brown, whom he considered little better than liars and traitors. His annoyance with Congress was compounded when he learned that it had also praised and promoted John Sullivan, the foolish and arrogant officer who had ignored Benedict's advice and attacked a clearly superior British force.

Benedict could not understand—and would never understand—how this body of representatives failed over and over to provide adequate supplies to its army, or why it accepted the word of corrupt, self-serving individuals over his. He was actually on Lake Champlain, nervously anticipating a British attack, when he finally let his frustration show. "I hope to be excused," he wrote to Gates, "if with 500 men, half naked, I should not be able to beat the enemy with 7,000 men, well clothed, and a naval force . . . near equal to ours." The failure to take and hold Canada, Benedict was saying, and to adequately arm and feed the army, rested on the shoulders of Congress alone. "I am surprised at their strange economy or infatuation below [in Philadelphia]," he went on. "Saving and negligence, I am afraid, will ruin us at last." Benedict's belief that Congress was a fair-minded and patriotic body, that it had the best interests of the country and its army in mind, would continue to deteriorate over the months and years ahead.

When he penned his angry words about Congress, Benedict was aboard a ship ironically named the *Congress,* which was anchored on the southern side of Valcour Island. During his scouting of the lake, Benedict had spotted the heavily wooded two-mile-long island and noted its military advantage immediately. A half-mile-wide harbor was tucked in behind the island and completely shielded on the north by a tall ridge. He could, he realized, hide his entire fleet there from approaching British ships.

Snow began falling in September, and by October 10 the surrounding mountains were completely white. At last, Benedict had reason to be optimistic. A week more of the cold, snowy weather and Carleton wouldn't be able to sail against him until the following April. Even the wind had cooperated, blowing from the south so strongly that no British ship could make headway against it.

But then on October 11 the wind shifted, and the British fleet set sail.

When Benedict learned this, he called a hasty council of war aboard his ship and asked his senior officers for suggestions. General David Waterbury, his second in command, advised that the American fleet sail immediately for Ticonderoga and make its stand there. Waterbury feared that otherwise they might be trapped behind Valcour Island.

Benedict thought this option undesirable. He wasn't certain they could outrun the British to Ticonderoga. And because his little fleet lacked quick, maneuverable ships to shield the slower boats, he worried that the British could swoop down and pick them apart with ease. Instead of fleeing, he told his officers, they would stay tightly packed in the harbor and wait for the British to sail past them. Then, when the enemy finally spotted them and began turning to sail back against the wind, the American ships would sail out and open fire.

Just after nine o'clock in the morning the British fleet was spotted. An additional four hundred Native American warriors, under the direction of Carleton's younger brother, were trailing the warships in birch-bark canoes.

Once again luck seemed to ride Benedict's shoulders. Carleton had turned command of the fleet over to a young, zealous naval officer, Captain Thomas Pringle. Pringle had dismissed the rebel sailors as inept and called Arnold "a horse jockey." He was so eager to take them on that he had all sails set to take full advantage of the strong northerly wind. In fact, his ships moved so quickly that he couldn't even send scouting vessels ahead to locate the enemy fleet.

At ten o'clock the lead British vessels sailed past the southern tip of Valcour Island, completely oblivious of the American ships there. It took nearly an hour before they realized their mistake and began to come about into the wind. At this point, Benedict ordered the *Congress* and three other ships to sail out to engage the enemy. The four vessels rushed toward the slowly turning British ships and began firing cannons at them. The enemy quickly responded with shots of their own.

Then Benedict ordered his ships to return to the harbor and rejoin the closely arrayed line for the battle. Such a formation would give the Americans a formidable wall of cannons to bombard the enemy. One American ship, the *Royal Savage,* had its rigging shot up and one of its masts badly damaged, and finally ran aground near the southern tip of the island. Its gunners kept up a lively fire until enemy gunboats maneuvered into range and blasted away at the helpless ship. Finally, the crew and captain abandoned the *Royal Savage* and took small boats to the rebel fleet, with only a few casualties.

The smaller British gunboats were able to come about and move within firing distance of the American fleet, but only one of the larger enemy ships, the *Carleton,* was able to maneuver into the battle line. The *Carleton* and the swarming gunboats then opened fire. "The engagement," Benedict would later write to Gates, "became general, and very warm." The booming roar of cannon fire echoed off the steep banks of the island as a choking cloud of acrid white smoke enveloped both lines of vessels.

Benedict moved about his ship as quickly as his leg allowed him, encouraging the men and even "point[ing] most of the guns on board the *Congress*" for his inexperienced artillery crews. Soon his face and uniform were covered in black soot from the spent gunpowder.

As the battle stretched into the afternoon, Benedict noticed that redcoats and their Native American allies had landed on the island. Others were moving down the western shoreline of the bay as well. Musket fire and arrows were soon pouring in on the American ships, but Benedict had anticipated this development and wisely positioned his fleet far enough from the shore to minimize the damage. He had also had his men tie thick bundles of sticks, called fascines, around each ship to form a five-foot-tall fence that protected them from enemy shots and arrows.

British and American ships firing at each other during the Battle of Valcour Island.
FORT TICONDEROGA MUSEUM

Still, casualties began to mount on both sides. Aboard the *Carleton* the captain was knocked senseless by a large piece of flying debris, while her second in command lost a hand to a cannonball. On the American side every officer except the captain aboard the gundalow *New York* was wounded, while a lieutenant on the row galley *Washington* was killed and its captain and first mate severely injured.

The damage inflicted on both fleets was severe. British and American ships had rigging swept away and masts splintered. A cannonball found its way into the powder magazine of a Hessian-manned gunboat and caused an ear-shattering explosion that sank the craft. Meanwhile, the *Carleton* took several hits below the water line and suddenly lurched and rolled, as if it might sink at any minute. Benedict's ship was hit over a dozen times and was taking on water as well. Four American gundalows were barely afloat (one would sink an hour after the fighting ceased), every row galley except one was shot up badly, and the *Royal Savage* had been set on fire by a detachment of enemy marines.

Despite the damaged and bloodied decks, amid the chaos and confusion of guns firing and orders being screamed, the battle raged on until about five o'clock in the afternoon. Then once again luck was with Benedict. The British ships began to run low on ammunition just as darkness descended on the bay. They backed off from the American fleet, indicating that the fight was over for the day.

Benedict and his men had fought a superior force to a virtual standstill, but they were still in grave danger. The British fleet—including its big, heavily armed ships—was now lined up at the mouth of the bay and waiting for the morning to finish off the crippled rebel ships. Valcour Island and the New York shoreline swarmed with enemy soldiers and Native American warriors. Not only were the Americans surrounded, but a quick inventory told Benedict his ships were almost out of ammunition.

Benedict knew that if they stayed in the bay until morning, they would either have to surrender to the British or stand and fight and be annihilated. He chose a third option—to make a run for it.

Wounded crew members were taken below decks so the British wouldn't hear their moans. All lamps were extinguished except for a tiny light at the stern of each ship. Oars were muffled to silence the creaking of wood on wood. And once again fortune smiled on Benedict as a thick fog rolled in to conceal their movements. Single file, each boat following the dim stern light ahead, the American ships were gently rowed out of Valcour Bay and past the British fleet. Benedict Arnold in his battered flagship, the *Congress*, was the last to leave.

It wasn't until eight o'clock in the morning, when the fog lifted, that a dumbfounded Carleton beheld an empty body of water in front of him. Furious, he ordered Pringle to get his ships under full sail to hunt down the rebels. Eight miles south, Benedict and his captains were hastily patching holes, mending sails, and fixing masts on the vessels deemed salvageable. The three that were beyond repair were set on fire to keep them out of British hands. It was vital, Benedict stressed, that what remained of the fleet make it to Ticonderoga, some thirty-five miles away. To ensure this would happen, Benedict assigned the *Congress* and Waterbury's ship, the *Washington,* to perform rear-guard duty.

For the rest of the day and through the night, both fleets made slow progress as squalls of rain and sleet pounded them from the south. On the morning of October 13 the wind shifted, and a northeast breeze filled the sails of Carleton's ships. The wind had not yet reached Benedict's little fleet when he realized the enemy was closing fast. He would have to do something dramatic or lose his entire fleet.

Waterbury was so alarmed by the fast-approaching enemy ships that he asked if he could run his badly damaged row galley ashore and strike his colors (lower his flags), signaling that he intended to surrender. Benedict refused this request and ordered him to stand and fight. Waterbury maneuvered about, but as thirteen-year-old American seaman Pascal De Angelis later testified, "after four or five shots from the [British ship], the *Washington* galley struck [their colors and surrendered] without firing one gun, General Waterbury being on board."

Benedict could have used the loss of the *Washington* as an excuse to strike his own colors, but he didn't. He had promised to delay the British, and that is exactly what he intended to do.

Three enemy ships converged on the *Congress* and began pounding away at her. "Two [were] under our stern," Benedict would report later, "and one on our broadside, within musket shot." The British ships had five times the firepower of Benedict's, but still Benedict's men stayed at their guns, returning fire for two straight hours. By two o'clock "the sails, rigging, and hull of the *Congress* were shattered and torn to pieces" and the ship was listing badly. Four more British ships arrived and joined in what can only be described as a slaughter. Still, Benedict would not give up the

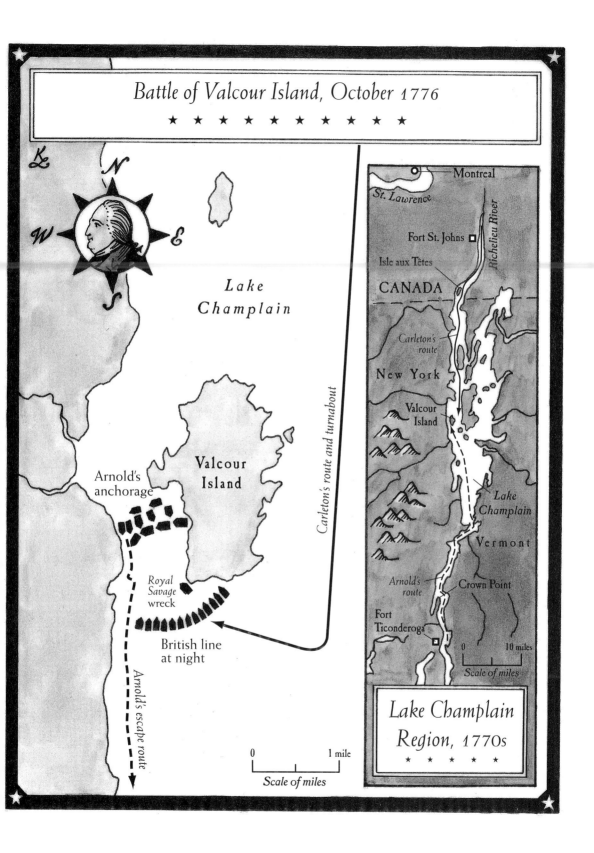

Battle of Valcour Island, October 1776

★ ★ ★ ★ ★ ★ ★ ★ ★ ★ ★

Lake Champlain

Carleton's route and turnabout

Valcour Island

Arnold's anchorage

Royal Savage wreck

British line at night

Arnold's escape route

0   1 mile
Scale of miles

Montreal

St. Lawrence

Richelieu River

Fort St. Johns ▫

Isle aux Têtes

CANADA

Carleton's route

New York

Valcour Island

Lake Champlain

Vermont

Arnold's route

Crown Point

Fort Ticonderoga ▫

0   10 miles
Scale of miles

Lake Champlain Region, 1770s

★ ★ ★ ★ ★

fight. Every minute he delayed the British was additional time for the rest of his fleet to escape.

During the entire battle three American gundalows had hovered in the water near the *Congress.* The British never bothered with them, hoping to bombard the *Congress* and its commander into submission. They had no idea just how tenacious and clever Benedict Arnold could be. Even as the end was drawing near for his ship, Benedict was searching for another miraculous escape. He saw his opportunity on the eastern shore of the lake and immediately ordered what was left of his crew to their oars. The *Congress* lurched forward, followed by the three gundalows. With the men paddling furiously, musket and cannon fire flying at them, the four vessels once again managed to slip between the British ships.

The startled British did not dare follow, not knowing how deep the water near shore was. With the enemy still lobbing shots at them, Benedict was able to run all his vessels aground. He got the injured safely ashore and set his ships on fire, refusing to the very end to strike his flag in surrender.

Benedict then shepherded his surviving crew members past British land patrols and rejoined his six remaining ships as they retreated to Ticonderoga. He was greeted there warmly by Gates, who praised him lavishly. Gates publicly thanked "General Arnold, and the officers, seamen, and marines of the fleet for the gallant defense they made against the great superiority of the enemy's force. Such magnanimous behavior will establish the fame of American arms throughout the globe." In addition to remaining commander of the rebel fleet, Benedict was assigned to command the advance fortifications to the north of the fort, the spot where the British were expected to launch their assault. This unusual double command was clear proof that Gates was very pleased with what Benedict had accomplished.

Aside from a brief and feeble cannon barrage, the British never attacked. Carleton was still wary enough of what remained of the American fleet that he did little but cruise the lake through the rest of October and negotiate a prisoner exchange. He would write the head of the king's cabinet, Lord George Sackville Germain, to explain that while they had defeated the enemy fleet, "[the] season is so far advanced that I cannot yet pretend to inform your lordship whether anything further can be done this year." Carleton began withdrawing his forces at the beginning of November to spend the winter in Canada, feeling he had done everything he could.

For Carleton the victory was clear. He had killed or wounded 80 rebels, captured another 120, and destroyed eleven of their seventeen ships. To his superiors in London, however, it was anything but a victory. While the Americans no longer controlled the lake, they were still at Fort Ticonderoga and able to prepare a stiff defense against any future invasion. Carleton would eventually be knighted for his defiant stand against the rebel invaders at Quebec. But he was also relieved of his command duties, which were handed over to General John Burgoyne.

In fact, Benedict Arnold came in for greater praise in England than Carleton. He had, a noted British journal reported, "not only acted the part of a brave soldier, but . . . also amply filled that of an able naval commander." Not even "the most experienced seamen could have found a greater variety of resources . . . to compensate for the want of force, than he did." Benedict had "raised his character still higher than it was before with his countrymen."

12

BY HEAVENS I WILL HAVE JUSTICE

While Benedict and the Northern Army had managed to hold the British in check, things were going very badly to the south, where George Washington had the main Patriot army. As expected, British ships of war began to appear off Staten Island, New York, in late June 1776, under the command of General William Howe. By August the British had 32,000 men under arms, supported by a fleet of 30 warships with 1,200 guns and over 15,000 sailors. It was the largest British invasion force ever assembled.

Against this formidable army George Washington had at most 19,000 troops on Manhattan Island and at Brooklyn Heights, with only a few pieces of light artillery and no naval support. His men were poorly armed, equipped, and trained, and few had any real experience in battle. This same sort of amateur army had humiliated the British in Boston, mainly because they held strong defensive positions on high ground. On New York's relatively flat, exposed terrain, the rebel army didn't stand a chance.

Washington personally directed the retreat from Brooklyn. His army would eventually be driven from Manhattan Island and forced to march to Pennsylvania to avoid complete annihilation. THE BROOKLYN HISTORICAL SOCIETY

In late August the British began a carefully planned and executed attack that drove American troops off Brooklyn Heights and up Manhattan Island to Harlem Heights, and eventually sent them retreating into New Jersey. What remained of Washington's army scampered south through New Jersey in November, littering the countryside with discarded guns, ammunition pouches, cooking kettles, and exhausted soldiers. By the time they made it to the safety of Pennsylvania, Washington had only 3,400 men left under his command.

With one more concerted attack Howe very likely could have wiped out Washington's bedraggled army and pretty much ended the rebellion. Instead of an offensive action, Howe decided to go into winter quarters, believing he could easily crush whatever was left of the rebels in the spring of 1777. Washington, however, had no intention of calling it quits for the winter. He planned a bold attack on British forces in New Jersey and called on both General Horatio Gates and General Charles Lee to hurry their troops to unite with his.

Gates and Lee knew that Washington's army—and the Revolution—hung in the balance, yet they procrastinated in moving troops to Washington's aid. Both Gates and Lee thought Washington was an inept bungler and should be relieved of command; each man felt that he would make a better commander of all American forces. Lee even went so far as to write to Gates criticizing Washington. "A certain great man is damnably deficient," Lee wrote, adding that Washington's poor generalship had "unhinged the goodly fabric we had been building." When Washington asked, then ordered, both generals to move their men south to him, neither budged. Gates and Lee saw in the rout of Washington's troops a chance for their own personal advancement, even if withholding support put the Revolution in jeopardy.

In any light, their refusal to follow the direct commands of a superior officer would have been enough to initiate court-martial proceedings. Though George Washington was furious with them, neither was ever disciplined for insubordination. Both had strong political supporters in

Congress who agreed with their appraisals of Washington and would battle any attempt to punish them. More important, Gates and Lee were among the few trained and experienced military men in the American army. Many in Congress were willing to put up with their dangerous antics because they did not want to see qualified leaders from other states (such as Benedict Arnold) promoted to fill their places.

Initially, Horatio Gates worked very well with Benedict, but Gates resented Washington's friendship with Arnold and eventually turned against them both.

Charles Lee might have kept his troops out indefinitely, except that on December 13 (twenty-two days after being first ordered to bring his men south) he blundered and was captured by the British. Major General John Sullivan took command of Lee's 2,000 men and had them across the Delaware in three days.

As for Horatio Gates, he eventually arrived in camp, and he immediately objected to Washington's plan to counterattack. Gates urged his commander to retreat farther into Pennsylvania, and when Washington made it clear that he intended to launch an offensive operation, Gates once again abandoned him. This time he claimed he was too ill to join in the surprise attack. He then left camp without authorization and went to Baltimore, where the Continental Congress had relocated itself temporarily. While there he managed, despite his "illness," to attend a number of parties and dinners where he lobbied to replace Philip Schuyler as head of the Northern Army.

Gates was up to more than just self-promotion. In the pocket he carried a petition written by Benedict Arnold's avowed enemy John Brown, and Gates presented this document to Congress. In the petition Brown listed thirteen alleged "crimes" committed by Arnold and urged Congress to arrest and court-martial him. Brown also included the names of witnesses to Arnold's "unjustifiable, false, wicked, and malicious accusation" that Brown had stolen property while serving under Ethan Allen. The witnesses included himself, Moses Hazen, James Easton, and all the officers who had turned Hazen's court-martial into a mockery.

Gates never revealed why he turned on his junior officer. He had never questioned Benedict's character or his military decisions before this (and had, in fact been lavish in his praise). It seems likely that Gates had grown envious of the great acclaim Benedict was suddenly receiving for his valiant defense of Lake Champlain.

Brown and Gates weren't the only Patriots to attack Benedict. Brigadier General William Maxwell wrote to the governor of New Jersey, William Livingston, condemning Benedict as "our evil genius to the north" who had foolishly gotten the American fleet destroyed. Maxwell was a retired British officer who habitually attacked his more celebrated fellow officers and younger officers who were promoted ahead of him. Benedict, unfortunately, fell into both categories. Maxwell claimed that the American fleet was larger than the British fleet (which wasn't true), that Benedict's desperate fighting was of no strategic value to the forces at Ticonderoga (also not true), and that Benedict had violated Gates's orders by sailing so far north and bragging that he intended to attack St. Johns (both incorrect and showing that Maxwell had no knowledge of the overall plan devised by Gates and Benedict).

Maxwell's comments eventually reached Congress, where they were echoed by two other officers. David Waterbury, worried that he would be condemned for surrendering his ship so quickly, wrote to John Hancock, the president of Congress, griping that Benedict had made his retreat "as fast as [he] could, and left me in the rear, to fall into the enemy's hands." Benedict's own aide, James Wilkinson, chimed in as well. In August, while still on Benedict's staff, he had praised his commander effusively and condemned those who were trying to blacken his name. When he jumped to Gates's staff in the autumn of 1776, his tune changed abruptly. Benedict's defense of Lake Champlain had occurred because of an "excess of rashness and folly" in order "to exalt his character for animal courage, on the blood of men equally brave."

Finally, a Virginia congressman, Richard Henry Lee, condemned Benedict in a letter to Thomas Jefferson as having acted in a "fiery, hot, and impetuous" way in his naval battles on Lake Champlain. This was a curious shift for Lee; just ten days before, he had praised Benedict and his officers and men because they had "bravely maintained the unequal contest, conducting themselves with valor."

In a matter of days Benedict's actions on Lake Champlain had been transformed from a heroic stand against superior odds into dangerous, useless, self-aggrandizing glory hunting. Because Benedict wasn't there in person, and because he had few political supporters in Congress, the backstabbing went on unchecked, gathering momentum as the days went along.

Where was Benedict? When the British on Lake Champlain had withdrawn to winter quarters, Benedict decided to return to New Haven. He had been away from home for over sixteen straight months, during which time he'd been severely wounded. He needed to rest his body and mind, and to become reacquainted with his young sons. His namesake, Benedict, was nearly nine years old, Richard was seven, and Harry a very lively four. He worried that they had grown so much, he wouldn't recognize them.

His sister, Hannah, had done everything in her power to keep his business going, selling just about every item in the store. British warships had effectively blockaded the coast, making it impossible for Benedict's ships to sail to his commercial contacts in the West Indies. Without an inventory of goods to sell, Hannah had to inform Benedict, prospects were gloomy. "If you ever live to return," she wrote him bluntly, "you will find yourself a broken merchant."

Benedict had made it as far as Albany when he learned of Washington's defeat in New York and his narrow escape through New Jersey. Instead of going home, Benedict rode south immediately, managing to pass the slow-moving Horatio Gates and reaching Washington's headquarters on December 21.

Benedict had a brief meeting with Washington, during which he offered some positive advice on the upcoming counterattack on British positions in New Jersey. He probably also offered to stay and help, but the commander in chief had other plans for him. The British had landed 7,000 troops in Rhode Island, and Washington wanted his young commander to hurry there and prepare to defend that colony. Benedict set out immediately, stopping for less than a week in New Haven.

While many in Congress felt that Benedict was a reckless commander, Washington saw his military decisions as levelheaded and cautiously aggressive. An indication of his confidence in Benedict can be found in Washington's orders to General Joseph Spencer, the aging and somewhat inactive commander in Rhode Island. Spencer outranked Benedict, but Washington pointedly instructed Spencer that he was to "cooperate with" Benedict rather than direct him.

The military situation in Rhode Island might have been much worse if the British had taken the initiative. They captured Newport and the surrounding territory very easily, but then the commander of the British there, General Henry Clinton, called a halt to operations for the winter.

Benedict's instinct was to attack Newport and drive the enemy from the state. He was bolstered in this plan by the stunning success Washington had in striking at Trenton (on December 26) and then Princeton (January 2), catching the British completely unprepared. Unfortunately, Benedict had only 5,000 men in camp, almost all of them raw recruits. His plan to assault Newport was finally dropped when it became clear that very few additional citizens were volunteering for the fight.

It seemed that enthusiasm for the Revolution had faded. The running battles at Concord and Lexington, and the Battle of Bunker Hill, had bolstered Patriot passions and prompted many to enlist in 1775. But the arrival of Howe's massive invasion force and the crushing defeat in New York had taken the edge off the average citizen's desire to fight. Not even Washington's victories in New Jersey drew in many new recruits. It seemed that the Revolution might be defeated not because of British military might but because of a lack of patriotic enthusiasm.

When the year ended and enlistments ran out, soldiers headed home in droves. Washington went into winter quarters in Morristown, New Jersey, with only 1,400 men, almost half of them ill and unable to serve. Benedict's troops also withered away. Even when the Rhode Island Assembly chastised Spencer and Benedict for leaving the British "long unmolested" and ordered them "to attack . . . immediately," Benedict prudently refused to fight until his troop strength was adequate.

This didn't mean Benedict had no battles to wage early in 1777. His adversaries, though, were people on his side of the conflict.

In January of 1777 George Washington sent a message to Congress asking that additional officers be appointed to the army. He assumed that with the Revolution on the brink of collapse, seniority and merit would be the criteria for promotion. Politics, regionalism, and cronyism, he hoped, would be put aside, at least until the current crisis had passed. Without doubt Benedict had proven himself a superior commander on both land and water and should have been promoted to major general. Instead, Congress passed over him completely in favor of five less senior officers.

Washington was shocked and embarrassed when he learned this. Of the five men made major generals, only one, William Alexander (who claimed to be a British earl and so called himself Lord Stirling), had served with any distinction. The others were mediocre officers at best, and Washington knew that Benedict would take their promotions as a direct insult. He was fearful that Benedict would summarily resign his commission in the army and head home, just as many others had done before him. He knew, too, that Benedict would be absolutely justified if he decided to leave.

Washington's first response was to write a soothing note to Benedict, telling him he hoped he had been "omitted through some mistake" and suggesting that he shouldn't take any "hasty steps in consequence of it; but allow proper time for recollection, which, I flatter myself, will remedy any error that may have been made." He immediately began working behind the scenes to get Congress to right the wrong. In a letter to Richard Henry Lee he was more direct and forceful than usual with a congressman: "I could wish to see Arnold promoted to the rank of major general," he told

Lee, adding that he also wanted Benedict to have seniority over the officers recently elevated to that rank. "It is by men of [Arnold's] activity and spirit the cause is to be supported."

Next, George Washington wrote again to Benedict, thanking him for staying at his assigned post and mentioning that he had asked General Nathanael Greene to find out why Benedict hadn't been promoted. Greene reported to Washington that he was told it was because Connecticut already had two major generals. "I confess this is a strange mode of reasoning," Washington admitted in a follow-up letter to Benedict, but "it may serve to show you, that the promotion which was due to your seniority, was not overlooked for want of merit in you."

Unfortunately, Benedict had also learned about John Brown's petition (though not that Gates had been the one to deliver it) and saw a direct link between the false charges and his failure to be promoted. In his reply to Washington, Benedict promised not to leave his position while the enemy was near, but added that "in justice, therefore, to my own character, and for the satisfaction of my friends," he couldn't continue to hold his commission without "a court of inquiry into my conduct."

Benedict was even blunter in a letter to Horatio Gates. "I am conscious of committing no crime since in the public service that merits disgrace, except it be a crime to have sacrificed my interest, ease, and happiness in the public cause." He then proclaimed, "By heavens I will have justice, and I'm a villain if I seek not a brave revenge for injured honor."

Benedict found men like Brown, Easton, and Hazen contemptible, evil, and cowardly, but the real culprit was Congress. As a representative body, Congress should have been above the pettiness that infected some individuals; it should have been able to see through the lies and reward men (like him) who had sacrificed and shown true courage for the cause of liberty. By failing to promote him, and by taking seriously Brown's ridiculous charges, Congress had made an "implicit impeachment of my character."

One phrase that Washington had used in his latest letter stood out for

Benedict. In describing public bodies of governance, he had said there was no immediate way to hold them responsible for their actions; therefore, they could "place and displace at pleasure." This made Benedict wonder whether, in joining the Revolution against Great Britain, he had been fooled into substituting one form of petty tyranny for another.

Benedict left Rhode Island in mid-April, intending to ride to Philadelphia and demand a court of inquiry. He stopped at New Haven, but within days a courier arrived with shocking news. A large British detachment had landed near Norwalk, Connecticut, just over thirty miles away, and was marching toward Danbury.

Benedict had suggested in a letter to Gates that he wouldn't fight again until his name had been cleared. In a similar situation many other officers would have opted to defend their honor before defending their neighbors. But with the enemy close at hand, that emotional ultimatum was forgotten, and Benedict prepared once again for battle.

13

A DEVILISH FIGHTING FELLOW

*B*enedict rode hard toward Redding, Connecticut, collecting about 100 militiamen on the way, as well as one of his neighbors, Brigadier General David Wooster. At Redding he joined forces with approximately 500 local militia and their general, Gold S. Silliman.

Benedict was disappointed with these meager numbers. He had assumed that thousands of men would pour out to defend their homes, as had happened in 1775 when the British marched on Lexington and Concord. Why weren't more people willing to make a sacrifice for their freedom? Benedict wondered.

He learned from Silliman that the British, now under the command of the ex–colonial governor of New York, William Tryon, had taken Danbury that morning without a fight. They had then proceeded to ransack the town, destroying supplies of food, arms, ammunition, and tents, and burning nearly every house. Once this had been accomplished, Tryon had his column marching south, hoping to reach the safety of the coast before the rebels could organize a counterstrike.

When Benedict learned which road the British had taken, he divided up his small army and planned to attack. Wooster would trail the British column and harass the rear. Meanwhile, Benedict and Silliman would hurry cross-country to Ridgefield and form a defensive line to block the road. They would be outnumbered twenty to three, but Benedict felt that the British had to be shown that they couldn't attack a defenseless town without paying a steep price.

Two hours later Wooster caught up to and attacked the rear guard of the British. Tryon didn't hesitate; he halted and ordered a strong counter-attack, accompanied by the massed firing of six artillery field pieces. The Americans panicked and fled, and Wooster fell, mortally wounded.

Wooster's attack hadn't hurt the British very much, but it did delay them long enough to allow Benedict and Silliman to find easily defensible high ground at Ridgefield and throw up a hasty barricade of earth, stone, logs, and wagons. The small Patriot force was ready when the British came marching down the road three abreast. Tryon wasted no time in drawing up a complicated battle plan. He ordered the center column to make an all-out frontal assault on the barricade, and he was shocked when the vastly outnumbered Americans not only held their ground but drove the British back, killing 80 of his men. The British would make three more charges and be repulsed each time.

While this was taking place, Tryon sent two companies of 100 men to work their way around both sides of the American line. Soon one of these groups was pouring in heavy fire from the side, and when Tryon called for a bayonet charge, the rebels broke and ran.

Benedict was riding back and forth, waving his sword and trying desperately to hold his defensive line together. It was no use. A group of British soldiers fired a volley at him, and his horse went down, shot nine times. Benedict was trapped under his thrashing animal. As he struggled to pull his leg free, a redcoat ran toward him, shouting, "Surrender! You are my prisoner." At that moment Benedict yanked his leg from under the horse, retrieved his pistol from its saddle holster, and according to legend replied, "Not yet." He then fired, killing the redcoat instantly, before fleeing to a nearby swamp.

The day's fighting had exhausted the British troops, so Tryon decided to camp for the night. While the enemy rested, Benedict rode through the countryside, rallying men for another crack at the British column. By morning he had his defensive line in place and ready, now at a spot two miles north of Norwalk. This time, however, Loyalists tipped off Tryon about the trap awaiting him, and he was able to march his men around it. Benedict was never one to let an enemy off without a fight, so he had his troops trail the fleeing British for the rest of the morning, firing into the column of red uniforms. As always, he was in the thick of the fighting. One witness was amazed that Benedict constantly "exposed himself, almost to a fault" to enemy fire, and repeatedly "exhibited the greatest marks of bravery, coolness, and fortitude."

As had happened at Ridgefield, Tryon sent out a massive charge to scatter the Patriot snipers. Almost immediately, the American lines began to crumble, and Benedict was once again seen everywhere trying to rally them to hold firm. While he was moving along his line, a musket ball ripped through the collar of his coat, and another struck his horse in the neck. This time Benedict was lucky; when the horse toppled over, he received only minor cuts and bruises and was not pinned beneath the dying beast. But the effect of seeing their commander fall was devastating to his men. They broke and ran.

Benedict had taken on a far superior force and dealt it a severe blow, but he wasn't satisfied with what had taken place. The turnout of militiamen had been pathetically small, and those who did show up had twice broken ranks and run from the fight. "I wish never to see another of them again," a disgusted Benedict would write later.

Word of Benedict's actions in Connecticut spread very rapidly. Newspaper accounts praised him lavishly, and army regulars were saying that he had "fought like Julius Caesar." Even the British were impressed by his

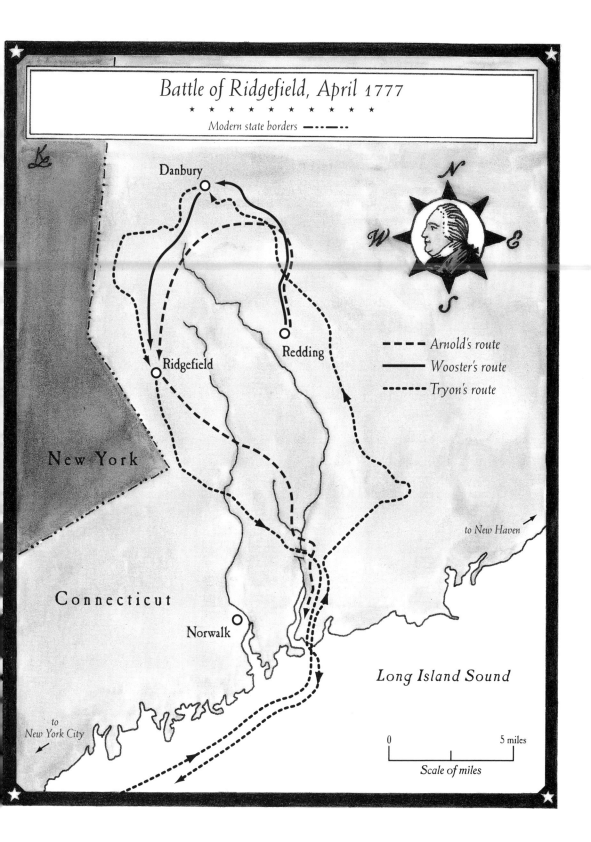

Battle of Ridgefield, April 1777

★ ★ ★ ★ ★ ★ ★ ★ ★ ★

Modern state borders —·—·—

Danbury

Redding

Ridgefield

New York

---- Arnold's route
—— Wooster's route
········· Tryon's route

Connecticut

Norwalk

Long Island Sound

to New Haven

to
New York City

0   5 miles

Scale of miles

quick actions and gallant stand, saying he had "the character of a devilish fighting fellow."

Members of Congress couldn't help becoming aware of Benedict's leadership—and feeling very embarrassed for having denied their best field general his promotion. Suddenly, John Adams, who not long before had said he would be happy to see Benedict resign, praised him highly for "his vigilance, activity, and bravery in the late affair at Connecticut." John Hancock stated that his actions were "highly approved of by Congress." They then reversed themselves and elevated Benedict to the rank of major general.

George Washington was happy to see that the members of Congress had come to their senses but noticed that they'd also created a new problem. They hadn't confirmed Benedict's seniority over the five other new major generals. This was no small matter, Washington knew. Many an officer would summarily resign rather than submit to orders from "those he commanded but a few weeks ago." The commander in chief was worrying about this and thinking up a new assignment for Benedict when Benedict himself appeared unexpectedly in Morristown to request a leave of absence. He wanted to go to Philadelphia and confront Congress, to clear his name once and for all and to settle his accounts for the Canadian campaign.

Washington would have tried to persuade his newest major general to stay in the field, but Benedict produced a recently printed handbill that had been circulating throughout the north. It was a rehashing of John Brown's wild accusations that Gates had delivered to Congress. Washington considered the charges false and scandalous. He had, in fact, refused Brown's direct request for a hearing in February, after which Brown had resigned his commission. Washington sent Benedict off to deal with Congress, cautioning his fighting general to hold his temper in check.

Benedict's meetings with Congress began well. He asked that Congress investigate Brown's charges and exonerate him, and he resubmitted his accounts for approval. His petitions were greeted warmly by delegates, and the next day Congress voted to give him a horse to replace the two shot out from under him. It put off any discussion of his rank, however, and turned Brown's charges, as well as Benedict's accounts for the Canadian campaign, over to a committee named the Board of War for review.

Members of the Board pored over the pile of documents Benedict had presented to substantiate his expenses and a week later issued their opinion. The Board expressed its "entire satisfaction . . . concerning the general's character and conduct, so cruelly and groundlessly aspersed [by John Brown's] publication." The full Congress voted its agreement with these findings and had the report published. The members did not promise to pay Benedict what he claimed to be owed, but they did say they would come to a decision about this as quickly as possible.

Congress had sidestepped completely the issue of Benedict's seniority, which annoyed him and made him feel his acquiescence had been bought off with a mere horse. He thought again of resigning, then remembered Washington's advice about holding his anger in check. He knew he did not want to leave the army. He had a natural ability to size up a battle situation and make fast, accurate decisions about troop placements and tactics. He also saw a successful military career as a way to repair his family's reputation and create a legacy truly worthy to hand down to his descendants.

The British army was at a complete standstill, so there was no need for Benedict to return to Connecticut. He stayed in Philadelphia, talking privately with members of Congress in the hope that he could advance his cause.

Meanwhile, Benedict's friend and mentor, Philip Schuyler, asked that a committee be formed to review his handling of the Northern Army. Schuyler heard that some Congressmen from New England blamed him for losing Canada and were suggesting that Horatio Gates should take over as commander. Schuyler was not only the commander of the Northern Army, he was now a member of Congress for New York and had many friends there. In a close vote (five states to four, with four abstaining), Congress voted to fully exonerate Schuyler and allow him to continue his command. The four that voted against him were all from New England. The deciding vote in favor of Schuyler came from Pennsylvania. Schuyler told Benedict that Pennsylvania had backed him because he was willing to go along with their choice for commander of Ticonderoga, Major General Arthur St. Clair. Benedict liked Schuyler and felt that the decision was just, but it was unsettling to know that politics and not merit were what counted most to Congress.

This was emphasized a month later when Gates stormed into Philadelphia to complain. Gates made it clear that he had no intention of serving under Schuyler or Washington and demanded to be heard by the full Congress. He then presented a long, rambling speech on military affairs in upper New York, made up largely of self-praise. When a supporter of Schuyler asked Gates to get to the point, he became incensed, and a shouting match followed.

Despite the fact that his troops in New Jersey were on full alert, Gates stayed in Philadelphia to lobby for himself. Even when Congress ordered him to return to headquarters and "follow the directions of General Washington," Gates refused to obey. Instead, he announced that he was going home to Virginia to visit his family. To Benedict's amazement, Congress did nothing to chastise Gates. While Gates had not vanquished Schuyler, he still had enough political clout to avoid being punished for what amounted to insubordination and desertion.

A month later Philippe Charles Tronson de Coudray, a French officer, appeared before Congress claiming that Silas Deane, Benedict's Connecticut ally and recently appointed ambassador to France, had promised him the rank of major general in the Continental Army. Such a commitment was not unusual at the time. To curry favor with various European countries, and to add experienced military men to the American ranks, Congress had given numerous European officers American army commissions, including France's Marquis de Lafayette, Prussia's Baron von Steuben, and Poland's Tadeusz Kościuszko, to name just a few.

In addition to being pompous and arrogant, Coudray presented a serious problem for Congress. If granted his commission, he would outrank many other major generals, including Benedict. When Coudray was given his commission, Benedict was as miffed by it as anyone but wisely kept quiet. But three other major generals—Henry Knox, Nathanael Greene, and John Sullivan—charged into Philadelphia to express their outrage. Each made angry statements to Congress, with Knox's capturing the collective tone perfectly. "I wish to know," he demanded, "whether this information be true; if it is, I beg the favor of a permission to retire, and that a proper certificate for that purpose be sent to me immediately."

A British drawing of Benedict done in 1780.
THE LIBRARY OF CONGRESS

Congress reacted swiftly and angrily. It sent a formal protest to George Washington, instructing him to reprimand his officers for their "attempt to influence [Congress's] decisions, and an invasion of the liberties of the people, and indicating a want of confidence in the justice of Congress." They also demanded an apology from Knox, Greene, and Sullivan, and stated that either the officers must accept the "authority of Congress" or they could resign their commissions and go home. Eventually all three apologized and returned to their commands.

These events confirmed a sobering reality. If politics and whim ruled the decisions of Congress, how could someone like Benedict—with few political allies and more than enough enemies—ever hope to get ahead?

Finally, on July 10, Benedict took pen in hand and began to write a letter he really didn't want to write. He wished to resign his commission, he told Congress, not "from a spirit of resentment (though my feelings are deeply wounded)," but because of a "real conviction that it is not in my power to serve my country in the present rank I hold." Holding him at this level was an "implied impeachment of my character and declaration of Congress that they thought me unqualified for the post that fell to me in the common line of promotions." He did not want to resign; more than anything he wanted to fight to become "a free citizen of America," but he couldn't, not without surrendering his honor. "Honor is a sacrifice no man ought to make, as I received [it] so I wish to transmit [it] inviolate to posterity."

Benedict handed in his letter on July 11 and then began preparing to leave Philadelphia, assuming his military career was over.

14

YOU WILL HEAR OF
MY BEING VICTORIOUS

While Benedict was still in the vicinity of Philidelphia, a message arrived from George Washington containing grim news. In New York General Howe had loaded 15,000 regular troops onto 260 transport ships, ready to sail at a moment's notice. Unfortunately, Washington could not be certain where this enemy force was going to strike. He saw two likely possibilities. Either Howe would lead his troops up the Hudson to cut off the New England states from those to the south, or he would head down to Philadelphia to capture the Patriot capital. Washington marched his few available troops—some 7,500—to a position along the Hudson and waited for Howe to move.

While he was camped there, more bad news arrived: Fort Ticonderoga had been surrendered to British troops who had come down from Canada. This second British force of 10,000 soldiers was now under the command of General John Burgoyne. Washington assumed that Burgoyne would continue marching south, "determined, if possible, to

General John Burgoyne strikes a dashing pose. His oversized ego and driving ambition led him to ignore sound military advice before and after the Battles of Saratoga.

possess himself of our posts in that quarter and to push his arms further."

Schuyler's Northern Army was undermanned and no match for the on-coming British. And Washington, with his eye on Howe, couldn't spare any of his men to help Schuyler stop Burgoyne's march. So on July 10, 1777, he turned to Congress for additional soldiers. He understood the crisis he and the Revolution faced. If Howe went up the Hudson and these two formidable British armies controlled the Mohawk Valley, they could choke off vital supply lines, starving out the Continental Army, and "the most disagreeable consequences may be apprehended."

Washington even broke from normal protocol and asked for a specific fighting general to take charge of these new recruits. "If General Arnold . . . can be spared from Philadelphia," he wrote to John Hancock, "I would recommend him for this business. . . . He is active, judicious, and brave, and an officer in whom the militia will repose great confidence. Besides this, he is well acquainted with the country and with the routes and [the] more important passes and defiles in it."

For once, Congress understood that the rebellion was in immediate danger and put aside petty politics to act quickly. It authorized the recruiting of 6,000 new troops from the New England states. As for Benedict, they simply disregarded his letter of resignation and ordered him to report to General Washington immediately.

Many other officers would have used the situation as leverage to have their rank changed. But Benedict asked that his resignation be accepted, and added that he would "be happy as a private citizen to render my country every service in my power." As a civilian, he would no longer be under the command of Congress. He then mounted his horse and began traveling north to meet with George Washington.

Congress saw no reason to honor Benedict's request, especially since he was dutifully following its orders anyway. It once again ignored his attempt to resign, though Hancock did write back, promising that Congress would reconsider having Benedict advanced in seniority at some time in the future.

Having dealt with many generals who were slow to respond to his commands, it pleased Washington a great deal to see how quickly Benedict appeared in camp. After they discussed the military situation in detail, Washington asked a favor of Benedict. Benedict might find himself under the command of General Arthur St. Clair, one of the less qualified junior officers who had been advanced in rank ahead of him. If this happened, Washington asked that Benedict waive "for the present, all dispute about rank." This was an awkward situation, and Washington knew it. Benedict had every right to refuse to serve under someone he considered his inferior in accomplishment and rank. Washington may have strengthened his position by telling his young general that St. Clair had surrendered Fort Ticonderoga without a fight, and that he'd probably be recalled to Philadelphia for an investigation into his conduct. In any case,

Benedict "generously," in the words of George Washington, agreed to "create no dispute should the good of the service require them to act in concert."

Understanding the urgency of the situation, Benedict left Washington's headquarters on July 19 and rode nonstop until he reached Fort Edward, which was just above Saratoga, New York, on July 22. There he met with Schuyler and was briefed on the situation.

Burgoyne had left Canada with approximately 10,000 well-trained and well-equipped troops, plus nearly 500 Native American scouts and 138 pieces of field artillery. His was such an intimidating force that St. Clair had taken one look and fled Ticonderoga on July 5 without firing a shot. Burgoyne had then halted at Skenesboro to await supplies.

The apparent ease with which the British troops moved concealed a number of serious problems Burgoyne was facing. Once Ticonderoga had been taken, Burgoyne had requested that Guy Carleton in Canada send him 3,000 soldiers to man the fort. Carleton, miffed at being replaced as commander of the invading army, refused to release any of his troops, claiming he needed them to defend Quebec. Burgoyne had no choice but to leave behind nearly one third of his army to hold the fort. In addition, Burgoyne was finding it hard to move such a large body of soldiers, all their equipment and baggage, plus gunboats, bateaux, and artillery, through an unforgiving wilderness.

The stop at Skenesboro cost Burgoyne three weeks' time and allowed Schuyler to formulate a thoughtful plan of response. But even if Schuyler had known of Burgoyne's difficulties, his options were limited. Few local militiamen had responded to the call to arms, so he had just under 6,400 soldiers in camp, with over 1,900 of them ill and unfit for duty. He had only two functioning pieces of artillery and not enough trained men to operate them effectively. And, as always seemed to be the case, the majority of his soldiers were untrained and ill supplied.

This ruled out a direct attack on Burgoyne. So while the British dawdled in Skenesboro, Schuyler sent hundreds of woodsmen from New York and Massachusetts into the vast forest that separated the two armies. Their assignment was to make the roads and footpaths as difficult to travel as possible. To this end they burned every bridge they found, cut down huge trees to block paths, rolled boulders into fordable streams, and diverted water to flood low-lying ground.

Benedict was ordered to lead a squad of soldiers that would act as advance scouts. Their chief job was to monitor the enemy's movements and relay this information to Schuyler. They were also expected to harass British troops with sniper fire whenever possible. Schuyler, meanwhile, would slowly withdraw his main army as the British advanced toward Albany, taking along any excess provisions that might be useful. The idea was to stretch the British supply line out and then attack it at several points in an effort to cut off and isolate Burgoyne's lead troops. It was a defensive plan that implied weakness and fear, but it was the only option Schuyler had.

When Burgoyne finally got his troops moving again, his progress was less than one mile a day. This slow pace was due in part to the excellent job Schuyler's woodsmen had done in ripping up and littering the winding forest path. Another reason for the sluggish march was the weather, which had turned foul and rainy. Still, the British commander was pleased that the rebels were retreating before him and was supremely confident. In a letter to the British foreign minister, Lord Germain, he sneered at "the perseverance of the enemy in driving both people and cattle before them as they retreat." And while there was some Patriot resistance, he felt "it cannot finally impede me."

Burgoyne was so sure of himself that he issued a public proclamation urging all rebels to lay down their arms, or "I shall stand acquitted in the eyes of God [in] executing the vengeance of the state against the willful outcasts." The commander of the hired Hessian soldiers, Major General Friedrich von Riedesel, shared Burgoyne's confidence, referring to Burgoyne's campaign as "the march of annihilation."

Burgoyne never lost his swagger or his determination to reach Albany before the end of the summer. He pushed his men south even as supplies ran low and exhausted soldiers began dropping out of the line of march. He kept them moving even when an expedition he had ordered to obtain desperately needed cattle, horses, and carriages resulted in more than 200 British killed and 700 taken prisoner at Bennington, Vermont.

As the days dragged along, Burgoyne's Native American scouts grew bored with the discipline of a military campaign and began drifting home. By the end of August fewer than 100 of them were left. Yet Burgoyne was as determined as ever to push on, at one point proclaiming, "This army must never retreat." In fact, it seemed to onlookers that Gentleman Johnny, as Burgoyne was known to his troops, was making a party of the entire affair. General Riedesel's wife, the Baroness von Riedesel, recalled Burgoyne "having a jolly time" during the campaign, "spending half the night singing and drinking and amusing himself in the company of the wife of a commissary, who was his mistress and, like him, loved champagne."

If he had known what was happening in Congress at that moment, Burgoyne might have been even more confident. As Washington had anticipated, Congress addressed the issue of the surrender of Fort Ticonderoga. New England delegates, spearheaded by John Adams, saw an opportunity to expand the inquiry to include "the general officers who were in the Northern [Army] at the time of the evacuation." The phrasing of the resolution was a sneaky way to once again examine Schuyler's military tactics in New York, even though Schuyler was not at Fort Ticonderoga when it fell.

Because Congress had already reviewed Schuyler's military decisions in Canada and given him a ringing endorsement, this sly move by the New England delegates should have been voted down easily. However, the members of Congress were extremely nervous and looking for a scapegoat. They had been getting reports that Burgoyne would soon occupy Albany, and they were also edgy over whether General Howe and his 15,000 troops might attack them in Philadelphia. The frightened representatives decided to investigate both St. Clair and Schuyler, and ordered Washington to appoint Horatio Gates as the new northern commander.

Benedict already saw Congress as politically driven and biased against him. But at least he had had Schuyler to look after him and to promote his interests there. With Schuyler gone, there was no one in Congress to act as his spokesman. What's more, Congress was still not supplying enough men to fight the war, or adequate supplies and ammunition to those already in the field. To Benedict, Congress seemed even less trustworthy than it had previously.

Another factor also weighed heavily on him. Even though one British army was approaching from the north and another was poised to strike, few Patriots were flocking to defend their farms or families. If people weren't willing to fight for their homes, what sort of future would the Revolution have?

Benedict could have sidestepped many of these issues by following the example of General John Stark. Stark had, like Benedict, been passed over for promotion when Congress elevated the five junior officers in 1777. Instead of staying in the Continental Army, he resigned his officer's commission and accepted the position of major general in the New Hampshire militia. Militia units were raised, supplied, and commanded by each state, which freed them from any obligation to obey the orders of either Congress or George Washington. Stark could nonetheless still make a contribution to the Revolution. It was Stark and his militiamen who had shortly before, on their own initiative, routed Burgoyne's supply expedition in Bennington, Vermont.

But Benedict once again did not insist that his resignation be accepted, as Stark had. He stayed, against his better judgment, because Schuyler "advised him to delay," worried that with both him and St. Clair being called down by Congress, the Northern Army would be short of experienced, skillful officers.

The fact that Horatio Gates would be replacing Schuyler may have also been a factor in Benedict's decision to stay. Benedict had as yet no idea that his former commander had turned against him, or that Gates and at least one member of his staff, James Wilkinson, were actively working to undermine Benedict's credibility with Congress. As far as Benedict knew, Gates was still a trustworthy friend.

In late June another British threat emerged. Lieutenant Colonel Barry St. Leger left Montreal with over 750 British regulars, Hessians, and Loyalists, and marched south to reinforce Burgoyne. He was joined along the way by nearly 1,000 Native American warriors. This was a formidable force, and St. Leger's troops easily trapped and routed almost 800 rebel militiamen at Oriskany, New York. They then laid siege to Fort Schuyler, which guarded a strategic portage at the headwaters of the Mohawk River.

Schuyler, still in charge while awaiting the arrival of Gates, knew the fort could not hold out very long. Once it fell, there would be no way to stop St. Leger's march down the Mohawk River on his way to Albany. The Northern Army would then face attack on two fronts, with the distinct possibility that Howe would travel up the Hudson and attack on a third front.

Schuyler's only hope was to send a small detachment up to delay St. Leger so that he, Schuyler, could deal with Burgoyne's main army separately. Because this was such a risky assignment, he asked for a volunteer from his senior officers to lead this expedition. Of all his field generals, Benedict Arnold was the only one who stepped forward.

Benedict's actions during this campaign are instructive and weigh against accusations that he craved physical danger and was ready to sacrifice his troops for personal glory. Before he left, a communication arrived from Horatio Gates, announcing that Gates would be in camp soon to assume control of the Northern Army. Benedict was ordered to "immediately return to the main army with all the force you carried with you" just as soon as "you have put a happy finishing to our affairs to the westward."

Benedict's answer was energetic and meant to show his determination to succeed for his new commander. "Nothing shall be omitted that can be done to raise the siege. You will hear of my being victorious, or no more;

and as soon as the safety of this part of the country will permit, I will fly to your assistance."

When Benedict's detachment was a few miles from Fort Schuyler, he called a meeting of his officers to discuss strategy. Even though scouting reports told Benedict that the enemy outnumbered him, he was for attacking St. Leger's troops before St. Leger took Fort Schuyler. This would compel St. Leger to divide his army into two units, one to continue the attack on the fort, the other to deal with Benedict. Benedict's junior officers were clearly nervous and voted "not to hazard our little army" until several hundred additional militiamen could be rounded up. Benedict wasn't at all happy with their cautiousness, but he knew better than to force his opinion on reluctant officers.

By sheer chance, a local British Loyalist, Hon Yost Schuyler (who claimed to be a cousin of Philip Schuyler), was about to be executed for recruiting local men to fight with St. Leger. Through his mother, Hon Yost begged for an interview with Benedict, claiming he had a plan that would help defeat the British and that he would reveal it to Benedict in exchange for his life. Benedict agreed to see the man.

The plan was quite simple. Hon Yost would make his way to St. Leger's camp, where he was considered a loyal and honest supporter of the king. Once inside, he would spread rumors that a rebel force of more than 2,000 was fast approaching with the much-feared Benedict Arnold in command. Hon Yost was certain the Native Americans with St. Leger would choose to flee before being drawn into a fight against such a powerful army.

Fortunately for the condemned man, Benedict knew that Hon Yost was a very unusual sort of person, having, as Benedict's great-nephew the historian Isaac N. Arnold later reported, "a singular combination of cunning and shrewdness in some things, with a want of sense approaching idiocy in others." The Native Americans in the region regarded such individuals as "stricken by the Great Spirit" and treated them with a "mysterious respect and wonder." Crazy or clever, Hon Yost seemed to have the ear of local Native American warriors.

So, while another commander might have dismissed Hon Yost as naïve and unreliable and sent him to the gallows, Benedict decided he had nothing to lose by going along with the man's plan. Wisely, Benedict held Hon Yost's brother, and even, according to some sources, his mother, hostage to make certain he wouldn't betray the Americans.

Hon Yost played his role to the hilt. He shot holes in his clothes to suggest he'd just barely escaped the rebels. Then he ran all the way to the British camp, where he arrived gasping for breath and trembling. Evidently, he increased the size of the approaching American army each time he retold his story, but he was convincing enough that over the following days more and more Native American scouts took off. Five days after Hon Yost stumbled into camp, almost every Native American scout had abandoned the British and left for home.

By this time, St. Leger's troops were within two hundred feet of Fort Schuyler and about to launch a massive charge. When Benedict received word of this, he ordered his army to circle around and strike at St. Leger's rear, hoping to delay the surrender of the fort. At this point, the reality of the situation dawned on St. Leger. He was outnumbered by the combined American forces, those inside the fort plus Benedict's army. Overnight he folded up his tents and headed back to Canada. The surprised and happy commander inside Fort Schuyler sneaked a message out to Benedict that evening saying that "St. Leger with his army was retreating, with the utmost precipitation."

Having engineered an amazing—and bloodless—victory, Benedict expected to be greeted as a hero when he got back to headquarters. Instead, he learned that Congress had finally gotten around to debating a special amendment to elevate him in rank "on account of his extraordinary merit and former rank in the army." When the vote was finally taken, however, seven states opposed the measure, while only four were in favor, with the rest abstaining. Of the states voting in the negative, three were home to the officers elevated over Benedict. The vote was clearly tainted by personal animus and politics. One outraged delegate from South Carolina,

Henry Laurens, called Congress's "reasoning on this occasion . . . disgusting."

Just as upsetting, Benedict discovered that Horatio Gates had not spoken to any of the delegates on his behalf, even though Benedict had expressly asked him to. If Benedict clung to the idea that Gates was still his friend, he had to reconsider when the new commander sent to Congress his official report about St. Leger's withdrawal. Gates proudly proclaimed that *his* troops had achieved a "brilliant victory [that] gives the brightest luster to American arms, and covers the enemies of the United States with infamy and shame." While specifically lauding several officers, he never once mentioned Benedict by name.

Benedict had been passed over again for promotion by a politically motivated Congress; his friend and patron Philip Schuyler was gone; and now he was saddled with a commander who would not acknowledge his part in a stunning victory but who seemed happy to accept praise, though he had done absolutely nothing to earn it. Benedict might have despaired, except for one last glimmer of hope in his quest for military achievement. Burgoyne was still nearby, still inching toward Albany and a confrontation with the Patriot army. When that happened, Benedict was more determined than ever to be in the fight.

15

INSPIRED BY THE FURY OF A DEMON

here is no doubt that Benedict was eager to take on Burgoyne and his army. In a letter to Colonel John Lamb, a comrade from the Canadian campaign, he wrote, "Our people are in high spirits, and wish for action . . . . I heartily wish your regiment [was] with us, as a few days, in all probability, will determine the fate of General Burgoyne's army, or of ours."

For two years Benedict had battled superior British forces despite his own lack of men, supplies, and artillery. For the first time, their positions were reversed. Burgoyne had allowed his army to travel well beyond his supply lines and was now cut off. He faced shortages of food for his men, fodder for the horses, and even ammunition. His troop strength was down as well—fewer than 5,000 men were combat ready.

American forces, meanwhile, were increasing in number. As the summer wore along and word circulated that Burgoyne's army was experiencing problems, more and more soldiers began arriving. By the beginning of September there were between 6,000 and 7,000 healthy soldiers available

A contemporary view of Burgoyne's troops camped just outside Saratoga.
FORT TICONDEROGA MUSEUM

to fight. Adding real muscle to this force, a number of experienced artillery companies came into camp as well.

There was one other good reason to attack Burgoyne and do so as quickly as possible. General Howe had finally made up his mind about where he intended to take his 15,000 troops. Flying in the face of direct orders from England and also of military logic, Howe had sailed south. On August 22 his ships were spotted in Chesapeake Bay, making their way to Head of Elk, where Howe would establish his base camp. From there they began their march for Philadelphia.

Howe's plan was to capture the rebel capital and rout members of Congress, a victory that he hoped would demoralize the Americans and throw the Revolution into chaos. After this he would head back north to aid Burgoyne's army. Evidently, he saw nothing wrong with stranding Burgoyne in the middle of hostile territory for what might turn out to be several months.

Because Howe had abandoned him, Burgoyne did not have many options. He could call off the campaign and withdraw to a safer position, where he could resupply and rebuild his army (and possibly resume the offensive in the spring). His other choice was to press on with his invasion and hope for the best. Burgoyne was eager to win favor in England and to advance in rank, and he knew perfectly well that even a partial withdrawal would be viewed as a defeat. Besides, he had bragged too often and too publicly about how he would destroy the amateur Continental Army.

On September 13 Burgoyne's army moved across the Hudson River just north of the village of Saratoga. As the commander of the Hessian troops, Major General Friedrich von Riedesel, recalled, Burgoyne "burned with impatience to advance on the enemy." Benedict felt this was the perfect time for the Northern Army to strike. But instead of acting, Horatio Gates hesitated.

Gates had acquired his military training in the British army, which preached caution at all times. Gates also had very little battlefield experience and was unsure that his soldiers, especially those from militia units, could execute complicated maneuvers during the heat of battle. He had no intention of risking a fight and his reputation until he had an overwhelming advantage in troop strength. He decided to wait in Stillwater, behind wood-and-dirt fortifications, and let the enemy come to him.

While this cautious approach would minimize American casualties, Benedict considered it foolish. Keeping the American army stationary would allow Burgoyne to choose when to fight and where to strike. Benedict worried that, even tucked behind fortifications, the new recruits wouldn't be able to hold their positions against the seasoned British troops. Better that they venture into the woods, where the British couldn't maneuver as freely or make effective use of their artillery.

Gates's strategy also meant the Americans would essentially be fighting a defensive battle. Even if they drove off the British, Burgoyne could still take what remained of his army and escape north to await a better time to fight. Benedict could never consider this a victory; it would open the way for a future battle in which the odds might be against them.

Benedict urged his commander to bring the Northern Army out, but Gates put him off repeatedly. When it was clear that Benedict would bring

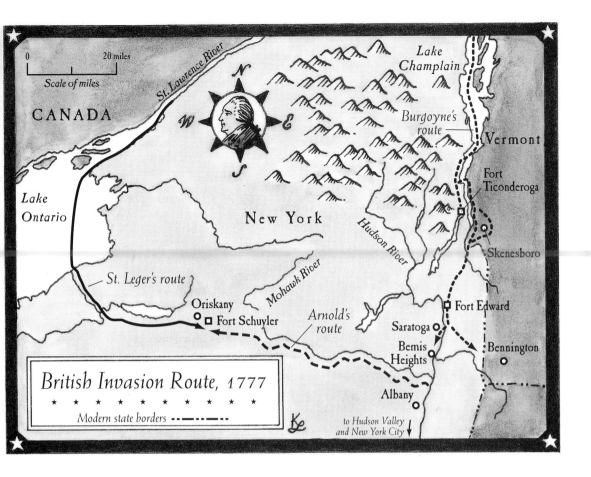

the matter up at every staff meeting, Gates simply didn't invite him to meetings anymore. Tensions increased when Gates arbitrarily reassigned several companies of soldiers under Benedict's command and failed to inform Benedict that he had done so. Benedict confronted Gates at headquarters, saying he had been "placed . . . in the ridiculous light of presuming to give orders" when "I had no right to do so, and having them publicly contradicted." Gates apologized for the mistake and promised to set the record straight in his next orders, but he never did.

Benedict also protested being excluded from the strategy meetings, and even named the person responsible. The "designing villain," Benedict insisted, was James Wilkinson. Gates dismissed Benedict's charge as nonsense, a move that reinforced Benedict's feeling that he was unimportant to his commander. But "Wilky," as Gates affectionately referred to him, was indeed actively plotting against Benedict whenever possible. Both in

private meetings with Gates and other senior officers and in letters to friends in Congress, he repeatedly questioned Benedict's loyalty and referred to Benedict's staff members disparagingly as that "New York gang."

Even as the relationship between Benedict and Gates escalated into open conflict, and even though Benedict did not approve of his commander's defensive strategy, he worked hard to make it as successful as possible. It was Benedict, along with the Polish engineer Tadeusz Kościuszko, who rode north in search of a more easily defensible campsite. Just four miles from the Stillwater camp they located Bemis Heights, a hill rising up three hundred feet that overlooked the Hudson River and the only road heading south. From this vantage point American artillery could easily shell enemy troops below and force Burgoyne to either retreat or attempt a charge up a very steep slope. At the time, Bemis Heights and the hilly terrain to the north were heavily wooded, with only a few open patches for crops at isolated farmhouses.

Benedict commanded approximately 2,000 men and was positioned on the left side of the American line, while Massachusetts general John Glover's men, plus most of the artillery, guarded the right side. Gates had the rest of his troops massed in the center behind crudely constructed breastworks and trenches.

The main body of Benedict's men was camped near Quaker Road, where they spent the days before the first battle hastily building-log-and-dirt fortifications. Benedict also placed riflemen at John Freeman's farm, with nearly 600 men under Daniel Morgan and Henry Dearborn just behind them. Morgan's group was composed of men from Virginia, Pennsylvania, and Maryland, all of them crack shots. Dearborn's men were fast-moving infantry assigned to protect Morgan's sharpshooters with muskets and axes.

As five days crept by with little activity, Benedict grew more edgy. The thick fog that began rolling in every morning did not help his disposition. The British could be moving troops through any one of the many ravines in front of him and he wouldn't know it. On Wednesday, September 17, Benedict begged Gates to order him forward to locate and assess the enemy's position, a petition Gates at first refused. Finally, after repeated requests, Gates allowed him to go out, though he warned Benedict not to initiate a general attack.

Benedict led his men out into the dense fog, groping their way through thick underbrush and down steep hills. Within two hours they encountered Burgoyne's advance troops repairing bridges. Because Gates had ordered him to stay clear of any sort of general battle, Benedict was careful only to probe the enemy lines with small-scale attacks. When he returned to camp that afternoon, he was able to tell Gates that Burgoyne planned to attack sometime in the next forty-eight hours and that the majority of his troops would probably strike at the left side of the American line. If this was true, it would require Gates to send out troops (most likely Benedict's) to prevent British artillery from taking a position on the high ground to the northwest that overlooked the American line.

Gates dismissed Benedict's prediction, saying Burgoyne would approach along the river road and attack from there. Two days later, on Friday, September 19, British soldiers came marching down the road. Gates must have been pleased to see a long line of soldiers approaching, trailed by provision wagons and, in the river, more than two hundred bateaux. It meant he could stay behind his barricades, as he'd planned, and pour fire down upon the helpless British soldiers below.

What Gates didn't realize was that this column, led by Riedesel, was made up of only about 1,100 men. Two other columns of Burgoyne's army, some 3,300 strong, had turned at a narrow, rutted wagon road just beyond Sword's farm to march west. They then split into two separate units. Burgoyne accompanied one unit toward Freeman's farm, with the intention of striking at the center of the American line. The other unit would do precisely as Benedict had predicted: swing wide to the west in order to establish a battery of artillery with which to rake the American camp.

Burgoyne's plan depended on the American forces never leaving their fortifications. He was fairly confident of this because, two days earlier, American deserters had told him exactly how Gates had positioned his troops as well as his plan to sit tight. Burgoyne decided to have the detachment from the river road engage the rebels first to distract them while the bulk of the army maneuvered into position, using the dense covering of shrubs and trees to conceal their movements.

The Americans might have been taken by complete surprise, except that rebel scouts stationed on the east side of the Hudson River had seen the two large British columns heading up the wagon trail. Word was relayed back to Gates, but he issued no new orders. He may have felt that the British were merely trying to entice him from the protection of his fortifications. He might also have been paralyzed with indecision or fear. For whatever reason, he did absolutely nothing to counter the enemy's advance, although any competent commander would have taken action.

Benedict sensed a massive flanking maneuver in the works, and as twenty-four-year-old Lieutenant Colonel Richard Varick later recalled, he "urged, begged, and entreated" Gates to act quickly. At least, Benedict asked, let him send out Morgan and Dearborn to probe and disrupt the advancing columns, with support from two other units. Gates hesitated and seemed confused, but eventually he gave in. Benedict could send out his troops, but, Gates warned, if they were overwhelmed by the enemy, Gates would not provide additional help.

Morgan's and Dearborn's men moved out first, followed by infantry. Benedict's job as field commander was to coordinate the movements of his troops for maximum effect, while his senior officers actually led the men in the field. Even so, Benedict rode between the two groups to maintain contact and issue orders. At a little past noon, cannon fire erupted from the

American soldiers firing on British troops from the safety of the thick forest.
THE ARMY ART COLLECTION, U.S. ARMY CENTER OF MILITARY HISTORY

British lines, the British signal that all three columns were in place and ready to advance on Bemis Heights. At around the same time, the "smart firing of small arms" was heard, as Morgan and Dearborn made their initial contact with the British at Freeman's farm.

The Americans rushed forward without hesitation, halting only long enough to aim and fire at the enemy. That first withering volley wounded or killed every British officer in the advance group, plus many of the men around them. Those who survived were so surprised to see rebels charging them that they turned and fled. Chaos ensued when their own troops began to "fire without orders (by which many of our own people were killed retreating)," recalled British artillery officer James Hadden.

Officers from following units soon regained control of the fleeing troops and managed to counter with their own sharp volley fired at the charging Americans. The wall of flying metal stopped the Patriot advance

Benedict (left, with sword in hand) directing his men on the battlefield.
THE NEW YORK PUBLIC LIBRARY

momentarily as Morgan hurried along his faltering line to encourage and reposition his men.

More pressure bore down on Morgan and Dearborn from the British column that had circled wide to the west and was now coming up the road near Freeman's. Benedict tried to help his outnumbered riflemen by attempting to outflank this column, but once again the British were able to react swiftly enough to halt the American charge.

After this initial charge failed, a strange quiet fell over the battlefield as the wounded were collected and taken to safety. It was during this lull that Benedict spotted a wide gap between the two British columns at Freeman's farm. If he could drive enough troops between the two columns, he realized, he could divide the enemy forces and attack each column separately. He immediately brought in more soldiers and launched an attack, which the British successfully repulsed. Benedict then focused his assault on the British center, and a series of at least six charges and countercharges ensued.

Benedict was everywhere, bringing more and more soldiers into the battle and directing troop placement until nearly all 3,000 of his wing were engaged. Captain Ebenezer Wakefield recalled that Benedict, "inspired by the fury of a demon," led at least one assault. "Riding in front of the line, his eyes flashing, pointing with his sword to the advancing foe, with a voice that rung clear as a trumpet, [he] called upon the men to follow him . . . and . . . hurled them like a tornado on the British line."

The fighting lasted over three hours, with Benedict either actively involved in the fray or urging his men forward throughout. "Nothing could exceed the bravery of Arnold on this day," Wakefield would remember. "There seemed to shoot out from him a magnetic flame that electrified his men and made heroes of all within his influence."

Late in the afternoon, Benedict peered through the smoke of battle and realized that the British line couldn't withstand another assault. Burgoyne had reached the same conclusion and sent a message to Riedesel that he needed fresh troops immediately. Riedesel responded quickly, dividing his force and sending 500 troops up the steep hill to attack the Americans.

Benedict dashed back to Gates and urged him to release some of the 4,000 men in camp. Gates refused, reminding him of what he'd said earlier. Finally, after much argument and wasted time, Gates ordered 500 men forward. Benedict rode off, promising, "By God I will soon put an end to it." But before Benedict could direct these fresh troops and organize a final assault, Gates ordered him to return to camp.

Gates's numerous blunders on September 19, 1777, cost the Americans a decisive victory. If Gates had supported Benedict sooner, the British center would have collapsed. At the very least, he should have sent troops to capture the British supply wagons, which were being guarded now by fewer than 600 men. Finally, by removing Benedict from the field, he left the American troops without anyone to direct their movements.

This analysis of the battle was later confirmed by Burgoyne, when he appeared before Parliament to explain why he had failed to reach Albany. He had expected that "Gates would receive the attack in his lines," which would have permitted Burgoyne to establish "a position he could have maintained." Unfortunately for him, "Arnold chose to give rather than receive the attack" and effectively disrupted his overall battle plan.

Burgoyne also admitted that he'd underestimated the fighting courage of the Americans, commending them for their "perseverance in the attack on his lines." A British officer, Lieutenant Thomas Anburey, went even further in his praise: "The courage and obstinacy with which the Americans fought were the astonishment of everyone."

With Benedict removed from the field, Burgoyne was able to move troops at will and drive back the remaining Americans. As the sun set, the British still held ground at Freeman's farm and could claim a technical victory. But it was a victory that came at a staggering price: nearly 600 of Burgoyne's soldiers, almost twenty-two percent of his troops, were killed, wounded, or captured that day. Patriot losses were substantially less, with 63 killed and just over 200 wounded.

When the battle ended, Benedict's immediate reaction was to urge Gates to mount a full-scale attack "on the 20th while the enemy was in confusion." He knew that the day's fight had stunned the British and thought the Americans should follow this up quickly before the enemy could regroup and put up strong entrenchments. Gates was not only cool to this suggestion, he simply turned his back on Arnold and ignored it.

Gates wasted no time in notifying Congress of the battle, however. His carefully phrased report proudly announced that Burgoyne's army had been stopped and mauled because of Gates's own fast action. He went out of his way to avoid mentioning that it was Benedict and his soldiers that had accomplished this. "To discriminate in praise of the officers would be [an] injustice," he said disingenuously, "as they all deserve the honor and applause of Congress." Gates's ally Wilkinson resorted to out-and-out lies

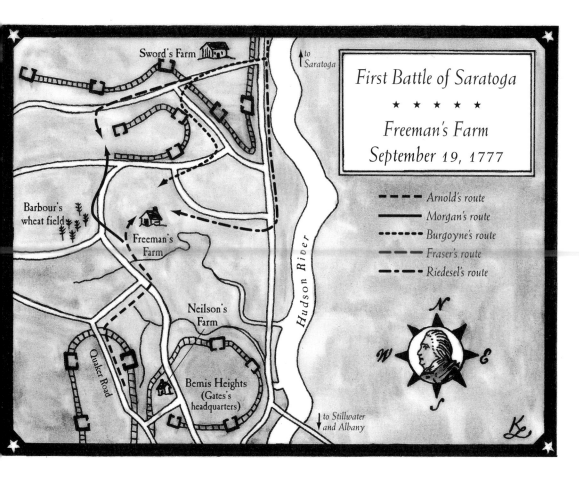

First Battle of Saratoga

★ ★ ★ ★ ★

Freeman's Farm
September 19, 1777

- - - - Arnold's route
———— Morgan's route
•••••• Burgoyne's route
- - - Fraser's route
-•-•- Riedesel's route

Sword's Farm

to Saratoga

Barbour's wheat field

Freeman's Farm

Hudson River

Neilson's Farm

Quaker Road

Bemis Heights
(Gates's headquarters)

to Stillwater
and Albany

to discredit Benedict, stating in a letter that "General Arnold was not out of camp during the whole action."

Most senior officers in the Northern Army and the soldiers who served under Benedict knew the truth. Captain Ebenezer Wakefield did not mince words when he stated, "Arnold was not only the hero of the field . . . but he had won the admiration of the whole army." Wakefield then criticized Gates for not acting quickly enough to reinforce Benedict, which would have "utterly routed the whole British army." Gates's failure was so widely known that "as an excuse to save himself from reproaches coming from every side . . . [Gates] gave out as the reason that the store of powder and ball in the camp was exhausted, and that the supplies of ammunition from Albany had not arrived." Wakefield concluded that "no one could dispute this, yet no one believed it."

Gates was unnerved by his sudden loss of popularity with his troops, and in the words of Lieutenant Colonel Richard Varick, he "seemed to be piqued that Arnold's division had the honor of beating the enemy." In a move that was clearly intended to reflect badly on Benedict's handling of troops in the September 19 battle, Gates took Daniel Morgan's regiment away from Benedict and reassigned Morgan to his own troops in the center of the American line. He made this move even though Morgan's riflemen were best used as snipers and fast-moving light infantry and should always have been on one or the other wing to attack the enemy's flank.

By the time this happened, Benedict knew that he and his men had been slighted in Gates's self-serving report. He confronted Gates at headquarters, and a loud, angry argument ensued. Before stomping out of Gates's tiny hut, Benedict requested a "pass to Philadelphia with my two aides-de-camp and their servants, where I propose to join General Washington, and may possibly have it in my power to serve my country."

The language used in the argument had been so nasty that one of Benedict's aides wrote to Schuyler, worried that "General Arnold is so much offended at the treatment Gates has given him that I [have] not the least doubt the latter will be called on [for a duel]." Schuyler promptly replied with what was certainly the truth: "Perhaps [Gates] is so very sure of success that he does not wish [Arnold] to come in for a share of it."

Gates wanted Benedict gone, but he did not want him telling what really happened at this first Battle of Saratoga. In granting Benedict permission to leave, he ordered that he report only to Congress, where Gates had enough support to suppress whatever account Benedict might submit. Benedict didn't want to leave under this sort of restraint. In addition, when word spread that he intended to leave, the officers and soldiers of the Northern Army became very upset. The British might launch another attack at any moment, and they didn't want to face it without their fighting general. In an unprecedented move, the majority of officers united to persuade Benedict that he was needed there. "They had lost confidence in Gates," Colonel James Livingston wrote, "and had the highest opinion of Arnold. To induce him to stay . . . a letter was written to Arnold, and signed by all the general officers . . . urging him to remain, for another battle seemed imminent." Soothed by the support and kind words of his fellow officers, Benedict decided to stay.

Gates then retaliated. He relieved Benedict of command, assuming command of Benedict's men himself. If Benedict objected, he would be arrested and charged with insubordination.

Benedict could have requested permission to leave again, but he didn't. Instead, he wrote a blunt letter to Gates documenting every slight inflicted on him, adding, "I have every reason to think your treatment proceeds from a spirit of jealousy." Benedict concluded, "I am determined to sacrifice my feelings to the public good, and continue in the army at this critical juncture, when my country needs every support."

Humiliated and feeling helpless, Benedict watched impatiently as September ended and Gates remained inactive. But if anyone thought Benedict would simply sit and take such abuse, they were sorely mistaken. He had never run from a fight in his life, and with Burgoyne less than a mile away, he wasn't about to run from one now.

16

WE'LL HAVE THEM ALL IN HELL

*W*hile Gates did nothing after September 19, Burgoyne dug in, throwing up earthworks, trenches, and protective fortlike timber enclosures, called redoubts, and positioning artillery in case the rebels launched an attack. He considered initiating his own assault, but his troops were exhausted, so he postponed any offensive move for a few days.

When a messenger arrived on September 21 with news that a relief column was finally headed up the Hudson, Burgoyne changed his plans. With Howe in Pennsylvania, General Henry Clinton was in charge of the British garrison in New York. He had over 3,000 men and estimated he could reach Burgoyne "in about ten days." Gentleman Johnny decided to sit tight and await Clinton, knowing full well that he couldn't wait very long. With provisions running low, he calculated that he would have to do something—either retreat or push on—sometime before mid-October.

However, Clinton did not hurry directly up to Saratoga as promised but stopped to fight rebels at both Peekskill and West Point. He then turned half his force around and marched back to New York City with them, ordering the rest of his men to proceed up the Hudson. They did, but at such a leisurely pace that they never met up with Burgoyne.

Meanwhile, as Burgoyne and his army waited behind their fortifications, morale began to slip. During the day Morgan's sharpshooters picked away at the British sentries. At night wolves prowled the no-man's-land between the armies, digging up the shallow graves. Lieutenant Thomas Anburey shuddered to recall that "when [the wolves] approached a corpse, their noise was hideous until they scratched it up."

Burgoyne noted that his troops and officers were drained physically. "The armies [were] so near," he would later write, "that not a night passed without firing and sometimes concerted attacks on our advanced pickets. No foraging party could be made without great detachments [of soldiers] to cover it. It was the plan of the enemy to harass the army by constant alarms and their superiority of numbers enabled them to attempt it without fatigue to themselves."

As October began and the trees turned vivid colors, Burgoyne realized he would have to act before the relief column arrived. On October 4 he held a council of war with his senior officers in which he argued for a massive assault on the left side of the American line. Most of his officers recommended caution, with Riedesel proposing a retreat across the Hudson. The Americans, Riedesel noted, had increased in number with the arrival of nearly 2,000 Continental soldiers from Lake Champlain, plus a huge influx of militia. Gates now had almost 11,000 soldiers in camp, while Burgoyne had fewer than 4,000.

Burgoyne did not want to hear talk of retreat because, according to Riedesel, he felt any "retrograde movement . . . disgraceful." He then ordered that a strong reconnaissance force find out if it would be possible to push through the American lines in order to get to Albany.

At around eleven A.M. on October 7, approximately 2,100 British soldiers set out. Burgoyne's orders had 1,500 taking the high ground to the west, while the remaining men were to circle wide of the American left "by secret paths in the woods to gain the enemy's rear," where they were to hold the Americans in check.

Almost immediately, American sharpshooters stationed in the woods began sending back word that a large number of British soldiers were approaching. The alarm was sounded, and men rushed to their places at the entrenchments, but Gates, true to form, did nothing else. No counterattack was ordered. No scouting parties were sent out. In fact, it was nearly three hours before Gates finally issued the order "to begin the game." This delay gave the British plenty of time to establish strong positions and prepare for battle.

At long last, the Americans slowly advanced, with three distinct groups closing in on their opponent from different directions. It took over an hour before the armies met and the fighting commenced. Benedict tried to watch the developing battle with a spyglass, though the battlefield was two miles away and his vision was obstructed by the rough rolling terrain and trees. As the firing intensified and acrid white smoke made seeing even more difficult, he grew increasingly anxious about his men, clearly itching to join them in the fight.

The American attack was well coordinated and effective. The British soldiers in Barbour's wheat field unleashed a musket volley at one group of advancing Americans and then made a bayonet charge. The Americans stood their ground, firing off two withering volleys of their own and sending the British into retreat.

As this was taking place, 300 sharpshooters under Morgan circled the British right and kept up a steady fire until the enemy began backing through the woods. A third American force caught these British soldiers in a killing crossfire until they dashed to safety behind a wooden fence. A large contingent of Americans regrouped and launched an unsuccessful attack on the British center, situated in a log fortification called the Balcarres Redoubt.

At this point the fight had been going on just over an hour, and Benedict could no longer be contained. He leaped onto his black stallion and rode to the ramparts, sword in hand. The men in camp cheered, thinking he was about to lead them into battle. Benedict only waved to them, then stared out at the chaos of the battlefield—wounded men being dragged back to safety, messengers dashing to and from the fighting, the flash of musketry and thundering report of artillery. To leave camp would be a direct violation of Gates's orders and surely lead to court-martial proceedings. But somewhere out there his men were in a fierce struggle. . . .

The next second Benedict yelled "Victory or death!" and put spurs to his horse, dashing headlong through an opening in the barricade. Gates, who was huddled inside his headquarters with his aides, heard that Benedict was leaving and ordered Major John Armstrong to fetch him back. Benedict managed to elude Armstrong and locate a regiment of Connecticut militia.

"Whose regiment is this?" he is said to have asked a soldier.

"Colonel Latimore's, sir," was the answer.

"Ah, my old Norwich and New London friends," Benedict replied. "God bless you! I am glad to see you. Now come on, boys; if the day is long enough, we'll have them all in hell before night." Benedict found the senior officer in charge, who graciously handed command of the men over to him. Benedict then realigned these soldiers for a second attack.

Next he dashed over to Morgan, who was locked in a fierce battle with a strong line of British regulars being urged on by General Simon Fraser. Benedict shouted to Morgan, "That man on the gray horse [Fraser] is a host in himself and must be disposed of." Morgan then ordered his best sharpshooter, Timothy Murphy, to bring the man down. Murphy's first two shots went wide, but his third shot hit Fraser in the stomach, and he slumped forward. An aide led him from the battlefield, and he would die of his wound the next day. Without their commander, the British began pulling back in disarray toward Freeman's farm and the safety of their fortifications.

The Americans had no orders from Gates to charge, and Benedict certainly didn't have permission to enter the fight or lead troops. But we can safely assume, based on his past performance, that Gates would not have ordered an attack even though the British were clearly in disorder. He was

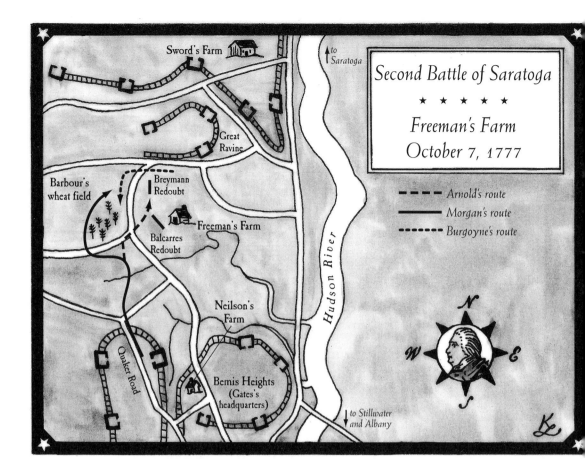

at best a conservative military leader and perhaps even a timid one; he would not have risked his reputation with a charge at well-established and well-manned fortifications.

"Fortunately for the Americans," military historian W. J. Wood writes, "Gates was not there, nor did he ever show himself outside his headquarters. Benedict Arnold *was* there, and that fact turned the next phase of Bemis Heights into a decisive battle." British historian Sir John Fortescue adds, "With true military instinct [Arnold] seized the opportunity to order a general attack upon the British entrenchments."

The British had two very strong redoubts in this part of the battlefield: the Balcarres Redoubt, which anchored the center of the British line, and, a half mile away to the northwest atop a slight knoll, the Breymann Redoubt. In between, two small but sturdy stockade buildings had been placed to protect the area separating the redoubts.

A nineteenth-century depiction of Timothy Murphy being ordered to shoot General Simon Fraser.
THE NEW YORK PUBLIC LIBRARY

Benedict spotted the Balcarres Redoubt first and, acting on his own authority, immediately led a massed charge on it. Despite constant fire from the British, Benedict managed to get his leading troops almost through the tangle of logs and sharpened sticks before severe losses forced them to withdraw. As he pulled back, Benedict surveyed the scene and tried to figure out his next move. That was when he realized his mistake. He had charged the strongest British position.

He wheeled his horse about and galloped after a column of American soldiers heading toward the log huts. Benedict's wild ride took him into a no-man's-land between the two enemy lines, some 120 yards apart. But despite an unrelenting barrage of musket shot and cannon fire, neither Benedict nor his horse was hit. Later, some would fault Benedict as "more like a madman than a cool and discreet officer," while others thought him drunk. He was neither. He sensed a weakness in the enemy line and was determined to exploit it no matter what the consequence to himself.

What Benedict had noticed was that the British and Hessian forces hadn't withdrawn to their original positions. Most of the Germans were inside the Balcarres Redoubt, while the Breymann Redoubt had only two hundred men. Benedict directed the American column past the lightly defended log huts and toward the Breymann Redoubt. The hastily devised plan called for him to circle around and attack the rear of the redoubt, while Morgan's men stormed the front.

*Benedict and his horse (center foreground) are both shot just as
they charge into the Breymann Redoubt.* THE NEW YORK PUBLIC LIBRARY

Inside, Colonel Heinrich Breymann screamed and slashed with his
sword to keep his men at their posts as two waves of rebel soldiers closed
in. It is alleged that he killed four of his own soldiers to keep them from
running. When the Americans were 50 yards from the redoubt, Breymann
let loose an artillery barrage that took one rebel's head clean off and
wounded several others. A second later, Benedict rode through the boiling
smoke and into the redoubt, followed by a regiment of Massachusetts soldiers. Breymann was dead, apparently shot by one of his own men, and
many of the Hessians began pulling back.

The retreating Germans stopped just long enough to fire off one
more volley at the Americans. A shot ripped into Benedict's left leg—the
same leg that had been so severely wounded at Quebec—while several
more struck his horse. The animal collapsed, and Benedict's newly
wounded leg hit the ground and shattered in several places as the horse
came down on it. From the ground, Benedict continued to shout orders
as Morgan's troops poured into the redoubt. Hand-to-hand combat en-

sued, but the Hessians had little fight left in them and soon began surrendering.

Benedict was pulled from under his dead horse and propped up nearby. No physicians were available, so all he could do was endure the blinding pain and watch as American troops secured the redoubt and took prisoners. Major Henry Dearborn came up to Benedict and "asked him if he was badly wounded." Shock was setting in from the wound, and Benedict's voice wavered when he allegedly whispered, "In the same leg. I wish it had been my heart."

Benedict was carried back to Gates's headquarters on a makeshift litter. Next he was loaded onto a wagon and transported thirty excruciating miles over rough roads to an army hospital in Albany.

His left femur had been broken in several places, and sharp bone fragments had penetrated the skin. Doctors worried that infection and gangrene might set in and advised that the leg be amputated immediately. Benedict refused the operation, which he called "such damned nonsense." This was a wise decision, since most amputations at the time ended in a slow and lingering death from infection.

Dr. James Thacher was with Benedict on the night of October 11 and recalled that he was "very peevish, and impatient under his misfortunes, and required all my attention during the night." There's little wonder Benedict was irritable. For one thing, the pain must have been unbearable, especially considering that the hospital—like everything else about the army—had been ignored by Congress and was short on supplies. For another, every doctor who attended him suggested he have his leg taken off. Finally, all the doctors could do to keep his leg straight was to construct a "fracture box" around it. This primitive form of wood cast forced the normally very active Benedict to lie on his back all day for weeks, completely immobilized.

Adding to his crotchety mood was the frustrating fact that his wound didn't heal properly or quickly. Weeks dragged along with his leg feeling better on some days, worse on many more. Benedict took his frustrations out on the doctors, whom he called "a set of ignorant pretenders." His leg didn't start to heal until the new year of 1778 began.

During his long recuperation, Benedict was visited by many friends, including a number of his staff. From them he heard about Burgoyne's fate.

Once Burgoyne realized that Benedict's troops had control of the Breymann Redoubt, he pulled his forces back across the Great Ravine. Horatio Gates did not follow up the success of October 7 by advancing toward Burgoyne. He was content to let sharpshooters pick away at the stationary British troops until Burgoyne removed his army to Saratoga, where he formally surrendered on October 17.

Gates wrote his official battle report to Congress, praising his troops and several officers and accentuating his own role in the fighting. He did note Benedict's "gallant" actions during the assault on the Breymann Redoubt, but did not mention that it was Benedict who had rallied the troops and led the charge.

Gates never thanked Benedict either in person or in writing for bringing about the victory and never inquired about his health. Instead, he heaped lavish praise on Wilkinson, calling him a "military genius" and suggesting that Congress elevate him in rank to general. Wilkinson, ever deceitful, insisted to friends that Benedict Arnold "neither rendered service, nor deserved credit that day."

Congress had fled Philadelphia in a panic when General Howe's army soundly beat Washington's troops at Brandywine, Pennsylvania, on September 11 and marched triumphantly into the rebel capital. The clear and decisive military victory at Saratoga put Congress in a mood to accept whatever Gates said without question. Congress offered "the thanks of Congress" to Benedict and another officer wounded in the battle, Major General Benjamin Lincoln. They also elevated Wilkinson in rank, as Gates had recommended. Finally, for Gates they voted to strike a gold medal to commemorate his great victory, an honor bestowed on only one other American officer during the war, George Washington. When the resolution was presented to Gates, the new president of Congress, Henry Lau-

Artist John Trumbull put Horatio Gates in the center of his painting of Burgoyne's surrender, even though Gates never stepped onto the field of battle. THE LIBRARY OF CONGRESS

rens, heaped on the praise: "Your name sir will be written in the breasts of the grateful Americans of the present age and sent down to posterity in characters which will remain indelible when [the medal's] gold shall have changed appearance."

Saratoga would turn out to be the decisive battle of the Revolution. Not only had the American soldiers thoroughly humiliated British regulars on the field of battle, but the stunning victory brought international recognition. After years of stalling, the French government officially recognized the new nation of the United States in February 1778 and pledged to aid it in its struggle against England with money and troops.

Benedict Arnold took the initiative that eventually routed Burgoyne at Saratoga, and he was actually in the fighting and sustained a grave wound. But it was Horatio Gates who would forever be called "the hero of Saratoga."

17

I AM HEARTILY TIRED

During his five months at the hospital in Albany, Benedict brooded in his bed. The lavish praise accorded Gates, plus Wilkinson's promotion, only confirmed for the twice-wounded general his worst fears about Congress. Toward the end of 1777, however, Congress began to appreciate Benedict's military skills. Even as the resolution praising Gates was being issued, many in Congress were having doubts about him. They questioned his desire to see Wilkinson promoted over so many other established and deserving officers. They also thought that the surrender terms Gates had worked out with Burgoyne—in which he agreed to let Burgoyne and his entire army sail back to England if they promised not to reenter the war—were foolishly lenient. And word about Benedict's real role in the battle was beginning to reach their ears as well. Even Burgoyne was publicly giving Benedict full credit "for the successes obtained over him."

Late in December, it dawned on Congress that the Americans needed a strong and active field general like Benedict. A resolution was passed to advance him in seniority over the other major generals who had been promoted ahead of him. Still, Congress refused to acknowledge it had done anything wrong when it originally passed over Benedict. The very carefully worded promotion papers made it clear that this promotion was not in recognition of Benedict's heroism at Saratoga or elsewhere; it was nothing more than a "legal correction." Finally, to add insult to injury, Congress made no public announcement of his change in rank. On the contrary, they guaranteed it would happen as quietly as possible by having "General Washington regulate the rank of Major General Arnold." In other words, Washington would inform Benedict of the change either by letter or in person.

Despite the fact that Gates didn't want to share credit for the victory at Saratoga with Benedict, the truth soon spread. This French painting of Benedict suggests that he played a significant role in defeating the British.
FORT TICONDEROGA MUSEUM

Benedict seems to have changed during his long period of recuperation. He apparently lost his passion for the Revolution, wondering what good it would do to replace one unfair government with another. If he had been able to shrug off the long list of slights and move on, he probably would have come down to us as one of our greatest patriots. Instead, he continued to see Congress as duplicitous and unchangeable, and he concluded that his hope that military success would restore the luster to the Arnold name would never be fulfilled.

Benedict was able to sit up for the first time in January, but the effort reopened his wound, and he flopped back down in agony. It would be more than two months before he could attempt to get up again. Trapped inside his hospital room by his shattered leg, inactive and often alone, he brooded about the slights and the shabby way he'd been treated.

Washington wrote Benedict late in January 1778, informing him of his change in rank. The letter was warm and friendly, and in it Washington asked Benedict "whether you are upon your legs again, and if you are not, may I flatter myself that you will be soon?" The commander stated an "earnest wish to have your services [for] the ensuing campaign" and promised his fighting general "a command which I trust will be agreeable to yourself and of great advantage to the public."

This was precisely the sort of praise Benedict had been longing for since the beginning of the conflict, and the kind of invitation he would have leaped at previously. Yet he did not respond to Washington's letter for over a month and a half.

When he finally answered it, he told his commander that he would not be physically able to take the field, and that his leg would probably require another five or six months to fully heal. He then concluded, "It is my most ardent wish to render every assistance in my power, that your Excellency may be enabled to finish the arduous task, you have with so much honor to yourself and advantage to your country, been engaged in, and have the pleasure of seeing peace and happiness restored to your country on the most permanent basis."

These words are a far cry from those he used when retreating from Canada back in 1776. "I am content to be the last man who quits this country, and fall," he had written, "so that my country [will] rise." Even in 1777, after he was initially passed over for promotion, he declared that for "the safety and happiness of my country . . . I have repeatedly fought and bled, and am ready at all times to resign my life still." In comparison, his March 1778 letter to Washington was curiously distant and lacking in passion. He referred not to "my country," but to "your country." Benedict's goals had shifted. He was no longer invested in the Revolution as a way to restore his family name. From this point forward he would consider his and his family's interests a separate issue and pursue them first and foremost.

George Washington was aware that Benedict was upset, but he had no idea how deep that resentment went. In May he wrote again, telling Benedict he wished to give him a set of shoulder ornaments for his uniform and a gold silk ornament for his sword hilt "as testimony of my sincere regard and approbation of your conduct." These seemingly insignificant adornments were, in fact, an extraordinary gesture on Washington's part. He was a notoriously reticent man, and any sign of friendship toward one of his officers was considered a deep privilege. Along with these gifts, he expressed his eagerness to see Benedict return to active duty.

Two weeks later Benedict appeared unexpectedly at Washington's quarters in Valley Forge, Pennsylvania, having traveled the 170 miles from New Haven in a carriage. His presence was "a great joy to the army," according to one soldier, and especially to its commander, who needed all the fighting officers he could muster. But Benedict was still hobbling about with the aid of a crutch. His muscles had atrophied from lack of use, and the compound fracture had shortened his leg by two inches. It was clear he wouldn't be able to take on any assignment that was physically demanding. How then could a crippled warrior be of service to the Patriot cause?

After France officially sided with the young United States, British priorities shifted as they began preparing for a European war against France and its allies. British general Howe had entered Philadelphia in September 1777 and spent much of the winter attending balls and parties. He was not aware of the shift in policy when he informed the king and Parliament that he would need at least 80,000 additional soldiers to win the war in America. Howe was recalled to England and replaced by Sir Henry Clinton, who was told to protect the seaports in America at all costs. In June he began moving his army back to New York.

When Clinton left Philadelphia, hundreds of Loyalists went with him, fearful that returning Patriots would harass and possibly execute them. But many more stayed, feeling they had done nothing criminal in backing the king and wanting to guard their businesses and homes from what they viewed as arbitrary and unlawful seizure. It fell to Congress, the Pennsylvania Council, and a military commandant to govern the deeply divided city. As a way to reward Benedict and allow him to serve the Revolution, Washington appointed him commandant of Philadelphia.

Stationing Benedict in Philadelphia to deal with members of Congress, the very people he detested, was a sad mistake. Now that he had been elevated in rank and no longer sought their support, he had no intention of ever again being humiliated by them or anyone else. His leg still very painful, Benedict came to Philadelphia not seeming to care whose feathers he ruffled.

When he learned that the widow and children of a Patriot leader killed at Bunker Hill, Dr. Joseph Warren, were in desperate financial straits, he went into immediate action. He chastised the Massachusetts authorities, saying the family had "been entirely neglected by the state," and then challenged Congress to do the proper, decent thing by granting them a special pension. At the time, Congress was trying to avoid the expense of establishing similar pensions for the families of Washington's officers, in the event that any of them were killed or wounded in battle. To be openly taken to task put them in an awkward position, and a grouchy Congress turned a deaf ear to Benedict's request.

Benedict was not about to give up. He announced in the newspapers that he was going to start a private fund to aid the family, and even contributed $500 himself. Two years later an embarrassed and annoyed Congress finally granted an annual payment to Warren's widow and children.

Benedict also found himself at odds with local Patriots. When the Patriot population returned to the city, they immediately wanted known and even suspected Loyalists punished severely. One congressman suggested that these people should be made to pay a combined fee of £100,000 (about $3.5 million today), while another, Joseph Reed, provided a list of five hundred he wanted charged with treason and hanged.

The incident that provoked Benedict to action involved two Quakers. John Roberts and Abram Carlisle were put on trial for selling goods to the British occupying force, found guilty of treason, and ordered hanged. The harsh verdict shocked just about everybody; the entire jury had recommended a pardon, saying that Roberts had dealt with the British "under the influence of fear" and had, in fact, done frequent "acts of humanity, charity and benevolence" that had saved many American lives. Roberts's wife and his ten children went before Congress and literally begged on their knees for mercy, while a petition bearing the signatures of one thousand civic, military, and religious leaders requested a reprieve. Reed, as head of the Pennsylvania Council,

Benedict's chief nemesis in Philadelphia was Joseph Reed.
THE LIBRARY OF CONGRESS

turned down all requests and demanded "a speedy execution for both animals."

Because he had not yet taken office officially in May 1778, when the trial took place, Benedict could not stop the public hanging of these two men. But the moment he was legally able to, he put a halt to all additional executions. Personally, he believed that peace in the city would be achieved more quickly if a lenient policy were followed, and there was outside support for his decision. On June 4 Congress passed a resolution over the objections of several representatives that expressly forbade any "molestation or pillaging of the inhabitants" of Philadelphia. Two weeks later George Washington issued orders instructing Benedict "to preserve tranquility and order in the city and give security to individuals of every class and description."

Despite these clear instructions, Benedict came in for the most intense criticism for his policy of leniency, especially from Joseph Reed, who had taken a dislike to Benedict even before meeting him in Philadelphia. Reed had been an aide to George Washington but had resigned because he thought the commander an inept military leader. He became an ardent supporter of Horatio Gates, which meant he opposed George Washington and Washington's followers and friends, such as Benedict Arnold. Reed

Benedict set up his headquarters in this building,
which he had to pay for out of his own pocket.
THE NEW YORK PUBLIC LIBRARY

had also signed the petition to acquit Roger Enos of deserting during Arnold's march to Quebec.

Reed and other Patriots like him had more in mind than simply purging their city of Loyalists. They wanted the Loyalists' property as well.

It was a common practice for local governing bodies to seize the property of Loyalists, either those who had left out of fear or those whom they had banished. The lands and any buildings on them were then sold at a very low price, usually to the same Revolutionary leaders who controlled the local assembly or to their friends. Just prior to Benedict's arrival in Philadelphia, Joseph Reed had purchased the mansion of Joseph Galloway, a Loyalist who had held important government positions. Before moving in, Reed had the state militia evict Galloway's wife, Grace, by carrying her out in a chair.

To make matters worse, Benedict was not shy about demonstrating his sympathy for the city's Loyalists. He staged a public reception at City Tavern and personally invited many Quakers and Loyalists to attend. He was able to express his disgust over the eviction of Grace Galloway by sending his housekeeper over to help her pack and by allowing her to use his coach as well. These gestures of respect infuriated Reed.

Benedict further annoyed local Patriots by pursuing personal business interests while governing the city. As commandant of Philadelphia he was obliged to regularly entertain foreign dignitaries, members of Congress, high-ranking officers in the army, and local businessmen. This required a large house, servants, and generous quantities of food and drink, all of which he was expected to pay for out of his own pocket. When he wrote to his sister, Hannah, asking that she send him money, he learned that Congress hadn't paid him (or any other officer in the Continental Army) in nearly two and a half years.

In order to subsidize his official position, Benedict purchased a schooner and had it fitted out as a privateer. (Privateers were privately owned ships that were sanctioned by Congress to hunt down and seize enemy ships and whatever they were carrying, which the owner of the privateer got to keep.) Next, when Benedict learned about a warehouse in New Jersey filled with goods, including civilian clothing, wine, and medical supplies, he had government wagons transport the items to Pennsylvania, where they were sold, Benedict splitting the proceeds with two other men. A third business venture had Benedict and two other officers buying up nonmilitary goods confiscated from Loyalists (just a few days before Reed planned to) and selling them at a sizeable profit.

Technically, Benedict's use of his military office for personal gain wasn't illegal. Commanding generals frequently used their official positions to acquire property. Historian Carl Van Doren notes, "Other American generals besides Arnold . . . engaged in speculations, like many citizens whose love of country did not interfere with their love of profits." At that time there were no laws against such undertakings, and while George Washington had ordered a strict accounting of all goods that might be of military use, he never explicitly said that nonmilitary items could not be seized and sold by senior officers.

While Benedict had broken no laws, the practice was viewed as unseemly by some officers. Still, it's probable that nothing at all would have been made of his business sidelines if Joseph Reed hadn't disliked him so much and hadn't wanted all nonmilitary goods for himself and his friends. Reed reported Benedict's business dealings directly to George Washington. Washington frowned on this sort of activity and had, in 1775, referred to "a dirty, mercenary spirit" that had infected the Revolution. Yet he understood that it was a common practice and pointedly did nothing to interfere with Benedict's dealings.

This did not stop Reed. He and his friends continued to vilify Benedict behind his back. Meanwhile, a newspaper friendly to Reed's views, the *Pennsylvania Packet,* amplified the attacks by printing a letter from William Matlack, the son of a friend of Reed's. The letter reproached Benedict for "high living," and said, "When I meet your carriage in the streets, and think of the splendor in which you live and revel . . . it is impossible to avoid the question, 'From whence have these riches flowed if you did not plunder Montreal.'" There followed a long list of all the past, unproven charges against Benedict from the Canadian campaign, plus other accusations from John Brown's vicious broadside.

Benedict responded to the various charges, but this only intensified the assault. Reed even questioned Benedict's rank and seniority, suggesting that two of Pennsylvania's major generals should be promoted over him.

Once again Benedict's character and honor were being questioned (though this time his dabbling in business for personal gain clearly gave his opponents real ammunition). The attacks irritated him to the point of exasperation: "I am heartily tired with my journey and almost so with human nature. I daily discover so much baseness and ingratitude among mankind that I almost blush at being of the same species."

Despite the obvious tension such personal attacks engendered, Benedict had cause to be optimistic. For one thing, he still had friends who wanted to look out for him. In New York, Philip Schuyler and a group of other Patriot leaders suggested that the legislature should reward Benedict for his defense of the state in 1775, 1776, and 1777. They specifically proposed that he be given one of two large Loyalist manors confiscated in Skenesboro and Johnson Hall (both located near the southern part of Lake Champlain), along with over 40,000 acres of land. In writing a strong recommendation to the governor, John Jay said, "Major General Arnold had in contemplation to establish a [town] of officers and soldiers who have served with him. . . . To you, Sir, or to our state, General Arnold can require no recommendation. A series of distinguished services entitles him to respect and favor."

Moreover, the thirty-seven-year-old Benedict had fallen head over heels in love. "I must tell you that Cupid has given our little general a more mortal wound than all the host of Britons could," wrote Ann Willing Morris, wife of Patriot leader Robert Morris. "Miss Peggy Shippen is the fair one."

18

ON YOU ALONE MY
HAPPINESS DEPENDS

Margaret "Peggy" Shippen turned eighteen years old in June 1778, the month Benedict arrived in Philadelphia. Even at that age she was already widely known and admired in the city. Not only was her family one of colonial America's richest and most illustrious, she was, according to historian Willard Sterne Randall, "tiny, blond, dainty of face and figure, with steady, wide-set blue-gray eyes. . . . Appearing to be shy, she was bright and quick and capable of conversing at length about politics and business to anyone."

Peggy's great-grandfather, Edward Shippen, had immigrated to America in 1668, bringing along a small fortune of £10,000 ($795,000) in cash. He married a Quaker being persecuted by the Puritans and was granted sanctuary in Rhode Island by Benedict's great-great-grandfather, Governor Benedict Arnold (I). The couple moved to Philadelphia, where Edward thrived as an importer of goods. He became the city's first mayor and a trusted advisor to William Penn, the colony's founder.

The second Edward Shippen expanded the family business; he was mayor of the city and then a judge, as well as a founder of the University of Pennsylvania and Princeton University. Peggy's father, also an Edward, wasn't as outgoing as either of the other Edwards, but he was a solid businessman and held a remarkable number of well-paying if rather mundane public offices, including principal clerk and then recording secretary to the state courts and an admiralty judge.

This pencil drawing of Peggy Shippen was done in 1778 by Major John André while Philadelphia was under British control.
THE YALE UNIVERSITY ART GALLERY

It was from her Loyalist father that Peggy learned about Philadelphia politics and the Revolution. Like most young ladies from well-to-do families of the time, she received instruction in such things as needlework, drawing, dancing, and music. But Judge Shippen gave her newspapers and political tracts to read and schooled her in bookkeeping, accounting, investments, trading, and banking. "There was nothing of frivolity either in her dress, demeanor or conduct," recalled her good friend Rebecca Franks, "and though deservedly admired, she had too much good sense to be vain."

But Peggy Shippen was no stick-in-the-mud, either. During the British occupation of Philadelphia, Peggy, her two sisters, and her friends found themselves being invited out just about every evening. She was frequently escorted to these events by General Henry Clinton's dashing twenty-seven-year-old aide-de-camp, Major John André. Another British officer, Navy Captain Hammond, remembered, "We were all in love with her."

This was the remarkable young woman Benedict met at a dinner in Edward Shippen's house. He immediately found himself captivated by her intelligence and beauty and quick wit. By July 1778 he was in love and thinking of marriage. This was not a sudden idea for Benedict. It had been three years since the death of his first wife, and more and more he'd found himself longing for the companionship and settled comfort marriage would provide. Hannah, too, needed help in managing his business interests and caring for his three sons.

A marriage between an older man—Benedict was thirty-seven at the time—and such a young woman might scandalize us today but was not uncommon in the eighteenth century. The fact that no one expressed outrage over their relationship—not her parents or other relatives, not any of her friends, not even Benedict's political enemies—suggests it was not considered unusual or immoral.

Peggy's father and mother were at first uneasy about having Benedict courting their youngest daughter, but for other reasons. As Loyalists they viewed all Patriots, but especially one as famous as Benedict, as interlopers who were trying to destroy their way of life. In addition, Edward Shippen worried that Benedict would always be a cripple and unable to provide properly for his daughter.

In Benedict's favor, his public defense of Loyalists had a softening effect on Peggy's parents. It probably wasn't lost on Papa Shippen that having a famous and powerful rebel interested in his daughter would offer his family and property a degree of valuable protection. As for Benedict's health, he maintained an active enough schedule that Peggy's soon-to-be brother-in-law, Neddy Burd, saw no problem. "We have every reason to hope [his leg] will be well again," he wrote another relative, adding, "[He is] a well-dispositioned man, and one that will use his best endeavors to make P happy."

Benedict became a regular visitor at the Shippen mansion for afternoon tea and dinner. During these visits he and Peggy would be closely chaperoned by Mr. and Mrs. Shippen. Peggy and her sisters were also frequent guests of Benedict's at his home, and Peggy accompanied him to dances, music recitals, and the theater. By September Benedict was completely smitten by the young beauty and declared his intentions in two letters, one to Peggy, the other to her father.

Benedict's letter to Edward Shippen was brief and businesslike. He had a decent income, he told the older man, and was not expecting to receive a dowry; he wanted only to marry Peggy and hoped "[our] difference in political sentiments, will . . . be no bar to my happiness," since the war would soon be over and "peace and happiness [will] be restored to every one."

His letter to Peggy is altogether different. Passionate and personal, flowery and at times wildly dramatic, it reveals Benedict as both bold and vulnerable and willing to risk embarrassment in pursuit of happiness. In many ways it echoes his quest to reestablish his family name as preeminent in America, when he was willing to absent himself from his family for months at a time and risk his life and fortune to prove he was a hero.

"Twenty times have I taken up my pen to write to you," his letter to Peggy begins, "and as often has my trembling hand refused to obey the dictates of my heart—a heart which, though calm and serene amidst the clashing of arms and all the din and horrors of war, trembles with diffidence and fear of giving offence when it attempts to address you on a subject so important to its happiness. Dear madam, your charms have lighted up a flame in my bosom which can never be extinguished; your heavenly image is too deeply impressed ever to be effaced. . . . On you alone my happiness depends."

Peggy's father did not immediately sanction the marriage. He wrote to his own father asking what he should do about the situation, a correspondence that took weeks to complete. Meanwhile, Benedict continued to visit the Shippen home and to invite Peggy and her sisters to various functions.

As 1778 ended, Papa Shippen remained reluctant, though he was clearly softening in his attitude. "I gave my daughter Betsy to Neddy Burd last Thursday evening, and all is jollity and mirth," he wrote his father. "My youngest daughter is much solicited by a certain General on the same subject. Whether this will take place or not depends on circumstances. If it should, it will not be till spring."

Several things eventually won Peggy's father over. Mr. Shippen had to be impressed when Benedict continued to protect Loyalists despite increasing harassment from Joseph Reed and his friends. In addition, rumors were beginning to circulate around town—rumors that Mr. Shippen no doubt heard—that Benedict was about to be given a handsome reward by the state of New York. This would, at least, allay any fears Peggy's father might have concerning his daughter's financial future. Finally, in early spring 1779, Benedict purchased a ninety-nine-acre country manor called Mount Pleasant. Located just five miles outside Philadelphia on the Schuylkill River, Mount Pleasant was, as John Adams noted, "the most elegant seat in Pennsylvania." Then, as a kind of reverse dowry, Benedict deeded the estate to Peggy, a move that reassured her father that he was sincere and won his approval of the marriage.

Benedict was on the verge of achieving two other things elusive to him throughout his life—emotional happiness and financial security. To finalize the latter, he prepared to travel north in February 1779, to confer with Schuyler and his other New York friends about the estate and land he was hoping to receive.

When Reed and the Pennsylvania Council heard about his trip, they grew livid. Reed quickly filed formal charges against the military commandant, accusing him of eight crimes in connection with his use of a public office for personal gain and ordering that he stand trial in a state court. Reed then added muscle to the charges by having the Council issue a pointed threat to Congress: It would no longer call out the state militia to combat the British, or pay to supply the Continental Army, as long as Benedict was in command. To humiliate him further (and possibly to put a halt to the New York transfer of land to him), the Council sent copies of the charges to every congressional delegation.

Benedict had already left Philadelphia when he learned what the Council had done. Instead of returning to the city, he headed for the Continental Army's winter quarters in Morristown, New Jersey, where he met with George Washington. As Benedict later related to his aides, his commander was outraged by the charges and suggested that he ask for a congressional investigation into them. Benedict would have preferred a military court-martial hearing, where he might expect a more sympathetic response. But he knew better than to go counter to a pointed suggestion from Washington, who still had many powerful friends in Congress. Besides, he would have more of a chance in a congressional hearing than in a Pennsylvania court, where the odds would definitely be stacked against him.

The matter was turned over to Congress, along with a motion by Reed's friends in Congress that Benedict be removed from office immediately. Congress rejected the idea of discharging Benedict by a roll-call vote, in which only the delegation from Pennsylvania voted in favor of dismissing him. Then Congress referred the eight charges to a special committee headed by William Paca, a highly distinguished Maryland judge.

Paca immediately asked for evidence concerning the charges. Benedict responded in detail to each charge and turned over any relevant documents he had. Reed and the Council had no real evidence. In fact, they admitted that they had nothing other than "an opinion operative only as the world shall give it weight." In other words, because they thought Benedict had done wrong, they hoped everyone else would, too.

The Paca committee acted swiftly, clearing Benedict of the six charges they felt they had the power to rule on. Because the other two involved militia troops and wagons, they suggested that these counts be heard by a military court-martial. Benedict was elated by the decision, convinced the court-martial would clear him completely of the remaining charges. He was so sure of this that he resigned as military commandant and began preparing for his new life as a civilian.

However, the confrontation was no longer about whether Benedict had acted improperly. It was now a contest between the nation and one of its states. If the Pennsylvania Council's threat to withhold troops and money from the national army went unchallenged, other states might defy Congress as well.

Congress demanded that the threat be withdrawn, which the Council promptly rejected. The ensuing arguments became so intense that many in Congress wanted to move the federal government out of Philadelphia. To head off an open fight with Reed and the Pennsylvania Council, a dispute that might jeopardize the war against Britain, cooler heads in Congress sought a compromise. After a tempestuous all-night bargaining session that left the president of Congress, Henry Laurens, feeling "as if my life was breaking," a new committee was formed to investigate Benedict all over again. This committee's first action was to toss out the findings of the Paca committee and recommend a court-martial trial on four of the charges (even though doing this would mean illegally trying Benedict twice for two of them).

The news devastated and angered Benedict. He had wanted to clear his name as quickly as possible, but a new trial would mean gathering and debating more evidence, more time spent answering the same questions. Benedict also knew that while he awaited this second trial, Reed and his friends would continue to smear him in Congress and in the newspapers.

Benedict wrote to George Washington, hoping to speed the trial along, while Reed requested an indefinite postponement, saying he needed to collect evidence and interview additional witnesses. Washington had originally scheduled the court to convene on May 1, but he did not want it to seem as if he was rushing matters to clear his friend of the charges. For appearances' sake, Washington granted the postponement and informed Benedict of this in a brief note.

The delay left Benedict feeling shaken and anxious and very isolated. He was under daily attack from Reed and his friends, Congress had expressly turned its back on him, and now it seemed that his mentor and friend had doubts about his honesty and was willing to leave him twisting indefinitely. Nine days later he wrote a desperate and anguished letter to Washington: "If your Excellency thinks me criminal, for heaven's sake let me be immediately tried and, if found guilty, executed. I want no favor; I ask only justice. . . . Having made every sacrifice of fortune and blood, and become a cripple in the service of my country, I little expected to meet the ungrateful returns I have received from my countrymen; but as Congress

have stamped ingratitude as a current coin, I must take it. . . . I have
nothing left but the little reputation I have gained in the army.
Delay in the present case is worse
than death."

Adding to his anger was yet
another insult: His military accounts—which had been passed
from the Massachusetts Provincial Congress to the Northern
Army to Congress to the Board of
War—were now going to be reviewed yet again by a congressional treasury committee.

*This French engraving of Benedict, done from a
portrait by Pierre Eugene Du Simitiere, is considered
the only authentic representation of him.*
THE NEW YORK PUBLIC LIBRARY

While Benedict stewed, Reed
went into action, though not to
gather real evidence. He wrote what amounted to a threatening letter to
Washington, who was then preparing for a major spring offensive. Reed
pointed out, "Such is the dependence of the army upon the transportation
of this state, that should the court treat [Arnold's transgressions] as a light
and trivial matter, we fear it will not be practicable to draw forth wagons
in the future, be the emergency what it may, and it will have a very bad
consequence." Reed then fired off another letter to Congress saying that if
Congress should in any way favor Arnold, the newly formed nation could
look forward to "a melancholy prospect of perpetual disunion between
[Pennsylvania] and the other United States." Clearly, Reed and the Pennsylvania Council were determined to use any means, including blackmail,
to punish Arnold and take possession of Loyalist property.

As the days slipped by into weeks and the weeks into months, Benedict grew more incensed and angry at "a set of artful, unprincipled men in
office [who] misrepresent the most innocent actions."

In the midst of all this darkness, there was one constant light: Peggy Shippen. She supported him despite the uncertainty of his future and the swirling public accusations. At the Shippen house on the evening of April 8 Peggy and Benedict were wed in a quiet, private ceremony.

Theirs was a genuinely happy marriage. But without the distractions of a field command or his office as commandant, Benedict had a great deal of time to think about an almost endless list of past humiliations. At Fort Ticonderoga he'd had to deal with the likes of Ethan Allen, John Brown, James Easton, and Edward Mott, who slandered him and denied him his share of credit for the victory. He'd been betrayed by Roger Enos on the march to Quebec and by Moses Hazen during the retreat from Canada, only to see both exonerated. He'd been demeaned by Horatio Gates and James Wilkinson at Saratoga and now was under attack by Joseph Reed and the Pennsylvania Council.

Congress, meanwhile, had not paid him for over three years of faithful military service and had insulted him on numerous occasions concerning his rank and expenses, all the while failing to provide adequate supplies to his troops. For his part, Benedict had been away from his family for months at a time, spent his own money to supply his troops, and been severely wounded twice. It was almost too much to bear, especially with another possible humiliation staring him in the face.

Many men might have given up completely, resigned their commissions, and tried to rebuild their lives as best they could. Benedict, however, was not about to admit defeat. Instead, he looked to his enemies for the salvation he couldn't find with his friends.

19

BECAUSE I MIGHT
HAVE DONE WRONG

e will never know how many weeks or even months of thought went into Benedict Arnold's decision to forsake the American Revolution. We don't know whether he agonized over it, or whom (besides Peggy) he might have consulted before making his decision. All we know is that during the first week of May 1779, Benedict asked Joseph Stansbury, a Philadelphia businessman and Loyalist, to visit him at his home. There in a secluded back room the men sat down to talk, and, as Stansbury later recalled, "after some general conversation, [Arnold] opened his political sentiments respecting the war . . . between Great Britain and America, declaring his abhorrence of a separation of the latter from the former as a measure that would be ruinous to both." Benedict then offered to help defeat the American rebels and asked if Stansbury would communicate this to the officer in charge of British espionage, Major John André. Stansbury must have sensed the magnitude of Benedict's offer, because he packed his bags and headed for New York the very next morning.

John André was young, bright, sophisticated, and dangerously eager to advance his military career.
THE LIBRARY OF CONGRESS

Riding through war-torn New Jersey was dangerous in itself, and slipping past patrols to get into New York City took patience and guile. And once there, Stansbury couldn't just walk into British headquarters and demand a meeting with André, no matter how big his news might be. He needed to follow protocol and have someone reasonably important request an interview on his behalf. After conferring with a friend, who sent him to see an acquaintance of his, who in turn sent him to yet another person, Stansbury finally got his letter of recommendation and met with André.

At the time André was twenty-eight years old. He had risen in the military with amazing speed, having been made chief of the secret service just two weeks before his meeting with Stansbury. He had been born into a rich family and gone to Switzerland to study military drawing and mathematics, as well as art, flute, and dancing. He was fluent in German, French, and Dutch, which made him extremely valuable when German-speaking mercenaries were hired to fight alongside British soldiers. Perhaps more important to Benedict, André was a close friend of Peggy's, having met her while the British occupied Philadelphia.

The moment Stansbury told Major André of his meeting with Benedict, the young officer must have sat up straight in disbelief. Recently, André had drawn up a list of all the American generals he thought could be brought to the British side. But never in his wildest dreams had he thought to include the name of Benedict Arnold. He immediately went to confer with his commander, Sir Henry Clinton, after which he drafted a full but careful reply to Benedict's offer.

In his letter André welcomed Benedict to the British cause, gave instructions on how to send coded messages, and suggested several ways that Benedict could be of service to the king. He could, André said, turn over secret information concerning American and French troop movement and strength, help facilitate prisoner release negotiations, aid in the capture of leading rebels, or urge other important rebel leaders to abandon the Revolution.

The letter became vaguer when it came to what Benedict would receive for these services. Benedict had asked for £10,000 sterling ($145,000) in compensation (to cover what he stood to lose in personal property and other assets if the plot were discovered and he had to flee America). André would say only that Benedict would be rewarded in a way that would exceed "even his most sanguine hopes," but he did not specifically agree to the £10,000 amount. This letter began a long and frustrating negotiation over what service Benedict would provide and how much he would be paid. More than eighteen months would pass before these questions were resolved.

Because Benedict was insistent on ironing out the financial aspect of his deal, many historians have assumed that it was simple greed that made him switch sides. But the state of his finances suggests otherwise. Congress had not paid him in nearly four years and owed him almost £1,800. He had used just under £3,000 of his own money to feed and supply his troops in Canada. Customers in Connecticut owed him another £3,000. Add to this approximately £4,200 he had yet to collect from two of the business schemes he had arranged while serving as military commandant of Philadelphia. This comes to £12,000 he would never see if his betrayal of the Revolution were discovered or if the British were defeated. And this does not take into account the value of his homes and their contents, his warehouses, his wharves, and other possessions such as carriages, horses, and so forth that would be seized by authorities. Clearly, £10,000 was a handsome sum, but nowhere near enough to compensate him, should he lose everything he owned or was owed to him.

If greed was not the driving force behind his change of loyalties, what was? The fact that he was the sole support of six other people—his three

One of Benedict's coded letters to André, along with the decoded version. Benedict signed his correspondence to André with the name Moore.

sons by his first wife; his sister, Hannah; and Peggy and their soon-to-be-born baby—weighed heavily on his shoulders. Adding to the pressure was the ever-present specter of ruin and failure, a product of witnessing his father's descent into debt and alcohol. He would negotiate with stubborn determination to protect his dependents from the sort of shame and pity that he had felt as a boy.

Of course, he had other personal reasons for turning traitor. A variety of enemies on the American side had insulted and abused him, while others had denied him the credit due his military skills. And Congress had, again and again, insulted his sense of honor by denying him advancement while promoting clearly less talented and accomplished officers.

But it is a mistake to see Benedict's betrayal as a personal vendetta only. At the start of the war he believed passionately that the hold Great Britain had over the colonies had to be broken if people like him were to have a fair chance at succeeding and rising in the world. That is why he threw himself into the Revolution and fought with such reckless abandon. However, the people who controlled Congress came to seem even more petty and shortsighted than those in Parliament, while Joseph Reed and those on the Pennsylvania Council appeared more dangerous than any Loyalist ever had. The pure spirit that had marked the start of the Revolution—the notion that the government of the country would be run by educated, fair-minded men, and that merit, not heredity, would be how a person advanced and succeeded—had died and been replaced by something dark and venal.

There was also a very real sense in 1779 that the Revolution was about to collapse. Years of war and deprivation had worn down the fighting will of the people. Troop strength for the Continental Army had gone from a high of 27,500 in 1775 to just over 3,000. In addition, the character of its soldiers had changed dramatically. When the initial call to defend their country had gone out in 1775, thousands of solid, middle-class men (and a few women) had rushed forward to enlist. But a year of fighting, harsh discipline, lack of pay, and inadequate food had made them, as a group, unwilling to continue. When their enlistments ran out in 1776, most of them went home.

After that, the army had to rely on what Washington described as the "poorer sort" to fill out the ranks. This meant individuals who lacked property and had little prospect of advancing economically. Boys in their teens, elderly men, the unemployed, and the crippled came forward, not so much to defeat an oppressive enemy but because of the promise of decent food, clothing, shelter, and handsome land grants once the war was won.

Neither Congress nor its Patriot supporters ever adequately fulfilled the promises made to these new recruits. Food and equipment shortages were so severe during the entire war that one soldier, Joseph Plumb Martin, remarked in 1780, "We therefore still kept upon the parade in groups, venting our spleen at our country and government, then at our officers, and then at our imbecility in staying there and starving in detail for an ungrateful people who did not care what became of us, so they could enjoy themselves while we were keeping a cruel enemy from them."

Insubordination and desertion were commonplace by 1779, and the army's hostility toward Congress and the "ungrateful people" was so strong that British spy Elihu Hall predicted a mutiny. Several did occur, the most prominent being the uprisings of both the Pennsylvania and New Jersey troops in 1781. Not even the arrival of French soldiers and French money eased tensions. Many citizens suspected that the French had ulterior motives in aiding the Revolution—that once the British were gone, the French would assume military control of all of North America.

Benedict wasn't the only Patriot wavering in his support of the Revolution. Some of his closest friends and supporters were having doubts as well. Silas Deane and Philip Schuyler both felt that the rebellion had gone seriously astray and advocated reconciling with Great Britain. Even George Washington was beginning to question the way the Revolution was being handled. In a letter to a friend, he lamented, "Unless a system very different from that which has long prevailed be immediately adopted throughout the states, our affairs must soon become desperate, beyond the possibility of recovery. Indeed, I have almost ceased to hope."

Even before his command in Philadelphia, Benedict was, according to historian James Kirby Martin, "seriously questioning why anyone should adhere to a code of selfless dedication, since from his perspective Congress and the general population were making a mockery of that tenet." Benedict, ever the realist, wanted to control his fate and his family's future and not leave them in the hands of incompetent or malicious individuals. The best solution for everyone, he reasoned, would be for America to rejoin England, but with guaranteed liberties and representatives in Parliament. When Parliament passed a Reconciliation Act early in 1779, granting the American colonies everything they had petitioned for—short of independence—the path to ending the war seemed even clearer to Benedict.

After receiving André's initial reply, Benedict sent off another letter, hoping to move the negotiations forward as quickly as possible. To prove his sincerity, Benedict began revealing congressional and military secrets—such as the date when Washington would move troops, and the fact that Congress didn't plan to defend Charleston, South Carolina, if the British attacked it again. He also asked for a meeting with Clinton to discuss military strategy.

Because of the difficulty of wartime travel, Benedict would not hear from André for nearly six weeks. When he finally did, he was very disappointed. There was still no guarantee of what money he would receive, only reassurances that he would be rewarded. André was very clear, however, in stating that Clinton would not meet with Arnold. Nor would he share any information about how the British would use the secrets Benedict had sent them. Benedict, André implied, would not be treated as Clinton's equal. André concluded his letter by informing Benedict that he would be much more valuable to them if he surrendered a significant number of troops. "Accept a command, be surprised, be cut off. . . . A complete service of this nature involving a corps of five or six thousand men would be rewarded with twice as many thousand [pounds]."

Benedict was miffed by how long it had taken André to reply as well as by the condescending tone of his letter and the implication that Clinton did not trust him. He took his time to respond, and when he did, he didn't even bother to put it in writing. Instead, he summoned Stansbury to his home and told him to inform André that he wanted £10,000 for his services no matter what he did or how the war ended.

Even though Benedict also gave Stansbury some vital military information, André was upset by the way Benedict had delayed answering and by his belligerent stance. André sent Stansbury back to make sure Benedict still intended to switch allegiance, but Benedict refused to see him.

At one point Peggy stepped in to keep the negotiations alive, but both sides were adamant. The British weren't going to give Benedict any guarantees until they knew what he was going to deliver; Benedict wasn't going to continue negotiating (and thus risk being found out) until the financial details were finalized.

In October 1779 Benedict broke off all communications with André. The plot could have ended there had not several thousand French soldiers and sailors arrived in Philadelphia, all needing to be fed. In order to procure an adequate supply of food, French commissary officers paid local farmers higher-than-normal prices in gold. This caused the cost of food to go up in Philadelphia, and many people couldn't afford such basic items as grain, meat, and milk. Anger simmered for several months and eventually resulted in two days of food riots toward the end of 1779.

Joseph Reed, along with other radicals who wanted to purge Philadelphia of all Loyalists, came up with a plan to ease the food shortage (and seize additional property for themselves). They would arrest the wives and children left behind by Loyalists who had fled to New York and send them to that city. In October the talk suddenly turned to action when an angry mob of Pennsylvania militia surrounded the three-story brick mansion of James Wilson and threatened to storm it and banish Wilson and his family. It didn't matter that Wilson wasn't a Loyalist; he was, in fact, a staunch Patriot and a signer of the Declaration of Independence. He was targeted because he happened to be a skillful constitutional lawyer who had defied Reed by successfully defending Loyalists prosecuted by the Pennsylvania Council.

Wilson and about thirty other armed men decided to defend his home, which they dubbed "Fort Wilson." The group included two other signers of the Declaration of Independence, Robert Morris and George Clymer, plus General Thomas Mifflin. Also on hand to defend Wilson and his family was Benedict Arnold.

The battle that ensued was brief but deadly. Benedict was upstairs to direct the fire, while Mifflin remained downstairs. When the mob launched its first charge, the initial musket volley from "Fort Wilson" killed four and wounded twenty, and forced the attackers to make a hasty retreat. Inside the house three men were slightly wounded. A second assault proved more successful. The front door was battered down and one defender was run through with a bayonet. Then concerted musket fire from Benedict's men drove the mob off once again. A third charge was about to be launched when Continental soldiers arrived to disperse the mob for the night.

In the days to follow, Benedict found himself a target of these same mobs. People yelled at him when he went about town; stones were hurled at his coach. When a crowd appeared at his house and threatened to attack it, Benedict sent off a message to Congress asking for protection. Congress refused, saying it was up to the state government to protect citizens and directing him to apply to Joseph Reed for help. The real message was clear to Benedict. Not only was he out of favor with many in Congress and being dishonored and persecuted by Reed and others, he and his family were in physical danger and no one was willing to protect them.

If this wasn't enough to put him in the British camp, Congress handed him two additional reasons. The treasury committee finally got around to his financial records for the invasion of Canada and decided he owed the United States £1,000. It also denied him payment for most of the other expenses he claimed. When Benedict tallied up the numbers, he was out just over $9,000, which would be worth roughly $300,000 in today's money.

Then, in January 1780, the officers involved in Benedict's court-martial came to a decision on the four remaining charges. Going into the trial, Benedict had been confident that he would be cleared completely. After all, he had been acquitted of most charges once before by the Paca committee, which he assumed would have some influence on the officers hearing his case. On top of this, Benedict had conducted a spirited and detailed defense. He opened it with an eloquent reminder: "When the present necessary war against Great Britain commenced, I was in easy circumstances and enjoyed a fair prospect of improving them. I was happy in domestic connections and blessed with a rising family, who claimed my care and attention. The liberties of my country were in danger. The voice of my country called upon all her faithful sons to join in her defense. With cheerfulness, I obeyed the call. I sacrificed domestic ease and happiness to the service of my country, and in her service have I sacrificed a great part of a handsome fortune. I was one of the first who appeared in the field and, from that time to the present hour, have not abandoned her service." He then addressed each charge individually, going over the fine points of military and civil law very carefully to show his innocence. Reed and his Pennsylvania Council presented a few witnesses, none of whom had any direct evidence against Benedict.

The verdict handed down was therefore a shock. As historian Willard Sterne Randall points out, "The court acquitted Arnold of any intentional wrongdoing and all illicit private speculation," a finding that should have "resulted in an acquittal with honor." Instead, the court bowed to the political pressure of Reed and found Benedict guilty on two charges of using his military authority in an "imprudent and improper" fashion. They sentenced him to a written reprimand—a kind of official bawling out—from George Washington.

Benedict held out the hope that Washington would ignore the court-martial findings. In an anguished letter to Silas Deane he wrote, "I ought to receive a reprimand: For what? Not for doing wrong, but because I *might have done wrong;* or rather, because there was a possibility that evil might have followed the good I did."

Not even the birth of his first son with Peggy on March 19, 1780, nor the arrival of Hannah and his other sons, could ease the emotional pain when the reprimand was finally issued. In it, Washington praised Benedict's past valor and called him one of the country's "most valued commanders." But he chastised him for forgetting that "even the shadow of a fault tarnishes the lustre of our finest achievements." Washington's

A drawing of Peggy Arnold and one of her sons, copied from a 1783 portrait by David Gardner.
THE NEW-YORK HISTORICAL SOCIETY

wording was as generous and gentle as it could have been, but the fact that he chose to issue it—that he chose to accept the court-martial findings and therefore Joseph Reed's accusations over Benedict's word—was a crushing blow. Benedict's one constant supporter, the commander of the American army, now seemed to be siding with his enemies. If that was so, he truly had no place in the Revolution.

Benedict reestablished contact with André in late April 1780, pushing to finalize the negotiations and requesting a "conference with an officer of confidence." He also asked his old friend and comrade Philip Schuyler to help him obtain the command of a vital defensive position for the American side: West Point.

West Point consisted of four major forts (one, ironically, named Fort Arnold), a blockhouse, and a series of smaller hilltop fortifications and river-level gun sites. All these fortifications were in place to guard the Hudson River and the 1,097-foot-long iron chain that was stretched across it to stop enemy ships from moving along it at will. The garrison there consisted of 1,500 men.

With the arrival of French troops West Point had taken on additional

A 1778 watercolor by Pierre Charles L'Enfant showing West Point fortifications and soldiers. THE LIBRARY OF CONGRESS

importance. The main French force was camped in Rhode Island, while Washington had his men at Morristown, New Jersey. West Point stood almost equidistant between them. In American hands it allowed the easy movement of supplies, troops, and information between the two armies. If the British controlled it, they could disrupt this "highway" and divide their enemies' forces. West Point was, as Washington himself had noted, "the key to America."

Schuyler and several others, including New York's congressional delegate Robert Livingston, began lobbying Washington to give the command to Benedict. Washington never openly agreed, but he must have been positive enough in his responses that Benedict began to feel the post was his. He told André and Clinton that he would soon be taking charge of the fortifications and even began sending money to England through friends in New York—this in case the plot was discovered and he and his family had to flee the country.

Washington did indeed want Benedict back in action. And when Benedict met him at King's Ferry, on the Hudson just below West Point, in late July, Benedict fully expected to receive the assignment he wanted. He was startled then when his commander informed him that he wished him to take the field as divisional commander.

Benedict was so stunned that he couldn't even respond. The proposed command was a post of honor meaning Benedict would lead fully one half of all of Washington's best infantry—precisely the sort of position he had hoped to have throughout his entire military career. It would put him in the thick of the action and give him the chance to win eternal honor for his family's name. But, sadly, it had come too late.

"Upon this information," Washington would later recall, Benedict's "countenance changed and he appeared to be quite fallen, and, instead of thanking me or expressing any pleasure at the appointment, never opened his mouth."

Later, Benedict begged off the field command, claiming that his leg was not healed enough to withstand such physically strenuous duty. He again asked for the command of West Point, and a somewhat perplexed Washington finally granted his request. With this piece of the puzzle in place, Benedict put into motion his plan to end the American Revolution.

20

WHOM CAN WE TRUST NOW?

One of the first things Benedict did when he officially took charge of West Point was to tour the fortifications and buildings and do a detailed analysis of the complex's weaknesses. Simply put, the place was in wretched shape. Much of the construction work had been done hastily and carelessly, Benedict wrote in his report to Washington, and many design flaws were evident. The fort atop the highest hill, called Rocky Point, had solid six-foot-thick walls facing the river but was almost completely "defenseless on the back." A relatively small British force could land downriver and easily move heavy cannons up the back road and pound the fort into submission. The garrison at West Point, Benedict further noted, was too small by half to properly resist an attack, and many of the men were ill and unfit for duty. Besides, they couldn't withstand a prolonged British siege because "there is not ten days provisions."

When Benedict finished his report, he sent a copy of it to George

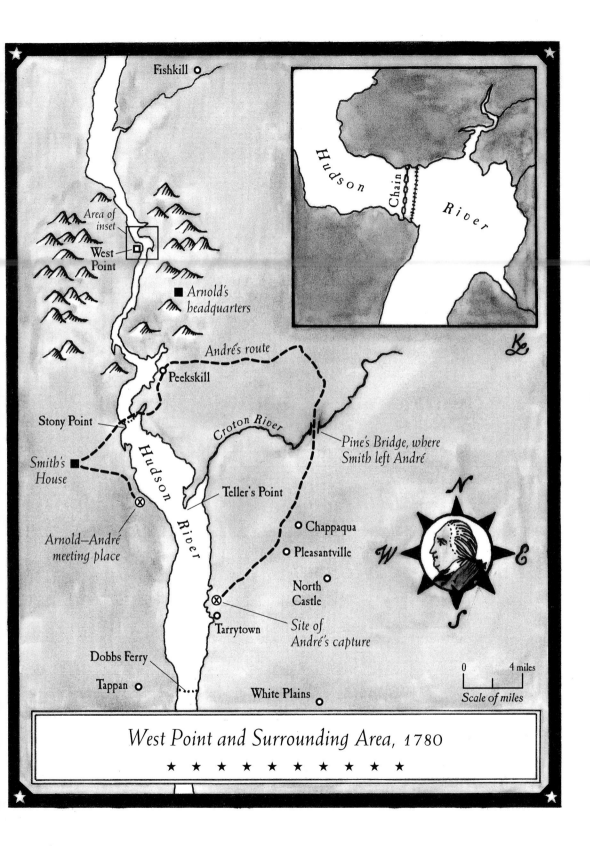

Fishkill ○

Area of
inset

West
Point

■ Arnold's
headquarters

Hudson

Chain

River

André's route

○ Peekskill

Stony Point

Croton River

Pine's Bridge, where
Smith left André

Smith's
House

⊗

Teller's Point

Arnold–André
meeting place

Hudson River

○ Chappaqua

○ Pleasantville

North
Castle ○

⊗

Site of
André's capture

Tarrytown

N

W   E

S

Dobbs Ferry

Tappan ○

White Plains ○

0   4 miles

Scale of miles

West Point and Surrounding Area, 1780

★ ★ ★ ★ ★ ★ ★ ★ ★ ★ ★

Washington and kept another, which he intended to hand over to the enemy. His communications with André were still frustrating. When he suggested that surrendering West Point and its garrison might be worth an additional £10,000, André answered in his usual vague way. In truth, Clinton was holding back agreement because he wasn't at all certain that Benedict really intended to turn traitor. He wanted some kind of independent verification that Benedict was sincere. The best André could do was have his own spies check as much of the information Benedict was supplying as possible, and verify that Benedict had been truthful about his movements between Philadelphia and West Point. Finally, in late August 1780, Clinton agreed to give Benedict £20,000 for the surrender of West Point, but stipulated that he wanted at least 3,000 troops captured as well.

This posed a bit of a problem for Benedict. To make it easier for the British to capture the fortifications, Benedict had been systematically depleting the 1,500-man garrison. He accomplished this by sending large groups of men off on various trivial assignments, such as chopping wood or escorting captured Loyalists to other prisons. He was still trying to figure out how to get troop strength up in time for the attack when George Washington unwittingly came to his rescue. He had read Benedict's report on the garrison's weaknesses and, as a show of support, had assigned an artillery corps to help protect West Point—just enough men to meet the 3,000-man quota.

Even with the financial aspect of his treason settled, Benedict was growing nervous. Negotiations had dragged along for almost a year and a half, slow by any standards, but to a person like Benedict who thrived on action, it must have felt like a lifetime. And with each passing day the chances of being caught increased. He kept insisting on a face-to-face meeting with a high-ranking official in order to turn over his description of West Point and the battle plan he'd drawn up.

André and Clinton were just as edgy. Having agreed to Benedict's terms and even advanced him £200, they wanted to seize West Point and the garrison before Benedict changed his mind. André was so desperate that he suggested he should meet with Benedict personally behind enemy lines. Clinton was much more cautious and wouldn't allow this. Going behind enemy lines in disguise would make André a spy, an offense that could get him hanged if he were caught.

In the end Benedict and André agreed to meet at Dobbs Ferry, in the neutral territory between the American and British lines, on Monday, September 11. Benedict left West Point on September 10 and was rowed down the Hudson to the home of a Loyalist merchant, Joshua Smith, where he waited impatiently for the next day to dawn.

On Monday morning André came up the Hudson aboard the sloop-of-war *Vulture*, accompanied by Loyalist Beverley Robinson. The pretext for getting André and Benedict together was quite simple: Robinson owned the house where Benedict had his West Point headquarters and had ostensibly come to ask permission to retrieve some personal items from the building. He had done this once before, so it wasn't altogether unusual. André accompanied Robinson as a guide and would be able to meet with Benedict on shore under a flag of truce.

While André and Robinson waited at Dobbs Ferry, Benedict was being rowed downriver for the meeting. Unfortunately, no one had bothered to tell the gunners of the *Vulture* or the gunboats accompanying it that a meeting had been planned. As soon as Benedict's barge came into view, at least one gunboat opened fire, forcing Benedict's unarmed crew to paddle with all their might for the safety of the western shore.

Only one mile of water separated Benedict and André, but neither made an effort to get to the other. André may have supposed that Benedict would find a way to complete his journey once the gunboats backed off. For his part, Benedict may have felt the cannon fire made the "secret" meeting too much of a public affair.

Benedict returned to headquarters that evening, understandably upset by the missed meeting. He was delighted, however, to be greeted at the door by Peggy and their infant son, Neddy. It had been two months since he'd last seen them, the longest separation he'd ever had from Peggy. But even as they were enjoying being a family again, Benedict arranged for another meeting with André on September 20.

In his letter to André he suggested that it would be safer for both of them if they met on land above Dobbs Ferry. He assured the spymaster that if he came inside the American lines, "you will be perfectly safe." Benedict would arrange to have a trustworthy fellow, Joshua Smith, meet André at night and have him rowed to where Benedict would be concealed for the meeting. Neither Smith nor the oarsmen would know who André was; they would be told only that they were meeting a man named Anderson and that the meeting was about private business matters. Keeping André's real identity secret would lessen the chance that they would be found out, either before or after the meeting. The catch, Benedict added, was that "it will be necessary for you to be disguised." To demonstrate his continued sincerity, Benedict also included information about the troop strength of Washington's army as well as the increased size of the West Point garrison.

Benedict was about to send off this message on Friday, September 15, when he received a confidential letter from Washington with stunning news. "I shall be at Peekskill on Sunday evening [the 17th]," Washington wrote, "on my way to Hartford to meet the French Admiral [François-Joseph-Paul de Grasse] and General [Jean-Baptiste Donatien de Vimeur, Count de Rochambeau]. You will be pleased to send down a guard of a captain and 50 [soldiers] at that time. . . . You will keep this to yourself, as I want to make my journey a secret." This news must have set Benedict's mind racing. Normally the commander in chief traveled with his army to avoid the chance of capture. But now he would have almost no guards—an easy target for capture, if the British could put together two or three hundred fast-moving mounted troops and sail them upriver by Sunday.

Benedict wrote a hasty note letting André know when and where Washington could be taken and had his courier rush it to New York. Luckily for the American cause, either this message didn't arrive in time or the British, ever deliberate, could not organize quickly enough to strike. On Sunday, Washington—along with his chief of artillery, Henry Knox; the Marquis de Lafayette; Alexander Hamilton; and a squad of only nineteen guards—was rowed safely across the Hudson within eyesight of the sloop *Vulture*. The British had missed an easy opportunity to thoroughly disrupt the American Revolution.

The meeting on September 20 between Benedict and André, though, was still on. Clinton, still very cautious, ordered that the meeting take place on board the *Vulture*, specifying that the sloop should be below Dobbs Ferry, between the British and American lines. But André was eager to push Benedict's betrayal of West Point forward, and so he disregarded these orders. He told Benedict he would meet with him wherever he wanted and then ordered the *Vulture* anchored off Teller's Point. This was fifteen miles below West Point, north of Dobbs Ferry and inside the American lines, but would make traveling quicker and safer for Benedict.

By seven o'clock on the evening of the meeting, André waited anxiously aboard the sloop for his ride. He wore his uniform (and a long, blue cape to conceal it), thus avoiding the danger of being captured as a spy. Several hours later Joshua Smith prepared to go downriver to get the businessman named Anderson and bring him to where Benedict said he would be waiting. Unfortunately for the scheme, Benedict had neglected to arrange for Smith's transportation, assuming Smith would have no problem in getting someone to row him down to the *Vulture*. Smith probably thought the same thing, and he asked one of his tenant farmers, Samuel Cahoon, if he would row for him that night. Cahoon recalled that "Mr. Smith was up at Fishkill, as he told me, and came down in the evening and . . . asked me to go that night a piece, he said, down river. I told him I had no mind to go, and did not want to go." Smith pressed the man to help him but eventually gave up. Once again the meeting—and a chance to finally set in motion the taking of West Point—was narrowly missed.

Both Benedict and André were annoyed and frustrated by this second delay, but it was André who took the next decisive step in the game of deceit.

Clinton had stated very clearly that if the meeting failed to take place, André should return to New York to report to him. But André did not want to lose what must have seemed like a golden opportunity to strike at the American rebels and advance his own career at the same time. So he delayed his return and arranged for yet another meeting with Benedict on Thursday, September 21.

On that day, near sundown, Smith approached Samuel Cahoon again. "Mr. Smith . . . told me to come up, as the general wished to speak to me. I went up with Mr. Smith in the room where General Arnold was, who asked me to go with [Smith] a piece that night." Benedict probably thought that revealing his identity would make Cahoon agreeable. To his surprise, Cahoon answered, "I said I could not go, being up the night before, and told him I was afraid to go; but General Arnold urged me to go, and told me if I was a friend to my country I should do my best."

Cahoon asked where the men wanted to be rowed to, and when they told him, Cahoon said he would need help rowing such a distance. "Mr. Smith desired me to go and fetch my brother [Joseph]. I went, and my wife being dissatisfied with my going, I went back to General Arnold, and told him that I did not want to go, and told him there were [American] guard boats out." Benedict tried to reassure Cahoon, telling him that he would see that the gunboats were alerted to their coming, but the man would not be persuaded.

Benedict had worked very hard so far to remain calm, but he was not (as either a sea captain or an army officer) used to having his requests denied. He ordered Cahoon to row Smith to the *Vulture* "and said if I did not go he would look upon me as a disaffected man. I then went and fetched my brother." But the argument was not yet settled. Joseph arrived and immediately peppered both Benedict and Smith with his own worries about the danger of the gunboats and the nature of the late-night visit. At one point Benedict must have grown very angry. When Joseph told him they would row the boat only in daylight, Joseph recalled that the commander

*A highly melodramatic drawing of the clandestine meeting between Benedict and André.
In case viewers missed the sinister nature of their talk, the artist has placed Satan
in the form of a snake on the branch just above them.* THE NEW YORK PUBLIC LIBRARY

of West Point began to yell that "if I did not assist when I was required for the good of my country and Congress he would put me under guard immediately."

Smith intervened to cool the situation, pouring out generous portions of rum for the brothers. The discussion took on a friendlier tone after this, and when Benedict offered each man a considerable amount of flour for the night's rowing, they finally agreed.

When they set out with Smith, it was around midnight, and the mission was already two hours behind Benedict's schedule. Smith made it to the *Vulture* somewhere near one o'clock in the morning, took "the man named Anderson" aboard, and set out for a spot on the river called the Old Trough, some two miles away. André had his uniform on but once again wore the cape that concealed it completely. Sometime later they landed, and Samuel Cahoon recalled that "I heard the noise of a man at a bank above, and Mr. Smith went up and returned immediately; and the person [Anderson/André] was brought on shore [and] went up, and Mr. Smith stayed with us."

André never revealed what was said during this meeting, and when Benedict later spoke about it, he said only that André had agreed to pay him £10,000 if the plot was discovered before West Point could be taken. At the meeting, Benedict turned over his military analysis of West Point, and in all probability the two men discussed the weaknesses of the fortifications, the distribution of troops, and how best to attack them. Benedict probably also told André that Washington would be stopping at West Point on Monday and that he would once again be vulnerable to capture. Whatever was discussed took almost three hours, and the meeting did not end until around four o'clock in the morning.

When André finally came back down to where the boat was, the sky was beginning to lighten. Smith, according to Samuel Cahoon, "asked my brother and myself if we would [row to] the vessel again that night. I told him I was fatigued . . . and could not go." Smith, of course, still did not know who André really was or the danger the man was in. As far as Smith was concerned, André was a businessman and in no urgent rush to get back to New York. So he told André he would be rowed to the *Vulture* later on Friday night and dismissed the Cahoon brothers.

Once the Cahoon brothers were out of sight, Benedict came out of hiding to join Smith and André, and all three went back to Smith's house. There Benedict and André waited in a second-floor room until darkness descended.

This delay might have had no effect on the plot except that fate once again altered the plan. Shortly after reaching Smith's house, the three men heard the distant rumble of cannon fire. Two American cannon crews on shore (without orders from Benedict) had opened fire on the *Vulture*. According to one witness on board the sloop, the "very hot fire . . . continued two hours, and would have been longer but luckily their [powder] magazine blew up. . . . Six shots hulled us, one between wind and water [that is, above the water line]; many others struck the sails and rigging, and boats on deck. Two shells hit us, one full on the quarterdeck, another near the main shrouds." No one was seriously injured, but it was enough to convince the captain that his ship was at risk. He withdrew ten miles downriver, leaving André behind.

News of what had happened created some tense moments for both André and Benedict. André still hoped to be rowed to the safety of the sloop, but Benedict worried that too many American gunboats would be patrolling the water to risk such a journey.

André may have wanted to protest but refrained from doing so. Smith still knew him only as a civilian businessman named Anderson, and André certainly didn't want his real identity to be known. He reluctantly agreed to travel to safety by land, and Benedict wrote out a pass to insure they wouldn't be stopped by American patrols. Because he would be riding in broad daylight, he would have to shed his officer's jacket and other military trappings.

Late on Friday, Benedict made his way home, while André and Smith mounted horses and headed south. Smith was in a lighthearted, talkative mood, and not at all concerned about being stopped by American patrols. If that happened, his traveling companion would simply show the pass signed by Benedict Arnold and they would ride on freely. André, on the other hand, was nervous and quiet during their journey.

André hoped to ride without interruption all the way to White Plains and safety, but around nine o'clock at night a party of New York militia stopped to question them. After a brief interrogation the captain of the militia advised the two travelers to put up for the night. "The reasons I gave Mr. Smith," the captain recalled, "were that riding in the night would be dangerous when they got below Croton river, from the Cowboys." "Cowboys" was the name given to nonmilitary groups of Loyalists who patrolled the roads looking for unsuspecting Patriots. André would have welcomed such an encounter, but he couldn't reveal this to Smith, so he reluctantly agreed to spend the night in a nearby farmhouse.

The two travelers were up before sunrise on Saturday, September 23, and rode south again, stopping briefly for a breakfast of cornmeal mush. At the bridge over the Croton River, Smith unexpectedly announced that he was turning back, but that André would be fine if he just followed the road. So André rode on alone down the twisting, unfamiliar route. He went through Chappaqua and then Pleasantville, where he learned from a boy that rebel scouts were patrolling the road into White Plains. To avoid them, André chose a different way and took the Tarrytown Road instead.

He was approaching Pine's Bridge over Clark's Kill, just a half mile from Tarrytown and safety, when three armed men emerged from the woods to confront him. The boy in Pleasantville had told André that Loyalists were roaming the area near Tarrytown. As if to confirm this information, the leader of the men was wearing a Hessian soldier's green coat. As André slowly neared the men, he told them he was a member of the "lower party," meaning a Loyalist from New York.

The leader, John Paulding, nodded, and André is reported to have blurted out, "Thank God, I am among friends, I am glad to see you. I am an officer in the British service, and have now been on particular business in the country, and I hope you will not detain me."

But André's—and, with him, Benedict's—luck had run out. "Get down," Paulding barked. "We are Americans." The three men were Skinners, roving bands of rebel militia who were as apt to steal from a Patriot as a Loyalist.

André, who had yet to tell them his name, tried to right his mistake by producing the pass written by Benedict for a man named Anderson. "Gentlemen," André is reported to have said, "you had best let me go, or you will bring yourselves in trouble, for, by stopping me, you will detain the general's business."

But Paulding was suspicious. "Damn Arnold's pass! You said you was a British officer. Get down. Where is your money?"

André told them he had only a few coins and a gold watch. The men

A nineteenth-century engraving of Major André's capture. THE LIBRARY OF CONGRESS

couldn't believe that a British officer had no real money, so they made André dismount and strip off his clothes. Naked except for his boots and stockings, André watched helplessly as they searched his clothes, then his saddle and other riding equipment.

One of the other men there, David Williams, later recalled, "We told him to pull off his boots, which he seemed indifferent about, but we got one boot off and searched [it], but could find nothing. . . . We found there were some papers in the bottom of his stocking, next to his foot, on which we made him pull his stocking off, and found three papers wrapped up." These, of course, were the papers Benedict had given him describing in detail the West Point fortifications and troop placement.

André promised, as a gentleman, that if the men released him, he would send them money from New York. But it was too late. They had bagged a spy and wanted to bring him in, hoping to receive a reward. They had André dress, then bound his hands behind his back, hoisted him onto his horse, and led him to an advance guard post at North Castle. The other militiaman recalled that André's mood changed dramatically. "You never saw such an alteration in any man's face. Only a few moments before, he was uncommonly gay in his looks, but after we made him prisoner, you could read in his face that he thought it was all over with him."

The commander at North Castle was Colonel John Jameson, a somewhat unimaginative, by-the-book sort of officer. When André was brought in, he did not suspect a conspiracy headed by Benedict Arnold. He believed only that André (who still had not revealed his real name) had stolen the papers. Jameson ordered that the prisoner be taken to Benedict's headquarters for further questioning, along with a list of the papers found on him. To inform Washington of the arrest, he then sent the papers to the commander in chief's headquarters (even though he knew Washington wasn't there).

There was still a chance that once André reached West Point, Benedict could intercede on his behalf and free him. But before that could happen, the second in command at North Castle learned about the capture.

In addition to being an officer in the Second Light Dragoon Regiment from Connecticut, Major Benjamin Tallmadge had also helped run George Washington's secret spy network on Long Island and in New York City. He knew that Benedict Arnold had been scheduled to meet a man named Anderson. Since Anderson had been caught with military secrets heading away from West Point, he concluded that Benedict had given him the papers. He begged Jameson to recall André and not inform Benedict of the arrest.

Jameson, nervous that such an action would imply he thought Benedict a traitor, wasn't about to go that far. He was willing, he said, to have André brought back, but insisted on sending a message to Benedict letting him know that "Anderson" had been arrested.

Benedict spent Saturday night at home with Peggy, his aides, and Smith, who reported that the businessman named Anderson had gotten off safely. For unknown reasons the messengers sent out on Saturday to both Benedict and Washington concerning the capture of André were delayed and could not proceed until Monday morning.

Benedict was expecting Washington for breakfast that day, but Alexander Hamilton and another aide appeared saying the commander in chief would be delayed and that the meal should go on without him. It was while the men were eating that Jameson's note telling of André's capture arrived. Benedict read the message at the door and told the messenger to say nothing about it to anyone, then sent him off to have his breakfast. A few minutes later he went up to Peggy in their bedroom. Since neither Benedict nor Peggy ever spoke or wrote about this brief meeting, we can only assume Benedict told her that the plot had been discovered and that he was going to flee. He probably assured her that because she was a woman and the mother of a young baby, she would be safe from prosecution.

While they were conferring, Washington's servant arrived to say the commander would arrive in a few minutes. "I went immediately upstairs," recalled Benedict's aide, David Franks, "and informed Arnold of it. He came down in great confusion and, ordering a horse to be saddled, mounted him and told me to inform his Excellency that he was gone over to West Point and would return in about an hour." Benedict then made his way to his barge on the Hudson and ordered the men there to row him downriver to the *Vulture*.

No one at West Point or at Benedict's headquarters suspected Benedict of treason—not his aides or any of the other officers present. Benedict's hasty departure was unusual, but not necessarily an indication of anything more sinister. Peggy knew, of course, but she stayed upstairs, possibly burning incriminating letters between Benedict and André.

Washington arrived, had breakfast, and then retired to his room to rest. It was almost noon when the messenger sent by Jameson finally caught up to Washington and handed him the incriminating papers. As Washington looked through them, the unbelievable, painful truth must have overwhelmed him. Benedict Arnold, his courageous, unstoppable

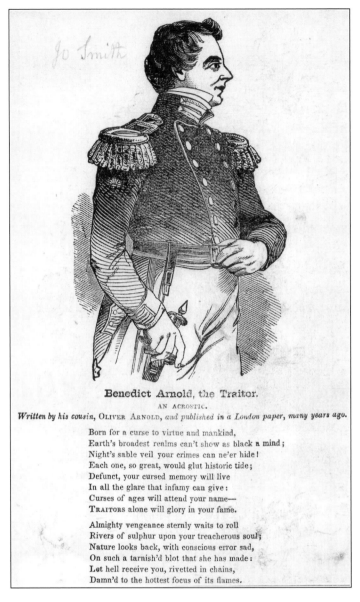

Benedict Arnold, the Traitor.

AN ACROSTIC.

Written by his cousin, OLIVER ARNOLD, *and published in a London paper, many years ago.*

Born for a curse to virtue and mankind,
Earth's broadest realms can't show as black a mind;
Night's sable veil your crimes can ne'er hide!
Each one, so great, would glut historic tide;
Defunct, your cursed memory will live
In all the glare that infamy can give:
Curses of ages will attend your name—
TRAITORS alone will glory in your fame.

Almighty vengeance sternly waits to roll
Rivers of sulphur upon your treacherous soul;
Nature looks back, with conscious error sad,
On such a tarnish'd blot that she has made:
Let hell receive you, rivetted in chains,
Damn'd to the hottest focus of its flames.

fighting general, the man he could always count on when others deserted him, had sold out to the British. The Marquis de Lafayette recalled entering Washington's room to find the commander in chief seated, head down with the treasonous papers in his shaking hands. "Arnold has betrayed me," Washington said quietly. "Whom can we trust now?"

21

NIL DESPERANDUM

Once the treason became known, pandemonium broke out at Benedict's headquarters. As shocked as Washington was, he was clearheaded enough to order Alexander Hamilton and another young officer to find and arrest Benedict. These officers galloped off, spreading word about what had happened as they hunted for the traitor.

Washington's numbed disbelief soon turned to anger, though he was very good at concealing it from those around him. A few days after Benedict's escape, Washington seemed almost philosophical about the incident. "Traitors are the growth of every country," he told French Admiral de Grasse on September 27, "and in a revolution of the present nature it is more to be wondered at that the catalogue is so small than that there have been found a few." Inside, however, the commander in chief was seething. On the day of his flight from West Point, while still onboard the *Vulture*, Benedict had sent a note to Washington. He knew, he said, that he would be condemned for his actions, but added, "I have ever acted from a princi-

One of the first things Benedict did after fleeing West Point was to write to George Washington to explain his actions and to say that Peggy had no knowledge of them.
THE LIBRARY OF CONGRESS

ple of love to my country, since the commencement of the present unhappy contest between Great Britain and the colonies. The same principle of love to my country actuates my present conduct, however it may appear inconsistent to the world, who very seldom judge right of any man's actions."

But to Washington, Benedict's actions were more than a political statement about Congress and the radical direction the Revolution had taken. Washington had gone out on a limb and risked his reputation numerous times for the controversial and outspoken Arnold. He had overlooked many instances of questionable behavior on Benedict's part because he felt the offenses slight when compared to his fighting general's overall contributions to the Revolution. No, Benedict's turnabout was more than one frustrated man's attempt to bring peace and justice to a very divided country. It was, for Washington, a deeply personal betrayal. When one of his aides suggested that Benedict must be "undergoing the torments of hell," Washington revealed the depths of his anger: "He wants feeling!" he snapped back. "From some traits of his character which have lately come to my knowledge, he seems to have been hackneyed in villainy, and so lost to all sense of honour and shame that while his faculties will enable him to continue his sordid pursuits there will be no time for remorse."

Washington then fixed upon capturing Benedict and even set in motion a plot to kidnap him from New York. In approving the plan, he stipulated that Benedict be taken alive. "My aim," Washington stated, "is to make a public example of him." Several months later, he changed his mind and ordered Lafayette to summarily execute Benedict should he ever be taken.

The commander in chief did not focus his anger on anyone else, though the temptation must have been great. In his letter to Washington, Benedict pointedly asked him to protect Peggy "from every insult and injury that a mistaken vengeance of my country may expose her to. . . . [She] is as good and innocent as an angel, and is incapable of doing wrong." Washington probably suspected that Peggy knew about the plot beforehand and might even have had a hand in arranging it. Her previous friendship with Major André was well known. At the very least, Washington must have considered holding her and six-month-old Neddy and offering their release in exchange for Benedict's surrender. In the end his sense of honor and chivalry prevailed. He allowed Peggy to return to her family in Philadelphia, and even provided an escort.

Washington did call for an investigation of Arnold's plot to see how widespread the conspiracy might be. This investigation included Joshua Smith, Benedict's two aides, and even Philip Schuyler and Robert Livingston, who had urged that Benedict be given the command of West Point. Statements were taken from those under suspicion and checked for accuracy. When rumors circulated that General St. Clair was somehow involved, inquiries were made regarding his loyalty to the Revolution. In very short order all those investigated were cleared. According to the official record, the only American involved was Benedict Arnold.

Benedict may have stood alone as a traitor, but it was André who would pay the ultimate price. André was taken to West Point for questioning, then rowed downriver to Stony Point, where a strong escort of mounted soldiers took him to Tappan for imprisonment at Mabie's Tavern. A board of fourteen officers was convened to examine and judge André. He admitted to having the military papers on his person and to traveling in disguise but vehemently denied being a common spy. He had arrived in uniform, he insisted, fully expecting to be rowed back to the *Vulture* in uniform. However, Benedict refused "to reconduct me back the next night as I had been brought. Thus become a prisoner, I had to concert my escape."

The board deliberated briefly, then issued its unanimous decision "that Major André, adjutant general to the British army, ought to be considered as a spy from the enemy; and that, agreeable to the law and usage of nations, it is [our] opinion he ought to suffer death." Washington approved the sentence and set the execution date as Sunday, October 1, at noon.

During his imprisonment, André's charm never deserted him. When told of his fate, he was visibly upset, one of his prosecutors recalled, "his flesh seeming to crawl upon his bones." He paced his small room for several minutes but managed to regain some of his composure. "I avow no guilt," he said in a shaky voice, "but I'm resigned to my fate."

His youthful spirit and open acceptance of the death sentence seemed to soften even the hardest of Patriots. Major Tallmadge, who had accompanied André from West Point to Tappan, found him "as cheerful as if he was going to [a meeting]. . . . I am sure he will go to the gallows less fearful for his fate and with less concern than I shall behold the tragedy."

The Marquis de Lafayette visited André on the day he was to be executed. "He conducted himself," Lafayette recorded, "in a manner so frank, so noble, so delicate that . . . I had the foolishness to let myself acquire a strong affection for him."

Alexander Hamilton was so taken by the young man that he wrote to General Clinton in New York. "Though an enemy," he said of André, "his virtues and his accomplishments are admired." Hamilton then went on to make a proposal that may have been approved by General Washington. "Perhaps he [André] might be released [exchanged] for General Arnold, delivered up without restriction or condition, which is the prevailing wish."

Clinton was terribly shaken by André's arrest and imminent execution, but he never considered turning Benedict over to the Americans. While his financial promises to Arnold had often been vague, he had clearly stated from the start that he would protect Benedict from harm. As a gentleman, he couldn't go back on his word, even if it meant the death of a valued and beloved member of his staff.

Everyone was sympathetic toward André, and no one, not even Washington, wanted to see him executed. But as Washington pointed out, to overturn the conviction or even to change the form of execution from hanging to death by firing squad (as André requested, considering it a more honorable way to die) would imply doubt about the verdict.

On Sunday, André's personal servant was allowed to bring him a fresh set of clothes—his full-dress British uniform. He spent time that morning meeting several visitors and sketching. At around ten thirty he was led from the tavern and down the street to the site of the execution. Soldiers lined the narrow road four deep, with civilians behind them. A fife-and-drum band playing the mournful "Dead March" led the prisoner to a flatbed wagon that held a coffin painted black. André mounted the wagon and then stepped up onto the coffin. When asked if he had any last words, André replied, "Only this, gentlemen, that you all bear me witness that I meet my fate like a brave man." He then removed his hat and placed the noose around his own neck.

At a signal, a whip cracked and the team of horses lurched forward. "The wagon was very suddenly drawn from under the gallows," a soldier recalled, "which together with the length of the rope gave him a most tremendous swing back and forth; but in a few minutes he hung entirely still."

The execution of Major André caused great upset in both the British and American armies.
THE CLEMENTS LIBRARY/THE UNIVERSITY OF MICHIGAN

Many of those who witnessed André's death were seen to be crying. John Hart, an army physician hardened to battlefield suffering and death, was moved to write, "Such fortitude I never was witness of, nor ever had I such disagreeable feelings at an execution, to see a man go out of time without fear but all the time smiling."

As André's death turned a charming, if headstrong and ambitious, young man into a folk hero, Benedict's betrayal of the Patriot cause made him a viper beneath contempt. When Captain Samuel Frost heard of Benedict's treachery, he wrote, "Treason of the blackest dye was yesterday discovered," a senti-

An effigy of a two-faced Benedict being carted to a bonfire to be burned.
He is accompanied by outraged Patriots and the Devil, who is prodding Benedict with
a pitchfork while offering him a sack of gold. THE NEW YORK PUBLIC LIBRARY

ment echoed a few days later by an indignant Colonel Alexander Scammell: "Treason! Treason! Treason! Black as Hell."

Many who had known Benedict for years refused to acknowledge any connection, worried that they would be dragged down by the association. Others diminished or even dismissed outright his courageous deeds as a cheap guise to cover, as Scammell put it, "a multitude of his villainous actions." Stories about Benedict focused on or exaggerated his less pleasant qualities (such as his outspokenness, his sensitivity to slights, and his forceful personality) and were often outright fabrications. It did not take long for friends and foes to link Benedict's treasonous actions with Satan himself. Nathanael Greene considered the esteem Arnold had once been held in by his military peers and the public and said, "Never since the fall of Lucifer has a fall equaled his."

Meanwhile, in Philadelphia, citizens staged a raucous parade in which a float was dragged up and down the crowded streets. On the float, reported the *Pennsylvania Packet* of October 3, was an effigy of Benedict having "two faces, emblematical of his traitorous conduct, a mask in his left hand, and a letter in his right from Beelzebub [Satan], telling him that he had done all the mischief he could do."

Standing next to Benedict was Satan himself, "shaking a purse of money at the general's left ear, and in his right hand [he held] a pitchfork, ready to drive him into hell as the reward due for the many crimes which the thief of gold had made him commit." To intimidate and discourage other would-be traitors and those Loyalists who might aid them, similar parades were held in other cities, including Boston and Providence, Rhode Island.

Benedict's personal history was quickly being rewritten. This revised story would state that he had been false and avaricious from the start. His support of the Revolution had been a sham, a sneaky way to gain favor, fame, power, and money. And money, this story claimed, was at the heart of his treachery.

On October 4 the Continental Congress ordered the Board of War to erase Benedict's name from its official rolls. His name was scratched out of the membership list at his Masonic Lodge in Connecticut. In Norwich, Connecticut, an angry mob stormed the local cemetery and destroyed the grave markers of Benedict's father and infant brother to obliterate the Arnold name. Some ardent Patriots even suggested making "the ever memorable 25th of September (the day when the blackest of crimes was unfolded)" a national holiday, so that Benedict's treasonous act could be "handed down to the latest posterity, to the eternal disgrace of the traitor."

Even young children were taught about Benedict's deception. A popular woodcut depicting Benedict and Satan in league also included this warning:

> Mothers shall still their children, and say—Arnold!—
> Arnold shall be the bugbear of their years,
> Arnold!—vile, treacherous, and leagued with Satan.

Very quickly, the real Benedict Arnold disappeared, replaced in history by a thoroughly untrustworthy, scheming, soulless creature.

In many ways it's understandable that Patriots of the time were so vicious toward Benedict. There was still a great deal of doubt and anxiety as to whether the rebellion would succeed. Emotions were running so high that even someone who was genuinely neutral about the outcome of the conflict would be suspected of Loyalist leanings and persecuted. Benedict offered an obvious target for anyone who claimed to be a Patriot, a handy way to unleash pent-up anger.

We have no way of knowing if Benedict heard or read any of the harsh statements about him. If he did, he probably dismissed them as the work of dishonorable liars, the sort of individuals who had soiled and perverted the Revolution. What we do know is that he seems to have been energized by his defection. The days following his flight from West Point he spent in New York with high-ranking British officers, discussing Washington's upcoming military strategy and the strengths and weaknesses of the Continental Army. When not in meetings, he was writing. He created a detailed report for the king's ministers in London that outlined the deteriorated condition of the American army, the general disenchantment with Congress, and the bankrupt condition of rebel finances. Next he published in a New York newspaper an open letter "To the Inhabitants of America" that explained the reasons for his defection and urged others to follow his example.

Within a week he drew up a bold military plan of action and sent it to Clinton. He wanted to lead a brigade of Loyalists south to drive Congress from Philadelphia and seize vast amounts of needed supplies; at the same time he began recruiting Loyalists in New York to fight his old allies.

Benedict also entered into intense negotiations with Clinton over his official military rank and pay as well as his financial reward for defecting. Clinton hadn't yet recovered from the execution of Major André and was justifiably miffed by how quickly after that event Benedict began these financial discussions. For the British commander, haggling over money was common and unseemly.

Benedict saw the situation differently. He had defected and given up everything based on a series of vague promises from Clinton and the word of a British officer who, unfortunately, was now dead and couldn't verify what he had agreed to pay Benedict. He pushed the negotiations to test just how committed the British were to him and to finalize a long and emotionally wrenching part of his life.

Clinton wasn't about to be rushed. Some issues, such as commissioning Benedict in the British army as a brigadier general and his annual salary of £450 ($25,600), were resolved fairly quickly. But the haggling over how much Benedict would receive for his defection was to stretch out over ten long years. The financial settlement would be less than Benedict asked for and did not cover the actual losses he sustained when his properties in Philadelphia and Connecticut were inevitably seized by Patriot officials. But the total, including his pay as a British officer and his pension, amounted to nearly $500,000 in modern terms, a considerable amount.

He had enough money to rent one of the finest townhouses in New York, right next door to British headquarters. He was joined there in mid-November by Peggy and Neddy, after his wife had been banished from Philadelphia as "dangerous to the public safety" by Joseph Reed's Council. (Benedict's sister, Hannah, also left Philadelphia, but went to New Haven, Connecticut, where she raised his three sons from his first marriage. While she chided him once for his constant complaining and "ill nature," she was faithful to her older brother for the rest of her life.)

Benedict pressed Clinton about a plan to attack Philadelphia, but Clinton rejected it. Instead, he sent Benedict to Virginia with 1,600 men to destroy American supply bases and retake Portsmouth. The British garrison at Portsmouth had recently left that town to support Major General Marquis Charles Cornwallis, who was trying desperately to maintain control of Chesapeake Bay.

Benedict approached this assignment with his customary zeal. Not only did he launch a successful surprise winter attack on Richmond, Virginia, but he was able to stage raids on Portsmouth, Westham, and Chesterfield. He then settled in for the winter to defend what he'd taken.

In June 1781 Benedict returned to New York and proposed that he take a force to Yorktown, Virginia, and link up with Cornwallis's troops in order to attack Philadelphia. This kind of aggressive strategy, Benedict argued,

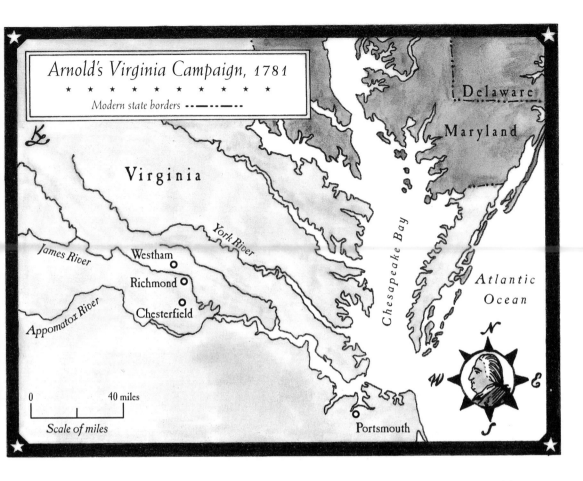

Delaware

Maryland

Virginia

York River

James River

Westham

Richmond

Chesterfield

Appomatox River

Chesapeake Bay

Atlantic Ocean

N

W   E

S

0   40 miles

Scale of miles

Portsmouth

would distress Congress and throw the Revolution into chaos. It would also have taken Cornwallis's army out of harm's way. Unknown to the British, Washington had begun assembling and moving troops in an attempt to surround the British at Yorktown, using the French navy to cut off escape by sea.

Once again Clinton refused to approve Benedict's plan. His differences with Benedict over finances had widened into a more general personality conflict. Benedict had begun complaining to anyone who would listen about Clinton's lack of initiative and overall indecisiveness. The American forces were vulnerable, he kept insisting. Clinton had to strike now, before more French troops arrived to reinforce Washington's army. Benedict was so upset by the situation that he went over Clinton's head to present his plan directly to London.

This breach of protocol was too much for Clinton, who countered with his own gripes about Benedict: that his defection was motivated by money alone and that he was an overly aggressive military leader. Even when it became clear that Cornwallis's army was in trouble in Yorktown, Clinton would not send Benedict with reinforcements. He did want to utilize his Loyalist officer (and probably wanted to get him out of town as well), so he ordered Benedict north to wipe out a privateering base at New London, Connecticut. Again Benedict demonstrated his superior skills as a military leader. He took New London easily and destroyed half of its shipping, plus the largest wharf and important warehouses.

In the eyes of many Patriots, however, the attack on New London was more than a daring military strike. During the burning of one ship, a supply of gunpowder exploded, sending tongues of flame into the sky. A change of wind "communicated the flames to part of the town," Benedict wrote in his report, "which was, notwithstanding every effort to prevent it, unfortunately destroyed." Many Americans felt he had torched the town on purpose to revenge past slights to himself and his family.

Another unfortunate incident during this raid would further stain Benedict's reputation. At one point he ordered that Fort Griswold be stormed and its cannons turned to destroy American ships trying to leave the harbor. Just prior to the assault, Benedict decided to call it off because he worried that the fort was so heavily manned that too many soldiers on both sides would be wounded or killed. But the officer in charge never received the order. During the bloody attack that followed, 113 of the 140 defenders were wounded or killed—many, it was claimed, after the fort had been surrendered. Despite the fact that Benedict had countermanded his original order and wasn't present when the assault went ahead anyway, he was accused of brutality.

Benedict returned to New York, more determined than ever to fight his American enemies. Then, several weeks after Benedict's Connecticut expedition, Cornwallis found himself trapped at Yorktown by a combined American and French force. On October 20, 1781, Cornwallis surrendered his 9,500 troops to George Washington. It would be another two

NARROW ESCAPE OF BENEDICT ARNOLD, WHEN
BURNING NEW LONDON, CONNECTICUT.

years before peace was officially declared, but keeping the thirteen colonies was no longer a priority for the British high command in London. This didn't stop Benedict from trying to persuade the king and his men to fight on. He and Peggy, along with Neddy and two of his sons, sailed to London, where he and Cornwallis (who had been released after promising not to reenter the war) tried unsuccessfully to wrest control of British troops in America from Clinton.

Benedict also continued to lobby for what he thought was a fair settlement for his defection and resulting loss of property. His testimony did help at least five other Loyalists receive increased compensation for their losses, but his own claims went nowhere. Ironically, Queen Charlotte was so taken by Peggy that she granted a £100 annuity to each of Peggy's children. Peggy went on to raise five children, and this additional £500 would eventually double her annual pensions to £1,000.

When the Revolutionary War finally came to an end and a peace treaty was signed in 1783, Benedict and Peggy found themselves shunned by a

A portrait of Benedict that shows him in his British brigadier general uniform.

The Library of Congress

number of factions. Many British citizens were not pleased that an American was allowed access to the king and his councilors, while others remained suspicious of his motives. British citizens and American Loyalists who wanted the war ended objected to his continued call for military intervention. A series of anti-Arnold letters appearing under the signature "R.M." began running in the London *General Advertiser and Morning Intelligencer*. One protested his access to the highest levels of the government and called him "a mean mercenary, who, having adopted a cause for the sake of plunder, quits it when he is convicted of that charge." Another said his courage in battle came more from "the brandy bottle [than] his heart." Still another condemned him as a common criminal and claimed "he stands [as much] chance of being hanged here as he does in America . . . [and] as to hanging, he ought not so much to mind it. He thought the risk of it but a trifle for his friend Major André to undergo."

Benedict continued to press the British government for compensation and compiled a list of lost assets amounting to £45,000 sterling ($3,300,000). While awaiting a determination on this, he applied for a post in India with the East India Company's private army. Three days later a director of the company, George Johnstone, sent him an icy rejection, specifically referring to Benedict's motives for switching sides when he said, "a fortunate plot holds you up as the savior of nations, a premature discovery brings you to the scaffold or brands your fame with dark and doubtful suspicions." Johnstone then added, "Although I am satisfied of the purity of your conduct, the generality do not think so. While this is the case, no power in this country could suddenly place you in the situation you aim at under the East India Company."

Benedict was forty-three years old at the time, not the sort of individual to settle for less than he felt he deserved or to give up without a fight. But with his and Peggy's combined annual income hovering at about

228 *The Real Benedict Arnold*

£1,500 and little prospect of improvement in England, he decided to try his hand in Canada. Tens of thousands of American Loyalists had fled to British protection in Canada at the end of the war. Established cities were growing larger, and new communities were being carved out of the wilderness. Benedict sensed economic potential and wanted to be a part of it.

In 1785 he withdrew his claims for payment and sailed to Canada's New Brunswick province aboard the *Lord Middleton,* leaving Peggy and their children behind in London. He brought along a shipment of butter, flour, beef, and pork, with which he planned to start his business dealings in his new hometown of Saint John. In a remarkably short time Benedict had a house, store, warehouse, and wharf and had established a vigorous trading business between New Brunswick, the West Indies, and London. He began buying land in other parts of Canada, amassing nearly 15,000 acres, where he set up stores, wharves, and warehouses to extend the reach of his business. He even managed, by using a middleman, to sell goods in New England. Within eighteen months of his arrival, writes Canadian historian Barry K. Wilson, "Arnold [had become] the most successful businessman and trader in early New Brunswick." His business prospects looking up,

A view of Saint John, New Brunswick, where Benedict established his primary Canadian business. THE NEW YORK PUBLIC LIBRARY

Benedict sent for his sister, Hannah, asking that she bring his three sons from his first marriage to Canada. He then sailed to England to get Peggy and their children.

He might have stayed in Canada for the rest of his life, but fate once again stood between him and happiness. After the war, British troops in Canada were called back to England to help fight the expanding war against France and its allies. This took hundreds of thousands of pounds out of the Canadian economy. Just as had happened in the American colonies after the French and Indian War, a severe depression descended upon Canada. A lawyer who had just seen one of his clients hauled off to jail for a debt lamented the terrible economic situation in Saint John. "Really," wrote Ward Chapman, "everybody is so poor. There is no such thing as money to be had."

Those who had purchased goods or land from Benedict on credit could no longer pay their accounts. At first, Benedict asked people very civilly to pay their debts. When they failed to respond, he began demanding payment. Soon he found himself involved in scores of lawsuits. And he did not bring suit against only common businessmen. He showed little concern for social status, taking three sitting legislators, a county sheriff, and even a venerable founder of New Brunswick, Edward Winslow, to court. Such dogged pursuit of justice did not win him any friends. Many of the people he sued considered him hardhearted and greedy (and spread rumors to that effect), even though they clearly owed him the money in question and were trying to welsh on their obligations.

One of Benedict's lawyers, Stephen Sewell, came closest to the truth about the difference between Benedict's outward manner and his true nature. He felt Benedict's "notions of propriety . . . often degenerates into pride and folly," such as when he insisted he was owed additional interest on debts even after a court awarded him a certain amount. But while Sewell saw that this aggressiveness gave a bad impression of his client, he also acknowledged that Benedict "is modest, true to his own interest but I think not further than is perfectly right and proper." What is more, Benedict could be generous when he chose. "When tenants reneged on notes," historian Willard Sterne Randall observes, "Arnold could not bring himself to dispossess men with families."

Benedict won most of these cases because the evidence was clear that those involved had failed to make good on their debts. But he rarely collected on these court awards. His creditors either fled the province or hid from sheriffs trying to enforce the court verdicts.

His dreams of a business empire thwarted, and his popularity lagging once again, Benedict took Peggy and his young family back to London in 1791. Two sons from his first marriage, Richard (who was twenty-one years old) and Henry (nineteen), stayed in Saint John with their aunt Hannah. They looked after his land holdings, attempted to collect debts, and did what they could to keep his struggling trading business afloat. His eldest son, Benedict (VII), enlisted in the British army to fight the French.

Benedict was fifty when he returned to a changed London. Those who had opposed the war with America were now in power, while those who had urged it to continue were pushed aside and ignored. Meanwhile, King George III, who admired and respected Benedict, was hovering on the verge of madness and was of little help.

Benedict tried to enlist in England's latest war against France but was rejected by political opponents and suspicious members of the military. He revived his falling income by outfitting a ship and sailing to the West Indies on trading voyages. On one voyage he was captured and held as a spy by the French, who considered selling the infamous traitor to America. He made a daring escape and then described his place in life to a friend in Canada. "My situation has often been dangerous and critical, my affairs sometimes have prospered and sometimes not. I have made and lost a great deal of money here but I hope to return to England in April a gainer upon the whole."

In an effort to raise cash, he continued in his attempts to collect debts owed him in Saint John, and to sell off pieces of his business there. These costly court battles produced little financial relief. He next outfitted a pri-

vateer, and almost immediately the hired captain captured a French ship with a cargo worth over £25,000 sterling—only to see it all lost because of the captain's "too free indulgence in his bottle."

As frustrations mounted and Benedict slipped deeper and deeper into debt, his health began to fail. His great-nephew, Isaac N. Benedict, wrote that "the bitter disappointments, cares and embarrassments of General Arnold pressed heavily upon him, and his strong physique and hardy frame began to show signs of breaking up." His two severe war injuries caused him constant pain, and he was plagued by bouts of dropsy, gout, breathing difficulties, and insomnia. On the 14th of June, 1801, Benedict Arnold slipped into a coma and died in his London home at the age of sixty.

Benedict was always confident in his ability to advance and succeed, always certain that whatever he was doing or about to do was what was best for himself, his family, and the community. He could be generous with friends and neighbors, but he responded quickly to any challenge or slight, whether to his business or his reputation, and would use any weapon at hand—legal, financial, or physical—to win his point.

In many ways Benedict was a very modern American capitalist, possibly too modern for an era that still clung to long-held notions of honor and proportion, where the aggressive pursuit of business and self-advancement was carefully concealed behind a very proper and reserved demeanor. Benedict's outlook and actions put him ahead of and at odds with his times.

Peggy Arnold was deeply devoted to Benedict, supporting and encouraging him through all his troubles with Congress and Joseph Reed's Council, keeping him calm during the long negotiations over his betrayal of the American cause, and relieving him of as much anxiety as possible when their finances were tight. Her letter informing his sons in North America of his death was bittersweet but deeply loving. "Your dear father whose long-declining state of health you have been acquainted with, is no more. In him, his family have lost an affectionate husband, father and friend and to his exertions to make provision for them may be attributed the loss of his life."

It may have been his love for Peggy and a desire to provide for her and their children that led Benedict to look to the British side for justice and respect; if either one of them ever regretted that decision, they left no word. Benedict did, however, leave an indication of the spirit that guided him throughout his turbulent life. One of the first things he did when he first arrived in England was to change his family motto. The old one was *Mihi gloria sursum* (Through glory yielded to me), an acknowledgment that their position in life had been the result of divine generosity. His new motto reflected his changed circumstances and his determination to overcome whatever stood in his path: *Nil desperandum*—Never despair.

NOTES, SOURCES, AND RELATED ASIDES

EPIGRAPH

From *To Begin the World Anew: The Genius and Ambiguities of the American Founders* (New York: Knopf/Random House, 2003). Bernard Bailyn is the Adams Professor Emeritus and the James Duncan Phillips Professor of Early American History at Harvard University.

1: THE MOST BRILLIANT SOLDIER

I have visited Saratoga National Historical Park twice, once long ago during the summer and again more recently just before the park closed for the winter. Both times I was struck by the beautiful, rolling terrain and the serene quiet of the countryside. The peaceful feeling of the hills is at odds with the hard fighting that took place there in 1777 and the terrible suffering of the wounded and dying.

Additional information about the park and these battles can be found in "Saratoga," a brochure issued by the National Park Service (GPO: 2003—496-196/40438); a virtual tour of the major battlefield sites as well as a history of the park and other information is offered on the Park Service website: www.nps.gov/sara. Also see the *National Geographic Guide to the National Parks of the United States*, edited by the National Geographic Society, National Geographic Society, Washington, D.C., 2006.

It wasn't easy piecing together information about the "Boot Monument," especially since it was erected nearly sixty years before the battlefield site became a part of the National Park system and accurate records were kept. What little I could discover was gathered during conversations with Eric H. Schnitzer, Park Ranger/Historian, Saratoga National Historical Park; Christopher Raab, Archives & Special Collections Librarian, Shadek-Fackenthal Library, Franklin &

Marshall College; Michael R. Lear, Archives & Special Collections Assistant, Shadek-Fackenthal Library, Franklin & Marshall College; and Christine Robinson, Curator, Saratoga National Historical Park.

John Watts de Peyster went to great lengths to ensure that his own name would be remembered. In addition to having buildings and statues erected in the memory of family members, each clearly bearing *his* name, de Peyster also had a biography written about himself: Frank Allaben, *John Watts de Peyster* (New York: Frank Allaben Genealogical Co., 1908). A number of de Peyster's statues were designed by American sculptor George Edwin Bissell (1839–1920), whose family ran a marble company in Poughkeepsie, New York. It is possible that Bissell also designed the "Boot Monument."

While de Peyster was a serious and scrupulous historian, he did get one fact wrong on the "Boot Monument." Arnold did not earn the rank of major general as a result of his actions at Saratoga. He had obtained that rank prior to the battles; what he did regain was his seniority.

The date of Benedict Arnold's birth that appears in *Vital Records of Norwich,* I:I53 is actually "January 3, 1740/41." This was at a time when the Julian calendar, first introduced by Julius Caesar in 46 B.C., was still in use. The British Empire switched to the more accurate Gregorian calendar in the 1750s, which automatically moved all dates, including Benedict Arnold's birthday, ahead by eleven days.

2: YOU ARE ACCOUNTABLE

The Arnold genealogy comes from Elisha Stephen Arnold, *The Arnold Memorial: William Arnold of Providence and Pawtuxet, 1587–1675, and a Genealogy of His Descendants* (Rutland, Vt.: Tuttle, 1935), and John Ward Dean et al., *Genealogy of the Family of Arnold in Europe and America* (Boston: Clapp & Son, 1879). Also of great use was Frances Manwaring Caulkins, *History of Norwich, Connecticut, From Its Possession by the Indians, to the Year 1866* (published by the author, 1866). This book provides a great deal of genealogical information, and also discusses the daily life of the town's people as well as its religious and business activity.

When towns were formed in colonial America, social position was often solidified by the way land was distributed. In Wallingford, Connecticut, every "high rank man" was able to purchase 400 acres, every "middle rank man" got 300, and those deemed from the "lower ranks" were allowed 200. Rank was determined by how wealthy a person was, the type of work he performed, his level of education, and his overall "usefulness either in the church or commonwealth." When Roger Williams founded Providence, Rhode Island, he insisted that every family receive the same amount of land. Benedict's town of New Haven, on the other hand, was one of the least egalitarian communities in the region, with most of the land and wealth in the hands of a very few. More about wealth and social rank can be found in David Hackett Fischer, *Albion's Seed: Four British Folkways in America* (New York: Oxford University Press, 1989), and William Haller, Jr., *The Puritan Frontier: Town-Planting in New England Colonial Development, 1630–1660* (New York: Columbia University Press, 1951).

Prior to the nineteenth century, dividing one's inheritance equally among children was not a regular practice. Most people with any sort of estate usually passed it all on to the eldest son, a form of inheritance known as primogeniture. A number of influential Revolutionary leaders felt that this was unfair because it helped maintain the financial and political power of a few very wealthy families. Thomas Jefferson feared such an aristocracy in the United States and proposed making division among heirs—partible inheritance—mandatory by law. In 1795 Thomas Paine urged that an inheritance tax be used to create a fund that would give £15 sterling ($932.40) to everyone on their twenty-first birthday, and £10 ($621.60) per year to everyone over the age of fifty. These efforts failed, but in 1916 an estate tax was passed that is still in effect today.

Fischer notes in *Albion's Seed* a humorous result of rigid adherence to partible inheritance. In England in 1585, Margaret Browne divided up her house among five children, giving the hallway and entrance to one, a bedroom to another, the kitchen to a third, the parlor to a fourth, and the attached shop to the last. All five shared the garden equally.

Information about eighteenth-century Norwich comes from Marian K. O'Keefe and Catherine Smith Doroshevich, *Norwich: Historic Homes & Families* (Stonington, Conn.: Pequot, 1967), and Bruce C. Daniels, *The Connecticut Town: Growth and Development, 1635–1790* (Middletown, Conn.: Wesleyan University Press, 1979). An overview of what life was like in a small town can be found in Robert J. Taylor, *Colonial Connecticut: A History* (Millwood, N.Y.: Kraus International, 1979).

Names were extremely important to pious people such as Hannah. As one

Puritan minister declared, "[A] good name is as a thread tyed [sic] about the finger, to make us mindful of the errand we came into the world to do for our master." How much a name weighs on a person is hard to say. Benedict's first name comes from the Latin *benedictus*, "blessed." His surname has two possible derivations. It could be from an ancient Germanic word that translates as "the eagle's power" or derived from a word in twelfth-century English that means "honor." More on New England naming practices and the use of a dead sibling's name can be found in David Hackett Fischer's "Forenames and the Family in New England: An Exercise in Historical Onomastics," *Chronos*, vol. 1 (1981), 76–111.

Quotes about Benedict's character come from Jared Sparks, *Life and Treason of Benedict Arnold* (New York: Harper & Brothers, 1848). Sparks also maligned Benedict's father by saying he was "a man of suspicious integrity, little respected, and less esteemed," and of his eldest son: "He was a violent, headstrong youth, and it is supposed he came to an untimely end." Sparks may have practiced questionable history when it came to Benedict Arnold, but he was a highly skilled historian nonetheless. He was one of the first to see the historical value of the writings of Revolutionary leaders, such as George Washington and Benjamin Franklin, and collected many of their letters and other writings. His valuable collection of manuscripts and papers is now at Harvard University, while his private library and maps can be found at Cornell University.

The account of Benedict Arnold's early years was pieced together from a number of sources that include Isaac N. Arnold, *The Life of Benedict Arnold: His Patriotism and His Treason* (Chicago: Jansen, McClurg, 1880); Malcolm Decker, *Benedict Arnold: Son of the Havens* (Tarrytown, N.Y.: William Abbatt, 1932); Charles Sellers, *Benedict Arnold: The Proud Warrior* (New York: Minton, Balch, 1930); James Kirby Martin, *Benedict Arnold, Revolutionary Hero: An American Warrior Reconsidered* (New York: New York University Press, 1997); Willard Sterne Randall, *Benedict Arnold: Patriot and Traitor* (New York: Barnes & Noble, 1990); Audrey Wallace, *Benedict Arnold: Misunderstood Hero?* (Shippenburg, Pa.: Bird Street, 2003); and Clare Brandt, *The Man in the Mirror: A Life of Benedict Arnold* (New York: Random House, 1994).

The Reverend Mr. Thomas Dilworth published *A New Guide to the English Tongue* in 1740 in London, England. Dilworth said his book was intended to rescue "poor creatures from the Slavery of Sin and Satan." To this end his text contained spelling, reading, and grammar lessons all generously "adorned with proper Scriptures." Chapter 1 has no word that is more than three letters long and contains thoughts such as: "No Man may put off the Law of God," "The Way of God is no ill Way," and "My Joy is in God all the Day." Dilworth's *New Guide* became an instant hit in England and in the American colonies. By 1765 every New England school had adopted it, and it was still in use when Abraham Lincoln attended school.

Edward Cocker was born in 1631 and seems to have been a genuinely talented individual. He was a skilled engraver, a teacher of writing and arithmetic, and the author of poetry and a number of popular writing manuals. His fame, however, lies in the publication of *Cocker's Arithmetic, being a Plain and Easy Method* in 1678, three years after his death. *Cocker's Arithmetic* became the most popular math book in history and gave rise to the phrase "according to Cocker," which meant "quite correct." In 1847 mathematician Augustus de Morgan offered proof that Cocker hadn't really written *Cocker's Arithmetic,* and that it was a compilation of other people's work, hastily slapped together by the book's publisher, John Hawkins. Even though Morgan condemned *Cocker's Arithmetic* as a "bad book," it still managed to go through well over 100 editions and was still in use fifty years after Benedict used it.

Information about the Great Awakening comes from several sources: Alan Heimert and Perry Miller, editors, *The Great Awakening: Documents Illustrating the Crisis and Its Consequences* (Indianapolis, Ind.: Bobbs-Merrill, 1967); Richard L. Bushman, *From Puritan to Yankee: Character and Social Order in Connecticut, 1690–1765* (Cambridge, Mass.: Harvard University Press, 1967); Gerald F. Moran and Maris A. Vinovskis, *Religion, Family, and the Life Course: Explorations in the Social History of Early America* (Ann Arbor: University of Michigan Press, 1992); and John Morgan, *Godly Learning: Puritan Attitudes Towards Reason, Learning, and Education, 1560–1640* (Cambridge and New York: Cambridge University Press, 1986).

Translating colonial currency to modern-day equivalents is a very tricky business, depending on whether we're talking about paper currency or hard currency (such as coins minted out of gold or silver), British pounds sterling or pound notes printed in the colonies. And since economies all over the world went through waves of growth and depression, the year under discussion is vital, too. I have made my calculations based on charts found in John J. McCusker, *How*

Much Is That in Real Money? A Historical Commodity Price Index for Use as a Deflator of Money Values in the Economy of the United States (Worcester, Mass.: American Antiquarian Society, 2001).

3: BE YE ALSO READY

The death rate among children was so high that the Puritan minister Cotton Mather once commented that a dead child was "a sight no more surprising than a broken pitcher." Information about mortality rates and the resulting emotional fallout can be found in Charles R. King, *Children's Health in America: A History* (New York: Twayne, 1993); William H. McNeill, *Plagues and Peoples* (New York: Anchor, 1976); Moran and Vinovskis, *Religion, Family, and the Life Course*; and Fischer, *Albion's Seed*.

Some writers have suggested that the fever that carried off Benedict's sisters in 1753 was yellow fever, but this isn't likely. The term Hannah used in her letters, "distemper," was commonly used by colonists to describe diphtheria, and the few symptoms mentioned fit the disease as well. See John Duffy, *Epidemics in Colonial America* (Baton Rouge, La.: Louisiana State University Press, 1953).

The discussion of the French and Indian War and the wide-ranging effect it had on the British and American economies comes from Walter R. Borneman, *The French and Indian War: Deciding the Fate of North America* (New York: HarperCollins, 2006), and Fred Anderson, *The War That Made America: A Short History of the French and Indian War* (New York: Viking, 2005). Both books discuss George Washington's part in the Battle of Monongahela and his subsequent leading of 1,000 men from the Virginia regiment. A concise overview of Washington's early military experience can be found in Joseph J. Ellis, *His Excellency: George Washington* (New York: Alfred A. Knopf, 2004).

Background information about Joshua, Daniel, and Jerusha Lathrop comes from the Lothropp Family Foundation website: http://www.lothropp.org.

The story of how Benedict was mistaken for "Benedick" was first reported by J. Flexner, *The Traitor and the Spy: Benedict Arnold and John André* (New York: Harcourt, Brace, 1953). Evidently, when Benedict did turn out for the general call-up of the militia in 1757 to halt Montcalm's advance into the colonies, he was one of about 5,000 men and boys, or twenty-five percent of Connecticut's available militia force. For more on this, see Harold E. Selesky, *War and Society in Colonial Connecti-*

cut (New Haven, Conn.: Yale University Press, 1990), and Francis Jennings, *Empire of Fortune: Crowns, Colonies, and Tribes in the Seven Years War in America* (New York: W. W. Norton, 1988).

The discussion of drinking in America is based on Peter Thompson, *Rum Punch & Revolution: Taverngoing & Public Life in Eighteenth-Century Philadelphia* (Philadelphia: University of Pennsylvania, 1999), and Mark Edward Lender and James Kirby Martin, *Drinking in America: A History* (New York: The Free Press, 1987). Also of interest is Alice Morse Earle, *Drinks and Drinkers in Colonial Massachusetts, Rhode Island and Connecticut (American History, 18th Century American Culture, Colonial America)*, 1893. Details about Benedict (IV)'s drinking and his run-in with church elders come from First Church of Norwich Records, I:46–47, Connecticut State Library, Hartford.

Three books proved to be helpful in retelling this segment of Benedict's life and the development of his personality: Randall, *Benedict Arnold: Patriot and Traitor*; Martin, *Benedict Arnold, Revolutionary Hero*; and Brandt, *The Man in the Mirror*.

4: A REPUTATION OF UNSULLIED HONOR

Background information on New Haven, as well as some of the questionable stories about Benedict, come from Edward E. Atwater, *History of the City of New Haven to the Present Time* (New York: W. W. Munsell, 1887).

What little we know about Benedict's sister, Hannah, comes from Isaac Arnold, *The Life of Benedict Arnold*. He quotes from a number of her letters.

Some very good information about Jared Sparks and his contributions to American history can be found at the Morristown National Historical Park website www.nps.gov/morr/index.htm under Jared Sparks Papers.

Information about Freemasonry comes from several sources: the official website of the Masons, www.co-masonry.org; Jon Butler's *Becoming America: The Revolution Before 1776* (Cambridge, Mass.: Harvard University Press, 2000); and Steven C. Bullock, *Revolutionary Brotherhood: Freemasonry and the Transformation of the American Social Order, 1730–1840* (Chapel Hill, N.C.: University of North Carolina Press, 1996).

Hiller B. Zobel's *The Boston Massacre* (New York: W. W. Norton, 1970) contains a fascinating history of colonial smuggling, including a glimpse into John Hancock's illegal activities and court cases, the practice of "compounding," and how Britain's continued efforts at tariff enforcement eventually led to violence. Also see John W. Tyler, *Smugglers and Patriots: Boston Merchants and the Advent of the American Revolution* (Boston: Northeastern University Press, 1986), and William M. Fowler, *The Baron of Beacon Hill: A Biography of John Hancock* (Boston: Houghton Mifflin, 1980).

Sources for the Boles incident include Lawrence Henry Gipson, *American Loyalist: Jared Ingersoll* (New Haven, Conn.: Yale University Press, 1920), and the *Connecticut Gazette*, Feb. 7, 14, and 21, 1766. Also see Martin, *Benedict Arnold, Revolutionary Hero*; Isaac Arnold, *The Life of Benedict Arnold*; and Randall, *Benedict Arnold: Patriot and Traitor*.

5: GOOD GOD ARE THE AMERICANS ALL ASLEEP?

A number of extremely interesting books were consulted for my discussion of the growing animosity the American colonies felt toward British policies and how this led to war, including James L. Stokesbury, *A Short History of the American Revolution* (New York: William Morrow, 1991); John R. Alden, *The American Revolution, 1775–1783* (New York: Harper, 1954); Robert Middlekauff, *The Glorious Cause: The American Revolution, 1763–1789*, vol. 2 of the *Oxford History of the United States* (New York: Oxford University Press, 1982); Bernhard Knollenberg, *Origin of the American Revolution, 1759–1776* (New York: Macmillan, 1960); Butler, *Becoming America*; and Pauline Maier, *From Resistance to Revolution: Colonial Radicals and the Development of American Opposition to Britain, 1765–1776* (New York: Knopf, 1972).

For more about secret Revolutionary societies, see David Hackett Fischer, *Paul Revere's Ride* (New York: Oxford University Press, 1994), and Esther Forbes, *Paul Revere and the World He Lived In* (Boston: Houghton Mifflin, 1942).

Guy Williams's book *The Age of Agony: The Art of Healing, 1700–1800* (Chicago: Academy Chicago Publishers, 1996) has a gruesomely entertaining chapter on venereal disease and its treatment during the eighteenth century.

Dueling to restore one's honor was quite common in the eighteenth century, though many prominent Americans opposed it, including Benjamin Franklin and George Washington (who urged his military aides to turn down duels because he did not want to lose their services to an opponent's bullet). One of the most famous duels took place in Weehawken, New Jersey, in 1804 between Aaron Burr and Alexander Hamilton. Hamilton had had many duels in his life but was not very skilled with a pistol, and he fired prematurely, allowing Burr a free shot at him. Hamilton was hit in the stomach and, after much agony, died the next day of his wound. Ironically, Hamilton's oldest son, Philip, had been killed two years before in a duel in the same location, using the same pistol as his father. For more on dueling during the eighteenth century, see Ron Chernow, *Alexander Hamilton* (New York: Penguin, 2004). Also a good source of information is J. G. Millingen, *The History of Dueling Including Narratives of the Most Remarkable Encounters that Have Taken Place from the Earliest Period to the Present Time* (first published in 1841 and reprinted by Kila, Mont.: Kessinger Publishing Company, 2004).

Lately, fascinating studies of George Washington have been published that paint a full and sometimes less than flattering view of how he conducted business and treated individuals who worked for him, including his slaves. Two of the best are Ellis, *His Excellency: George Washington*, and Henry Wiencek, *An Imperfect God: George Washington, His Slaves, and the Creation of America* (New York: Farrar, Straus & Giroux, 2003).

Studies of how the powerful East India Company influenced British politics can be found in Lucy S. Sutherland, *The East India Company in Eighteenth Century Politics* (Oxford, Clarendon Press, 1952), and Marc Aronson, *The Real Revolution: The Global Story of American Independence* (New York: Clarion Books, 2005).

6: NONE BUT ALMIGHTY GOD SHALL PREVENT MY MARCHING
The very best book about the Battles of Lexington and Concord is Fischer, *Paul Revere's Ride*.

For information on the "battle" at Fort Ticonderoga, I consulted Allen French, *The Taking of Ticonderoga in 1775: A Study of Captors and Captives* (Cambridge, Mass.: Harvard University Press, 1928), and Allen French, *The First Year of the American Revolution* (Boston: Houghton Mifflin, 1934). Also see Martin, *Benedict Arnold, Revolutionary Hero*, and Isaac Arnold, *The Life of Benedict Arnold*.

I've tried to treat Ethan Allen and his Green Mountain Boys as fairly as possible, and to be honest, there are different opinions about him and his actions on Lake Champlain. Michael A. Bellesiles, *Revolutionary Outlaws: Ethan Allen and the Struggle for Independence on the Early American Frontier* (Charlottesville, Va.: University

Press of Virginia, 1993) presents Allen and friends as stouthearted, well-intentioned Patriots. However, he never really refutes the facts as I've recounted them (and as Benedict insisted in letters to the Massachusetts Provincial Congress). Even Bellesiles admits that after taking Ticonderoga, Allen and his men went on a drunken spree and did little to get the desperately needed cannons to George Washington. Bellesiles adds that "Allen deserved his reputation as a scoundrel, a charismatic charlatan of enormous strength and courage, and a braggart of almost mythical proportions. In short, Allen was the ideal of the frontier redneck." Also see Charles A. Jellison, *Ethan Allen: Frontier Rebel* (Syracuse, N.Y.: Syracuse University Press, 1969).

7: I HAVE RESIGNED MY COMMISSION

Sources of information on the plan to invade Canada and take Montreal and Quebec included Justin H. Smith, *Our Struggle for the Fourteenth Colony: Canada and the American Revolution,* 2 vols. (New York and London: G. P. Putnam's Sons, 1907); George F. G. Stanley, *Canada Invaded, 1775–1776* (Toronto: A. M. Hakkert & Co., 1973); and Robert McConnell Hatch, *Thrust for Canada: The American Attempt on Quebec in 1775–1776* (Boston: Houghton Mifflin, 1979).

For more on Benedict's political troubles following Ticonderoga, see Martin, *Benedict Arnold, Revolutionary Hero.*

8: OUR GALLANT COLONEL

Dr. Benjamin Church was a highly trusted leader of the Revolution and counted among his friends such people as John Adams, Samuel Adams, John Hancock, and Paul Revere. It came as quite a shock, then, when it was discovered that he was in the pay of British general Thomas Gage and sending him confidential information about Revolutionary leaders and military plans. He was convicted of spying, but could not be hanged because Congress, in its haste to form the Continental Army, had forgotten to include a penalty for such an offense. Church was imprisoned in Connecticut and released at the end of 1777. The ship he was taking to the West Indies sank, and he was never heard from again, though his widow, who moved to England, did receive a £150 ($10,989) annual pension for "certain services" Dr. Church had provided.

The basis for my discussion of the trek through the Maine wilderness to Quebec is Justin H. Smith, *Arnold's March from Cambridge to Quebec* (Bowie, Md.: Heritage Books, Inc., 1998). This is a facsimile reprint of the 1903 book that traces the expedition in amazing detail and includes a reprint of the journal Benedict kept during the journey. In addition, other good sources for this information were the same author's *Our Struggle for the Fourteenth Colony*; Stanley, *Canada Invaded*; and Hatch, *Thrust for Canada*. To re-create elements of the march, I also used Kenneth Roberts, editor, *March to Quebec: Journals of the Members of Arnold's Expedition* (New York: Doubleday, Doran, 1938).

Roger Enos went before a court of inquiry on December 1, 1775. The reason he gave for abandoning the march was that he had only three days' rations for his men. He further claimed to have distributed all the food he had to his troops and Greene's. Not only did he have a great deal more food than he admitted, but he certainly didn't give Greene very much of it. Everyone who could testify against him was still up north struggling to survive, so the only people to speak were Enos's subordinates, who praised his skill in saving their lives. The hearing board decided to "acquit him with honor."

9: THE FORLORN HOPE

A very concise recounting of the siege of Quebec and attempted storming of the walled city can be found in W. J. Wood, *Battles of the Revolutionary War 1775–1781* (Chapel Hill, N.C.: Algonquin Books, 1990). Also see Michael Pearson, "The Siege of Quebec, 1775–1776," *American Heritage*, vol. 23, no. 2 (February 1972), and George F. Scheer and Hugh F. Rankin, editors, *Rebels and Redcoats: The American Revolution Through the Eyes of Those Who Fought and Lived It* (New York: Da Capo Press, Inc., 1957).

An interesting look at the military styles of both Guy Carleton and Benedict Arnold can be found in Paul David Nelson, "Guy Carleton Versus Benedict Arnold: The Campaign of 1776 in Canada and on Lake Champlain," *New York History*, vol. 57, no. 3 (July 1976), 339–66.

Evidently, David Wooster's ill treatment of Benedict at Quebec was not unusual; he exhibited deep and open contempt for Philip Schuyler (even though Schuyler was his commanding officer), and for every other officer in Montreal.

10: HE WILL TURN OUT A GREAT MAN

The retreat from Canada and Benedict's vital role in it are studied very nicely in Martin, *Benedict Arnold, Revolutionary Hero*.

The role played by Benjamin Franklin and his commission is discussed in some detail in Randall, *Benedict Arnold: Patriot and Traitor*. Also see Charles Carroll, *The Journal of Charles Carroll of Carrollton as One of the Congressional Commissioners to Canada in 1776*, edited by Allan S. Everest (Fort Ticonderoga, N.Y.: Champlain–Upper Hudson Bicentennial Committee, 1976).

11: THE GALLANT DEFENSE

Details about assembling the American fleet on Lake Champlain and Benedict's handling of it came from Gardner W. Allen, *A Naval History of the American Revolution*, 2 vols. (Boston: Houghton Mifflin, 1913); Harrison Bird, *Navies in the Mountains: The Battles on the Waters of Lake Champlain and Lake George, 1609–1814* (New York: Oxford University Press, 1962); William M. Fowler, Jr., *Rebels Under Sail: The American Navy During the Revolution* (New York: Scribner, 1976); Philip K. Lundeberg, *The Continental Gunboat Philadelphia and the Northern Campaign of 1776* (Smithsonian Publication 4651, Washington, D.C., 1966); and Oscar E. Bredenberg, "The American Champlain Fleet, 1775–1777," *Bulletin of the Fort Ticonderoga Museum*, vol. 12, no. 4 (September 1968), 249–63.

12: BY HEAVENS I WILL HAVE JUSTICE

Four books proved to be very handy for my brief account of the British victory over Washington in New York and Washington's stunning comebacks at Trenton and Princeton: Barnet Schecter, *The Battle for New York: The City at the Heart of the American Revolution* (New York: Walker, 2002); David Hackett Fischer, *Washington's Crossing* (New York: Oxford University Press, 2004); Richard M. Ketchum, *The Winter Soldiers: The Battles for Trenton and Princeton* (New York: Owl Books, 1999); and John Buchanan, *The Road to Valley Forge: How Washington Built the Army that Won the Revolution* (Hoboken, N.J.: John Wiley & Sons, 2004).

Readers will note that what were previously referred to as colonies are now called states. On July 4, 1776, Congress adopted the amended draft of the Declaration of Independence, declaring that "these united colonies are and of right ought to be free and independent states." The switch took some time to get used to, and many staunch Patriots were still using the word *colony* months later when writing about their home states. Of course, the British and Loyalists resisted the change for years.

The claims that Benedict was overly aggressive on Lake Champlain, and that losing as many ships as he did was not a wise military choice, have not stood up over time. Naval authority Alfred Thayer Mahan said, "Waterbury's advice evidently found its origins in that fruitful source of military errors of design, which reckons the preservation of a force first of objects, making the results of its action secondary. With sounder judgment, Arnold decided to hold on. A retreat before square-rigged sailing vessels having a fair wind, by a heterogeneous force like his own, of unequal speeds and batteries, could result only in disaster." From A.T.T. Mahan, *Major Operations of the Navies in the War of American Independence* (Cranbury, N.J.: Scholar's Bookshelf, 2005).

The passing over of Benedict for promotion is discussed in detail in Martin, *Benedict Arnold, Revolutionary Hero*.

13: A DEVILISH FIGHTING FELLOW

More information about the raid on Danbury and Arnold's stand at Ridgefield can be found in Richard Buel, Jr., *Dear Liberty: Connecticut's Mobilization for the Revolutionary War* (Middletown, Conn.: Wesleyan University Press, 1980); Robert F. McDevitt, *Connecticut Attacked, A British Viewpoint: Tryon's Raid on Danbury* (Chester, Conn.: Pequot, 1937); Paul David Nelson, *William Tryon and the Course of Empire: A Life in British Imperial Service* (Chapel Hill, N.C.: University of North Carolina Press, 1990); and Isaac Q. Leake, *Memoir of the Life and Times of General John Lamb* (Albany, N.Y.: Joel Munsell, 1850).

The bickering over Philippe Charles Tronson de Coudray's appointment to the American army was resolved by a clever bit of wordplay. Congress designated Coudray a "staff" major general whose duties included the inspection of cannons and other weapons. He would function only in an advisory capacity and have no authority over generals who were actually in combat. Less than a month later, Coudray dismissed the advice of fellow travelers that he should walk onboard a ferryboat about to cross the Schuylkill River, and instead he rode his horse aboard at a gallop. The horse panicked, then bolted straight forward and into the water, drowning Coudray before he could get his feet out of the stirrups.

14: YOU WILL HEAR OF MY BEING VICTORIOUS

Both Martin, *Benedict Arnold, Revolutionary Hero*, and Brandt, *The Man in the Mirror*, have discussions of Burgoyne's march and how Philip Schuyler was replaced as commander of the Northern Army.

Information about Hon Yost Schuyler is sketchy and comes from William L. Stone, *The Campaign of Lieut. Gen. John Burgoyne and the Expedition of Lieut. Col. Barry St. Leger* (Albany, N.Y.: Joel Munsell, 1877).

15: INSPIRED BY THE FURY OF A DEMON

Information about General Howe's southern strategy and Washington's response to it can be found in Christopher Ward, *The War of the Revolution*, 2 vols. (New York: Macmillan, 1952); Mark M. Boatner III, *Encyclopedia of the American Revolution* (New York: David McKay, 1974); Douglas Southall Freeman, *George Washington, A Biography*, vol. 4 (New York: Charles Scribner's Sons, 1951); and Wilmer W. MacElree, *Along the Western Brandywine* (West Chester, Pa.: published by the author, 1909).

Both the first and second Battles of Saratoga and Benedict Arnold's role in each are discussed in Wood, *Battles of the Revolutionary War*; John R. Elting, *The Battles of Saratoga* (Monmouth Beach, N.J.: Philip Freneau Press, 1977); Rupert Furneaux, *The Battle of Saratoga* (New York: Stein and Day, 1971); Hoffman Nickerson, *The Turning Point of the Revolution* (Boston: Houghton Mifflin, 1928); James Lunt, *John Burgoyne of Saratoga* (New York: Harcourt Brace Jovanovich, 1975); F. J. Hudleston, *Gentleman Johnny Burgoyne: Misadventures of an English General in the Revolution* (Indianapolis, Ind.: Bobbs-Merrill, 1927); James Graham, *The Life of General Daniel Morgan, of the Virginia Line of the Army of the United States* (New York: Derby & Jackson, 1856); Samuel White Patterson, *Horatio Gates: Defender of American Liberties* (New York: Columbia University Press, 1941); Joseph P. Cullen, "Saratoga," *American History Illustrated*, vol. 10, no. 1 (April 1975); and William Waller Edwards, "Morgan and His Riflemen," *William and Mary Quarterly*, vol. 23, no. 2 (October 1914).

Two articles were of particular help in writing about the Gates-Arnold relationship: John F. Luzader, "The Arnold-Gates Controversy," *West Virginia History*, vol. 27, no. 2 (January 1966), and Paul D. Nelson, "The Gates-Arnold Quarrel, September 1777," *New-York Historical Society Quarterly*, vol. 55, no. 3 (July 1971).

In addition to using material from the above histories of the battles, further personal accounts were taken from Thomas Anburey, *With Burgoyne from Quebec: An Account of the Life at Quebec and of the Famous Battle of Saratoga*, edited by Sydney Jackman (Toronto: Macmillan of Canada, 1963); Ray Raphael, *A People's History of the American Revolution: How Common People Shaped the Fight for Independence* (New York: New Press, 2001); Sheer and Rankin, *Rebels and Redcoats*; and Henry Dearborn, "A Narrative of the Saratoga Campaign, 1815," *Bulletin of the Fort Ticonderoga Museum*, vol. 1 (1928–1929), 8–9.

Information about the near rescue of Burgoyne by Clinton can be located in William B. Willcox, *Portrait of a General: Sir Henry Clinton in the War of Independence* (New York: Knopf, 1964). The Battles of Saratoga can be looked at from the Hessian point of view in William L. Stone, translator, *Memoirs, and Letters and Journals, of Major General Riedesel* (Albany, N.Y.: Joel Munsell, 1868). James Wilkinson's rather slanted view of Arnold and these battles is found in James Wilkinson, *Memoirs of My Own Times*, 3 vols. (Philadelphia: Abraham Small, 1816), while Burgoyne's take on the failed campaign is told in John Burgoyne, *A State of the Expedition from Canada* (1780, reprinted by New York: Arno, 1969). A good look at the strategies used at Saratoga is located in Max M. Mintz, *The Generals of Saratoga: John Burgoyne and Horatio Gates* (New Haven, Conn.: Yale University Press, 1990).

16: WE'LL HAVE THEM ALL IN HELL

In addition to the titles listed above about the Battles of Saratoga, several other titles proved helpful in re-creating the events of October 7: Martin, *Benedict Arnold, Revolutionary Hero*; Randall, *Benedict Arnold: Patriot and Traitor*; and Henry Steele Commager and Richard B. Morris, editors, *The Spirit of Seventy-Six: The Story of the American Revolution as Told by the Participants*, 2 vols. (Indianapolis, Ind.: Bobbs-Merrill, 1958).

17: I AM HEARTILY TIRED

One reason Washington was slow in responding to Benedict was that he was fighting to stay commander in chief of the army. Following Gates's triumph at Saratoga and Washington's defeat at Brandywine, a number of people, including members of Congress such as John Adams, Thomas Mifflin, James Lovell, and Benjamin Rush, began suggesting that Gates should supplant Washington. Major

General Thomas Conway agreed and sent a letter to Gates criticizing Washington: "Heaven has been determined to save your country; or a weak general and bad counselors would have it ruined." The ever-sly James Wilkinson repeated a version of this statement to other officers in October 1778. When Washington learned about the letter, he confronted both Gates and Conway, and by the end of the year what came to be called the "Conway Cabal" had blown over. Conway, as a way to bolster his status, offered his resignation and was shocked when Congress unanimously accepted it.

A great deal of information about Benedict's role as commandant of Philadelphia and his interactions with Joseph Reed can be found in Randall, *Benedict Arnold: Patriot and Traitor*.

18: ON YOU ALONE MY HAPPINESS DEPENDS

Peggy Shippen wasn't the only woman whom Benedict considered marrying. Before meeting her, Benedict had been infatuated with Elizabeth "Betsy" De Blois (sometimes spelled Deblois), the daughter of a wealthy Loyalist merchant from Boston. His romantic gestures were rejected by the young woman, allegedly because her mother did not want her associating with rebels.

Primitive medical knowledge, a lack of skilled doctors, and the dangers of childbirth meant that many women died in their thirties and forties. The surviving husbands often wanted their new wives to be young enough to care for the house and children and, possibly, to have more children. This was especially true if the man was wealthy and came from a distinguished family.

Background information about the Shippen family comes from Randolph Shipley Klein, *Portrait of an Early American Family: The Shippens of Pennsylvania Across Five Generations* (Philadelphia: University of Pennsylvania Press, 1975), and *Nancy Shippen, Her Journal Book*, edited by Ethel Armes (Philadelphia: Lippincott, 1935), as well as Randall, *Benedict Arnold: Patriot and Traitor*.

19: BECAUSE I MIGHT HAVE DONE WRONG

Information on Benedict's negotiations with André and the up-and-down course of his betrayal were found in Carl Van Doren, *Secret History of the American Revolution: An Account of the Conspiracies of Benedict Arnold and Numerous Others, Drawn from the Secret Service Papers of the British Headquarters in North America* (New York: Viking,

1941); William Abbatt, *The Crisis of the Revolution: Being the Story of Arnold and André* (1899, reprinted Harbor Hill Books, 1976); John Edwin Bakeless, *Turncoats, Traitors, and Heroes* (Philadelphia: Lippincott, 1959); Charles Swain Hall, *Benjamin Tallmadge: Revolutionary Soldier and American Businessman* (New York: Columbia University Press, 1943); and Benjamin Tallmadge (his speech to Congress about André's captors), Annals of Congress, 1817, 4474–75.

Incidentally, Benedict's initial request for £10,000 may have been more a matter of precedent than precise financial calculation. When General Charles Lee was asked to join the Revolutionary army, he asked Congress for and was granted a £10,000 bounty in case his Virginia estate was seized by the British. Benedict may have simply used this as a standard figure, assuming the British would agree that he was worth at least as much as Lee.

For additional specifics on Peggy Arnold's involvement in the plot, see Cokie Roberts, *Founding Mothers: The Women Who Raised Our Nation* (New York: William Morrow, 2004).

While some writers suggest that Benedict's treason was motivated by anger and a desire for money, one suggests there was at least another reason—genuine protest over the political direction the Revolution was taking. See James Kirby Martin, "Benedict Arnold's Treason as Political Protest," *Parameters: US Army War College Quarterly*, vol. 11 (1981), 63–74.

Joseph Reed explains his role in Pennsylvania politics in William B. Reed, *Life and Correspondence of Joseph Reed, Military Secretary of Washington* (Philadelphia: Lindsay and Blakiston, 1847). It is interesting to note that even though Joseph Reed came to despise George Washington, his relative understood that Washington was a favorite among readers and used his name to attract an audience.

There is a good description of the Philadelphia food riots and the battle of "Fort Wilson" in Randall, *Benedict Arnold: Patriot and Traitor*, which also discusses the court-martial verdict.

Details about Benedict's court-martial can be found in *Proceedings of a General Court Martial of the Line, Held at Raritan, in the State of New-Jersey: By Order of his Excellency George Washington, Esq. General and Commander in Chief of the Army of the United States of America, For the Trial of Major General Arnold June 1, 1779; Major General Howe, President: Published by Order of Congress* (Philadelphia: F. Bailey, 1780), and Isaac Arnold, *The Life of Benedict Arnold*.

The information about the West Point fortifications and their importance to the American Revolution is derived from Dave Richard Palmer, *The River and the Rock: The History of Fortress West Point, 1775–1783* (Westport, Conn.: Greenwood Press, 1969); Edward C. Boyneton, *History of West Point and Its Military Importance During the American Revolution* (New York: Houghton Mifflin, 1922); and Lincoln Diamant, *Chaining the Hudson: The Fight for the River in the American Revolution* (New York: Carol Publishing, 1989).

20: WHOM CAN WE TRUST NOW?

Many books and sources were used in my discussion of Benedict's long negotiations with André, their meeting, André's capture, and Benedict's escape. Among the most detailed were: Van Doren, *Secret History of the American Revolution*; Abbatt, *The Crisis of the Revolution*; Randall, *Benedict Arnold: Patriot and Traitor*; and Isaac Arnold, *The Life of Benedict Arnold*.

The three men who captured André, John Paulding, David Williams, and Isaac Van Wart, became instant heroes. George Washington went out of his way to shake their hands on the day of André's execution, and in a letter to Congress he praised their "virtuous and patriotic conduct." Washington also ordered "that each of them receive annually out of the Public Treasury Two Hundred Dollars in specie . . . and that the Board of war procure for each of them a silver Medal." They were also allowed to keep André's boots, watch, horse, and saddle, which they promptly sold. Benjamin Tallmadge was not as taken by them as his commander in chief. Tallmadge called them "plundering Cowboys" who were "roving and lurking above the lines, sometimes plundering on one side and sometimes on the other."

21 NIL DESPERANDUM

George Washington wanted Benedict captured and executed so urgently that he set in motion a complicated kidnapping scheme. He contacted a Continental colonel, Henry Lee, then stationed in New Jersey, and told him to arrange to get Arnold, with the only caution being that he should not be killed in the attempt. "[The] idea which would accompany such an event," Washington instructed the twenty-four-year-old officer, "would be that ruffians had been hired to assassinate him."

Lee then recruited Sergeant Major John Champe, who proceeded to make his way to New York City, where he claimed he had deserted the American cause in order to aid the British. After a few days he met Benedict "accidentally" on the street and was recruited into a unit of deserters Benedict was forming. Champe learned that Benedict came home every evening at around midnight and liked to walk in his garden before retiring for the night. Champe loosened the boards of Benedict's fence and had even recruited two men to help him kidnap Benedict and carry him to a waiting boat to be rowed across the Hudson. However, on the night before the kidnapping was scheduled to take place, Champe was ordered aboard a transport ship and ended up in Virginia as part of Benedict's campaign in Virginia. It took Champe several weeks before he could desert the British side and return to Lee in New Jersey.

A number of books and articles provided the details of André's trial and execution, including John Evangelist Walsh, *The Execution of Major André* (New York: Palgrave/St. Martin's Press, 2001); *Proceedings of a Board of General Officers, Held by Order of His Excellency Gen. Washington, Commander in Chief of the Army of the United States, Respecting Major John André, Adjutant General of the British Army. September 29, 1780, and printed by order of Congress* (Philadelphia: F. Bailey, 1780); Anon., "An Authentic Account of Major André's Death," *Political Magazine* (London), vol. 2 (1781) 171–73.

Martin, *Benedict Arnold, Revolutionary Hero*, shows a number of interesting ways in which Benedict was vilified and compared to Satan. He also suggests that many patriots may have heaped such hatred on Benedict because they themselves had been less than patriotic in their support of the Revolution and wanted to divert attention elsewhere.

Benedict's military career with the British and his life in England are discussed in Randall, *Benedict Arnold: Patriot and Traitor*, and Brandt, *The Man in the Mirror*. Additional details about Benedict and Peggy's time in England can be located in J. G. Taylor, *Some New Light on the Later Life and Last Resting Place of Benedict Arnold and of His Wife Margaret Shippen* (London: George White, 1931).

Benedict had eight children—three by his first wife, Margaret, and five by Peggy. His oldest son, Benedict, entered the British army and was wounded in Jamaica fighting the French. The wound became infected, and he died there in 1795. Richard became a successful farmer in eastern Canada and was elected a magistrate. He married a fifteen-year-old local girl, and they had nine children during a marriage that lasted twenty years. Henry was also a farmer in eastern Canada. He and his wife, Hannah, had eleven children, only one of whom survived childhood. He died in New York in 1826. Benedict's first child with Peggy, Edward, became a lieutenant in the 6th Bengal Cavalry and died serving in India in 1813. James became a distinguished member of the Royal Engineers, heading that unit in British North America, and was knighted by the king in recognition of his achievements. He died in 1854. George also joined the army and rose to become a lieutenant colonel in the Bengal Cavalry. He died at the age of forty-one in India. William, Benedict's youngest son, became a captain in the Royal Lancers and a justice of the peace in England. Benedict's only daughter, Sophia, married an army officer and died at age forty-two in England after giving birth to four children.

A fair-minded look at Benedict's years in Canada and his place in Canadian history can be found in Barry K. Wilson, *Benedict Arnold: A Traitor in Our Midst* (Montreal: McGill–Queen's University Press, 2001). Also consulted were Phyllis R. Blakeley and John N. Grant, editors, *Eleven Exiles: Accounts of Loyalists of the American Revolution* (Toronto: Dundurn Press, 1982), and D. G. Bell, *Early Loyalist Saint John: The Origin of New Brunswick Politics, 1783–1786* (Fredericton, N.B.: New Ireland Press, 1983).

The most famous case Benedict brought in Canada was against a former business partner named Munson Hayt. After Benedict got a legal judgment that said Hayt owed him over £1,500 sterling ($120,000), Hayt began telling people that Benedict had burned down one of his own warehouses to get the insurance money. Benedict sued him for slander. He won the case, but then the two judges involved awarded him only twenty shillings ($85.25), suggesting that they did not think his reputation was worth very much. The case was another indication of bias against Arnold. Several of the jurors had been on the losing end of lawsuits filed by Benedict, and the two judges were friends of Hayt.

Following her husband's death, Peggy Arnold found herself saddled with nearly £6,000 sterling ($368,000) of debt. By selling the family home and moving to a less expensive town, by applying for various pensions and moneys she felt her husband had been owed by the government, and by selling just about everything she could, Peggy managed to satisfy the debt inside eighteen months. Shortly after this she was diagnosed with "a complaint of the womb." By the summer of 1804 she was having trouble breathing and in so much pain that she had to take opium. "My only chance," she wrote to her sister, "is from an internal operation, which it is at present dangerous to perform." She died three years and two months after her husband's death. She was just forty-four years old.

What happened to some of Benedict's many enemies? After Ticonderoga, Ethan Allen did very little else to help the American cause. He staged a foolish attack on Montreal in 1775 and was captured and sent to England in chains. He was returned to America and formally exchanged for a British prisoner in 1778, after which he became the major general of Vermont's militia troops. He used this military position to drive off settlers from New York who had valid land grants, and later threatened to have the New Hampshire Grants rejoin the British Empire if Vermont was not designated as the fourteenth state. He died in 1789, two years before Vermont officially was granted statehood.

After sending his final nasty comments about Benedict to Congress in 1776, James Easton returned to Massachusetts and a tavern he kept in Pittsfield. Congress canceled his colonel's commission in 1779, and he died in obscurity and heavily in debt.

Following the Battles of Saratoga, John Brown returned to his law practice in Pittsfield, Massachusetts, became a judge, and won election to his state's General Court. He was also the local militia colonel and as such led his men against a combined Loyalist and Native American raiding force in the Mohawk Valley in 1780, where he was killed in a skirmish.

Roger Enos resigned from the Continental Army shortly after beating the court-martial charges for desertion. He returned to Connecticut and, as James Kirby Martin put it, "he never again had the opportunity to rise out of the historical obscurity into which he now so justifiably descended."

Moses Hazen continued to have problems with his military associates, being accused of stealing from his own regiment by subordinates. He beat the charges by accusing one of his challengers of insubordination. He served with little distinction at Yorktown, then left the army to focus on land speculation, which produced an endless number of lawsuits and ruined him financially.

James Wilkinson "led the life of a loutish scoundrel," in the words of James Kirby Martin. After being rebuked by Horatio Gates for leaking the Conway letter, Wilkinson turned on his mentor, and the two came very close to fighting a duel. Following this, complaints by fellow officers over his sudden elevation in rank after Saratoga escalated, and he eventually resigned his commission. In 1779 Congress appointed him clothier general for the army, only to remove him eight months later for embezzling public funds.

After the war Wilkinson turned his sights on the west. He took money from Spanish officials in the 1780s to encourage settlers to renounce their allegiance to the United States in favor of Spain. Then he and Aaron Burr concocted an elaborate scheme to create a vast empire in the southwest independent of the United States. He would eventually turn on Burr to help expose the scheme. He rejoined the army as a major general during the War of 1812, but his leadership of a force to invade Canada was so bad that he was recalled and discharged. He died (from either excessive drinking or an overdose of opium) in 1825 while trying to persuade the Mexican government to give him a large land grant in Texas.

Following Saratoga, Horatio Gates did nothing to suggest he was an able military commander. In 1780 Congress gave him control over an army operating in the southern states without bothering to consult George Washington. Gates then took 3,000 troops and, against the advice of his officers, marched them into a battle at Camden, South Carolina, against a sizeable British force commanded by Cornwallis. The Americans were routed, suffering 750 casualties. Before the fighting had actually ceased, Gates was riding fast to the north and safety, covering nearly sixty miles before midnight. Gates claimed he was seeking assistance, but most soldiers thought he had panicked in the face of the enemy. An embarrassed Congress immediately recalled Gates and refused to even hear his explanation. He retired from the army and eventually moved to New York City, where he died in 1806, seemingly happy with his place in history.

INDEX

Note: Page numbers in **bold** type refer to illustrations.

British navy, on Lake Champlain,
    105–10, **108**, **111**, 118
Brooklyn Heights, Battle of, 114–15,
    115, 119
Brown, John, 51, 56, 58, 61, 62, 83,
    100, 101, 105, 117–18, 122,
    128, 129, 177, 186, 254
Burd, Neddy, 180, 181
Burgoyne, John, **134**
    as British commander, 113,
        133–38
    in Canada, 96, 113
    march toward Albany, 136–38,
        140, 143, 144–46
    at Saratoga, 1, 146, 149–50,
        153–54, 158–59, 166, 167
    surrender of, 166–67, **167**,
        168
    at Ticonderoga, 113, 133–36
Burr, Aaron, 241–42, 255

Cahoon, Samuel, 205, 206, 208
Canada:
    attack on (map), **72**
    Benedict's move to, 229–31
    Benedict's plans to invade,
        54–55, 57–58, 60, 66–68
    boats for invasion of, 68–71, **70**,
        75
    British forces in, 54, 66
    colonial retreat from, 92, 93–98,
        99, 100, 112, 129, 186
    Congressional authorization to
        invade, 61–62
    march toward, 68–71, 73–77,
        74, 83, 92, 186

Carleton, Sir Guy, **81**
    at Lake Champlain, 103, 104,
        106, 109, 112–13
    at Montreal, 57, 80
    at Quebec, 81, 83–85, 88, 90, 96,
        104
Carlisle, Abram, 172–73
Cedars, fort at, 96–97
Charlotte, queen of England, 227
Church, Benjamin, 65–66, 243
Clinton, Henry:
    and André, 179, 188, 193,
        202–3, 205, 206, 219
    and Benedict's military proposals,
        224–26, 227
    and Benedict's rewards, 223–24,
        225
    and Benedict's treason, 188,
        193–94, 198, 202–3, 205,
        206
    and British military actions, 120,
        158–59, 171, 226–27
Cogswell, Rev. James, 10, 14, 17
Concord, Battle of, 48, 55, 60, 120
Continental Congress:
    and Benedict in Philadelphia,
        172–73, 182–85, 196
    and Benedict's army rank, 92,
        121–23, 128–29, 135,
        142–43, 169, 186
    Benedict's enemies in, 105,
        118–19, 121–22, 129,
        139–40, 184–85, 186, 195
    and Benedict's expenses, 66,
        128–29, 185, 186, 189,
        195–96

France (*cont.*)
    at war with Britain, 15–16, 17,
        171, 230
Franklin, Benjamin, 25, 95, 96, 98
Fraser, Simon, 161
Freeman, John, 1, 148, 151, 161
Freemasonry, 25–27, **26**, 36, 222
French and Indian War (Seven Years'
        War), 15–16, **16**, 17, 28–29,
        39, 43, 50, 81–82, 230
Frost, Samuel, 220

Gage, Thomas, 44, 47–48
Galloway, Grace, 174–75
Gates, Horatio, **117**
    as Benedict's enemy, 118, 122,
        128, 129, 140, 143, 146–50,
        153, 156–57, 168, 173, 186
    as Benedict's supporter, 101, 104,
        105, 112
    and colonial army in Canada, 68,
        104, 105
    and Congress, 101, 105, 116–18,
        128, 129, 130, 143, 154,
        166–67, 168, 255
    as northern commander, 129,
        139–40
    at Saratoga, 146–50, 153–57,
        158, 160–62, 166–67, **167**
    as Washington's enemy, 115–17,
        119, 130
George III, king of England, 47, 55,
    231
Germain, Lord George Sackville,
    113, 137
Goodrich, Samuel, 73

Grasse, François-Joseph-Paul de,
    204, 215
Great Awakening, 11
Great Britain, *see* Britain
Great Carrying Place, 71
Greene, Christopher, 74–75
Greene, Nathanael, 122, 131, 221
Green Mountain Boys, 50–54,
    55–56, 58
Grenville, George, 28

Hall, H. B., etching by, **4**
Hamilton, Alexander, 205, 213, 215,
    219, 242
Hancock, John, 25, 29, 118, 128,
    134, 135
Hazen, Moses, 98, 100, 101, 104,
    105, 118, 186, 254
Hessian (German) soldiers, 1,
    95–96, 137, 140, 146, 164–65
Hinman, Benjamin, 61, 62, 64
Howe, Sir William, 102, 114–15,
    120, 133–34, 138, 145, 158,
    166, 171
Hudson River, iron chain at, 197

Ingersoll, Jared, 31–32

Jameson, John, 212, 213
Jefferson, Thomas, 119, 236

Knox, Henry, 131, 205
Kościuszko, Tadeusz, 130, 148

Lafayette, Marquis de, 130, 205,
    214, 217, 219